Academic Rebels in Chile

SUNY Series in
Latin American and Iberian Thought and Culture

Jorge J.E. Gracia, EDITOR

ACADEMIC REBELS IN CHILE:

The Role of Philosophy in Higher Education and Politics

IVÁN JAKSIĆ

State University of New York Press

Published by
State University of New York Press, Albany

Printed in the United States of America

For information, address State University of New York Press, State University Plaza, Albany, NY 12246

Library of Congress Cataloging-in Publication Data

Jaksić, Iván, 1954
Academic rebels in Chile: the role of philosophy in higher education and politics / by Iván Jaksić.
p. cm. (SUNY series in Latin American thought and culture)
Bibliography: p.
Includes index.
ISBN 0—88706—878—2. ISBN 0—88706—879—0 (pbk.)
1. Philosophy, Chilean—History. 2. Education, Higher—Chile—History. 3. Political science—Chile—Philosophy—History. 4. Philosophy and religion—History. 5. Chile—Intellectual life. I. Title.
B1046.J35 1988
199'.83—dc 19 88—12675
CIP

10 9 8 7 6 5 4 3 2 1

To the memory of my father,

Fabián Sebastián Jaksić Rakela

Contents

Abbreviations

AUCH: *Anales de la Universidad de Chile*
FECH: Federación de Estudiantes de Chile
FFE: Facultad de Filosofía y Educación
FFH: Facultad de Filosofía y Humanidades
FRAP: Frente de Acción Popular
IN: Instituto Nacional
IP: Instituto Pedagógico
PC: Partido Comunista
PDC: Partido Demócrata Cristiano
RF: *Revista de Filosofía*
SCF: Sociedad Chilena de Filosofía
UC: Universidad Católica
UCH: Universidad de Chile
UP: Unidad Popular

Preface

Chilean secondary school students have been attending their weekly philosophy class in *Liceos* across the nation for the last 178 years of the country's independent life. I was one of their teachers in 1975, when the situation in the country, the school, and the discipline was hardly as normal as such a continuity would suggest. I talked to my students about logic, about Plato, and about philosophy up to Descartes. They nodded in apparent approval, but I had the unpleasant feeling of saying little of consequence to the young men and women who often missed class because they could not afford the bus fare, and who found it difficult on winter days to walk the long way from San Miguel and La Cisterna, where most of them lived, to Avenida Matta, where the school was located. By virtue of my abstruse subject, philosophical ideas, there was little that could pass as communication in our classroom. They changed this situation one day by asking me whether what I had said about Socrates had any applicability to Chile. I had no problem in responding that it did but did not know what to say when I was bluntly asked for my feelings about it. Was I to dismiss the question and stick to the philosophy curriculum, or was I to tell them about what I saw happening in my own Department of Philosophy at the University of Chile?

One day I ran into one of my students at a prison camp called "Tres Alamos" off Vicuña Mackenna Avenue one third of the way between downtown Santiago and Puente Alto. He was visiting a relative, and I was visiting my philosophy professor and mentor. We shook hands but did not say much. When I returned to the classroom, my students seemed to be more receptive and friendly than usual, no doubt because they had learned about my silent encounter with one of their classmates. From then on until they graduated at the end of the year, they told me of their experiences and feelings about military rule. I had little to give them in return except for what I believed to be the valuable insights one can gain from philosophy. After all, the tension between what one thinks the truth is and a repressive government's ultimate power to define truth as it wishes has been an old and familiar problem for philosophers throughout history.

My students taught me more than I could have possibly taught them. They led me to think about how Chilean philosophers in the past would have answered their questions. I certainly knew how Chilean philosophers reacted to the military coup, but I had no historical context to account for the ways in which philosophers confronted the country's most pressing social and political problems. With my students' questions in mind, I have since attempted to understand Chilean philosophy from the standpoint of the discipline's connection with larger national events.

Philosophy can be studied both as a discipline of universal validity and as a field that, like other academic endeavors, is influenced and sometimes limited by national circumstances. This book, in particular, suggests that in Chile even the claims to the universal validity of philosophical work have been related to national events. Therefore, the main focus of the book is not on how Chilean logic or metaphysics compares with logic and metaphysics elsewhere, but rather on how Chilean academics have used the tools of philosophy to address subjects of national relevance. Because of this focus, some attention is paid to the wider context of the philosophers' work, but this book pays primary attention to the philosophical treatment of the two major issues philosophers have encountered in the history of their discipline since independence from Spain: religion and politics.

I have incurred numerous debts to colleagues, friends and institutions during the writing of this book. I am particularly grateful to Jorge J. E. Gracia of the State University of New York at Buffalo. He encouraged my interest in the subject ten years ago and provided me with the wider context of Latin American philosophy without which any national case study is at fault. I am very indebted to him and to Juan Carlos Torchia Estrada of the Organization of American

States for their guidance and critiques since the inception of this work. I am also very grateful to the following scholars: Rafael Caldera, José Echeverría Yáñez, Edmundo Fuenzalida, Manuel Antonio Garretón, Mario Góngora, Charles A. Hale, Tulio Halperín Donghi, Daniel C. Levy, Solomon Lipp, Brian Loveman, Richard Morse, Guy Neave, and Sol Serrano for their advice and criticism at various stages in the writing of this book.

My colleagues at the Berkeley Center for Latin American Studies, Thomas Bogenschild, Andrés Jiménez, and Alex Saragoza, patiently discussed with me the central ideas of this book and provided me with editorial suggestions that improved the manuscript. In Chile, Raúl Allende, Mauricio Bravo, Erik Cortés, Miguel Da Costa Leiva, Eugenio Ponisio, and Rogelio Rodríguez provided me with published and unpublished materials essential for the writing of this book. Many of the philosophers discussed in this work generously provided me with comments and access to unpublished materials and personal files. They include Marco Antonio Allendes, Humberto Giannini, Gastón Gómez Lasa, Edison Otero, Juan Rivano, and Félix Schwartzmann. I am also grateful to the editors of *Latin American Research Review* and *Stanford-Berkeley Occasional Papers in Latin American Studies* for permission to use parts of articles published through their auspices. In addition, I am grateful to the American Council of Learned Societies, the Faculty of Arts and Letters of the State University of New York at Buffalo, and the Center for Latin American Studies of the University of California at Berkeley for travel funds that made this research possible.

My largest debt is to Juan Rivano, who was my professor of philosophy until his imprisonment in Chile in 1975. He introduced me to the discipline and has consistently been my mentor and critic since I first met him in 1971. I learned that philosophy could be much more than an academic exercise when I witnessed his deliberate decision to stand by his students and colleagues even at the cost of imprisonment and exile. His ability to withstand persecution, isolation, and banishment from his country has provided me with an example of how the discipline can guide and sustain someone's life. It is this understanding of philosophy—which, in Rivano's case, has meant a dedication to his country and his students—that has inspired me to undertake this examination of the history of Chilean philosophy.

The human race will never see the end of its evils until that class of men who philosophize with rectitude and truth obtain the government of political affairs, or until those who govern, by some divine endowment, become true philosophers.

—Plato, "Seventh Epistle," circa 354 B.C.

Introduction

Philosophical ideas in Chile, much the same as ideas in general, have been greatly influenced by European currents of thought. Major philosophical schools such as Scottish Common Sense, liberalism, positivism, existentialism and Marxism, among others, have all at one point or another been embraced by Chilean intellectuals. This is not to say that these schools have been adopted in a completely uncritical fashion, but rather that they constitute the world of ideas that Chileans have lived in during their educational and subsequent intellectual development. Philosophy scholars have adopted these schools not only for the practical purpose of informing their classroom lectures, but also for guiding the larger educational system and, not infrequently, the wider society.

The expectations Chileans have had about the discipline may seem rather grand, but it is not rare to find philosophers everywhere, and in different historical periods, who have made society and its politics the substance of their thought. In Chile philosophers have traditionally understood their role as one of utilizing the instruments of philosophy for addressing social and political problems. However, there has been a significant tendency within Chilean philosophy to attempt to free the discipline from social and especially political concerns. But even in this case philosophers have placed politics at the center of their attention. This close linkage between philosophy and politics constitutes the fundamental basis for understanding the history of the discipline in Chile and in many instances some of the most significant educational and political events of the nation.

The centrality of ideas for Chilean political history has been amply demonstrated by scholars such as Simon Collier, Ricardo Donoso, Mario Góngora, and Allen Woll, among others. There is also an important nineteenth-century tradition of Chilean historians who paid substantial attention to ideas, such as Miguel Luis Amunátegui, Domingo Amunátegui Solar, and Diego Barros Arana. Many of the ideas these scholars have discussed are philosophical, but philosophy per se has not received the attention that its contributions warrant. Perhaps the main reason for this dearth of attention concerns the lack of precise boundaries for the discipline, particularly in the nineteenth century. Also, philosophy as a recognized intellectual activity often seems to be found only in remote corners of a school's curriculum.

However, closer attention reveals that philosophy has enjoyed an important degree of continuity and latitude well beyond the classroom. This can be seen in the fundamental role played by philosophers in debating such issues as the role of religion, politics, and higher education in society since independence from Spain in 1810. Understanding the role of philosophy, then, is most important for understanding the nature of intellectual life in the modern history of Chile. Such an understanding can also help to account for the views and production of many Chilean thinkers whose philosophical contributions have been largely ignored. Few would think of Andrés Bello and Valentín Letelier as philosophers, yet their respective *Filosofía del entendimiento* and *Filosofía de la educación* represent not only important philosophical efforts in the context of their own work, but also pieces of note in the intellectual history of the country. Similarly, many other intellectuals who were occupied in various political and academic endeavors produced philosophical textbooks, shorter pieces for the periodical press, and participated in debates of a philosophical nature. All of this amounts to an important volume of philosophical activity that can both illuminate the larger concerns of various intellectuals and uncover works that remain thus far untreated in the literature on Chilean ideas.

Philosophy can also show the extent to which Chilean thought has evolved in direct contact with, or independently from, major organized political forces or institutions. There are deeply rooted liberal and conservative Chilean historiographical traditions that claim views and thinkers for their camps. Many intellectuals in the nineteenth century, such as José Victorino Lastarria, did in fact advance philosophical ideas informed by liberalism first, and positivism later. But it is far more difficult to understand Ventura Marín, Ramón

Briseño, and even Andrés Bello as either liberal or conservative—unless, of course, one overlooks their philosophy and focuses exclusively on their political or religious views. And yet it is in the context of their philosophical positions that one can fully understand their views on religion and politics. In the twentieth century, philosophers have developed clear sympathies for Marxism and Christian Democracy, as well as other major center and right wing movements. But they are far from being spokesmen for such groups. An examination of Chilean philosophical activity can help determine the allegiances of these intellectuals and assess the degree of their independence from organized political parties.

A study of Chilean philosophy can also shed light on significant developments in Chilean history. Philosophical activity demonstrates that there existed a significant degree of conflict between secular and religious thought long before the more overt confrontations that occurred in the area of church-state relations in the second half of the nineteenth century. As early as the 1820s, philosophy served as a vehicle for the discussion and evaluation of secular and religious interpretations of ethics and ideas generally. Philosophy played this role until the constitutional separation of church and state came about in 1925.

The discipline also helps in understanding the magnitude of the impact of populism and Marxism in Chile since the 1920s. Philosophers, reflecting in many ways the views of an alarmed elite, used the discipline to devise a response to the perceived threat of political mobilization in general, and Marxism in particular. Similarly, the role and attitudes of philosophers concerning the military coup of 1973 reveal the depth and extent of the transformations brought about by the collapse of the democratic political system.

Philosophers have not been leaders of large political movements, but the importance of their views should not be underestimated. Many have occupied key political positions. They have also written influential books. But most importantly, they have had significant influence over higher education. Traditionally an elite institution graduating the nation's leading intellectuals and politicians, the Chilean university has commanded a great deal of respect and influence over society as a whole. This has provided philosophers with an opportunity to transmit their views to important segments of society.

It is indeed in the context of higher education that one can observe the development and centrality of philosophy. Since early in Chile's independent life, philosophy was not just another discipline in a diversified curriculum, but rather a prime force behind the creation and the transformation of Chilean higher education institutions throughout their history, particularly the University of Chile, founded in 1842. The reasons for the preeminence of philosophy rest on the traditional importance accorded to the field during colonial times as well as on the perception of many that the ideals of philosophy were also the ideals of the university: a haven for the cultivation of reason and the source for the dissemination of enlightened thinking, scientific or otherwise.

Philosophy in Chile assumed a privileged position both at the University of Chile and in the writings and speeches of many prominent intellectuals who used the discipline as an instrument to deal with the central issues of their time. However, philosophy did not maintain this position unchallenged: the very incorporation of the discipline as an academic field subject to university scrutiny and regulation substantially eroded the role of philosophy as the guide for higher education in the nation. The university and the field of philosophy became something other than a haven for reason as both took on the practical endeavor of educating Chile's professionals, politicians, and intellectuals. Philosophy, in particular, underwent a process of specialization that was closely related to the academic demands of the university as well as the effort, encouraged by the state, to maintain higher education apart from politics.

Philosophy, however, did not yield easily to the pressures for specialization and depoliticization. Critiques of the discipline's alleged detachment from social and political issues were expressed early and frequently during the modern history of Chile. This book describes the numerous occasions when philosophers brought about significant changes in the academic orientation of the institution and became critical of the wider society. A historical tension can thus be seen between the outward, or political, and the inward, or academic, tendencies in Chilean philosophy. These tendencies have taken turns in dominating the field, and they reflect a larger conflict between politicization and academic specialization in the history of Chilean higher education.

It is also in the context of higher education that one can see the development of the main distinction among philosophers who, as mentioned above, waged politics even when they professed to be against it. In effect, the development of Chilean philosophy can be understood in terms of the tension between those philosophers who have viewed the discipline as an instrument for the analysis and ultimate change of society and those who have conceived of the discipline as primarily an academic field that, though certainly affected by larger social and political changes, depends on its own historical development for nourishment and further growth. The terms *critical* and *professionalist* will be used to refer to philosophers who have held these divergent views of the discipline and to underscore their positions with respect to the larger division characterizing the country's intellectual and academic life.

The distinction between professionalists and critics provides the underlying structure of this book. Both groups of philosophers have changed their specific educational, political, and philosophical stands over time, but the fundamental difference between the two groups remains the same and concerns the ultimate object of their allegiances. The professionalists are those who believe in the universality of their discipline, if not its timelessness, and therefore refuse to mix philosophy with the current and presumably fleeting problems of society. They are generally antagonistic to politics because they believe that the exercise of reason, which they view as central to the discipline, requires distance from mundane affairs. Yet they feel quite strongly that the discipline is perfectly capable of guiding society. In contrast, critics are those who, however similarly trained in the discipline, feel that in the context of Chilean ideas, philosophy must help elucidate the problems of the nation. They claim that this connection to society has always been present in philosophy, but that in Chile the professionalists have turned the discipline into an esoteric subject with little, if any, connection to the central issues of the time. Professionalists and critics have polarized along these lines throughout modern Chilean history, thus lending Chilean philosophy its confrontational character. The polarization between the two groups has carried over to specialized areas, as professionalists have shown a preference for metaphysics, while critics have chosen logic as their main field of study. Likewise, philosophers have made their attitudes to the discipline extensive to education and politics.

The university provides the clearest example of how professionalists have sought to keep the institution apart from politics, while critics have argued for the transformation of the university to conform to society's needs. Their views in this regard provide a basis for understanding an important body of work on Chilean higher education.

Another area in which philosophy can contribute to the understanding of ideas in Chile involves the interpretation of the immensely rich, if not unbridled, variety of foreign influences on Chilean education and culture. Chilean philosophers are among the intellectuals most sensitive to such influences, and perhaps most sensitive to the questions raised by the transfer of foreign models that accounts for the transformation of Chilean cultural institutions throughout the country's modern history. Through the field of philosophy, one can see how intellectuals have debated the questions concerning the dependence or independence of national thought. Certainly, the apparently esoteric veneer of Chilean philosophy belies the often dramatic concerns that have traditionally agitated the field. But when seen in the context of higher education and the country's social and political history, the field betrays an unparalleled level of concern for the relationship between national and international currents of thought.

Chile is not unique among Latin American countries, where intellectuals trained in philosophy have played an important role in the educational and cultural history of their nations. What distinguishes Chile, however, is the development of a rich philosophical culture, reflected in philosophical writings and debates, beginning early in the country's independent life. Also unique are the strength and continuity of the country's premier higher education institution, the University of Chile. University-based intellectual groups flourished in Chile due to the institutional stability of both the university and the nation. While other Latin American countries endured disruptions and frequent disintegration of their universities and intellectual communities, Chile maintained significant continuity in the evolution of its intellectual life. This allowed generation after generation of intellectuals, especially philosophers, to play out their differences and probe into the full range of social, political, and cultural implications of their various philosophical views. It was only under military rule beginning in 1973 that Chileans experienced the collapse of institutional stability that has been all too familiar in other Latin American countries. Yet even then continuities offset many of the obvious changes in philosophy and higher education.

The Chilean case is also meaningful in the context of the ongoing debate on the existence and nature of a "Latin American philosophy." The extremes of this debate range from the assertion that such a philosophy indeed exists to one that argues that philosophy cannot be anything less than universally valid and therefore independent of national circumstances.[1] Chile reveals that while one can talk about a distinctive Chilean philosophy, its distinctiveness rests more on the nature of the themes addressed during a given historical period than on any peculiarly different approach to the field. Chilean philosophers have relied on tradition to address specialized problems of the field as well as wider human and social issues, but the scope and tenor of their concerns has not necessarily been dictated by such a tradition. It is not what they say that is different about their philosophy, but rather when they say it and how.

ORGANIZATION OF THE BOOK

Six major periods characterize the development of modern Chilean philosophy; each one is covered by a separate chapter in this book. The first chapter covers the period from early independence through the death of Andrés Bello in 1865. This is the time when both Chilean philosophy and education, particularly higher education, sought to address the delicate issue of the relations between the emerging national state and the powerful Catholic church. Although conflicts between the two eventually burst into the open in the 1850s, both Chilean philosophy and higher education had already experienced numerous encounters with the religious issue. At stake was the nature of education and thought in the country. Philosophy served as a vehicle for the increasing secularization of educational and intellectual activities in the nation, secularization which the church viewed with understandable apprehension. The philosophers themselves were torn between their loyalty to a discipline that counted many secular thinkers among its European practitioners and their work in a Catholic nation as well as their own beliefs in Catholicism. The attempt to conciliate the two gave rise to forms of philosophical work that combined, often awkwardly, secular thinking and religious beliefs.

Philosophers were headed for significant trouble as some openly attempted to use the field for attacking the church and precipitating the secularization of society. Andrés Bello, however, managed to decisively control the field by turning it into an academic endeavor that avoided both overt religious and overt political advocacy. Bello's success in this regard was related not only to his impressive philosophical expertise, but to his success in impressing upon the University of Chile, which he helped to create, a similar academic character. During this period, the glimmer of a professionalistic attitude appeared as Bello emphasized specialization as a means to separate philosophy from political involvement. He could not do so entirely, as demonstrated by infrequent but significant attempts on the part of intellectuals to use philosophy politically. Far more frequent was the advocacy of Catholic beliefs through the philosophy textbooks sanctioned by the university for use in the secondary school system. Philosophy closely followed the vicissitudes of church and state relations during this initial period.

The second chapter covers the era of positivism from José Victorino Lastarria's encounter with the school in 1868 to its demise in the 1910s. This chapter describes how positivists promoted a rationale that was primarily anticlerical, first in small intellectual groups and eventually in the nation's educational system. Their impressive success in undermining Catholic influence in schools and in institutionalizing the teachings of scientific subjects could not help but affect the philosophical discipline. Initially, philosophy was completely concerned with the religious issue as battles between church and state raged on regarding control over education during the last quarter of the nineteenth century. As the Catholic church lost significant influence not only over education but also over cemeteries, marriages, and other civil issues, philosophical concern with religion tended to die away and concentrated instead on positivism's preferred themes. Not without a battle that was waged primarily in textbooks, positivist philosophers managed to replace religiously inclined works with others that brought the field to a nearly total identification with logic and scientific methodology. The positivists' emphasis on logic, philosophy of science, and experimental psychology, however, failed to capture the interest of philosophers who were soon to stage a philosophical rebellion that had significant implications for higher education as well. European influences played a substantial role in the demise of positivism, but such national circumstances as the end of the overt clashes between church and state in the first quarter of the twentieth century provided the decisive factor. Positivists had taken a leading role in secularizing society through the educational system but in the process invited challenges to their alleged effort to transform Chilean culture. Ironically, the challenges came from the same philosophical discipline that the positivists had used to promote their own views.

The third chapter covers the period from 1920 to 1950. This is the period when, much as it happened in the rest of Latin America, philosophers in Chile rebelled against positivism and successfully institutionalized a new, metaphysically oriented philosophy that earned them the name of "founders" on account of the novelty of their work. In Chile, philosophers who reacted against positivism found that this school had simply outlived its usefulness and had left them without a central issue to devote their energies to. That issue was soon provided by the arrival of Marxism and the threat that many believed it posed in the form of the politicization of society and its institutions. They countered by making spiritual concerns—as opposed to the alleged materialistic interests of the Marxists—the center of philosophical inquiry. These philosophers turned the field into a highly specialized endeavor almost exclusively focused on metaphysics and the theory of values. Philosophy became an active promoter of antipolitics, though not necessarily by becoming apolitical itself.

The fourth chapter covers the period from 1950 to the onset of the university reform movement of 1968. This is a period when philosophers consolidated their antipolitical philosophical concerns and established the foundations of a professional philosophical community. Philosophers were able during this period to develop a highly specialized type of philosophical work enhanced by both the arrival of foreign professors and a significant increase in international philosophical contacts. Intellectually, Chilean philosophers found inspiration in and devoted their energies to the massive flow of European philosophical currents, particularly phenomenology and existentialism. They effectively cut the already tenuous ties that existed between the discipline and larger educational and political events.

Philosophy during this period appeared to have little to fear from political disruptions, to a great extent because the policies of the

Carlos Ibáñez del Campo administration (1952–58) kept a tight lid on political dissent. Philosophers became accustomed to carrying on their philosophical interests in isolation, and thus reacted with shock as the 1960s brought not only a high level of political mobilization but also the first critiques against their professionalistic orientation, which was alleged to be a rationale for detachment from social and political concerns. This chapter discusses how philosophers polarized, first along specialized philosophical lines, and then along political ones as they held contending views about the commitments the discipline should have with respect to university and national affairs.

Chapter 5 covers the period from 1960 to 1973. This is a period when philosophers, either willingly or unwillingly, were drawn into the intense political battles that characterized the era. Philosophers could not but move out from what many called their ivory tower in order to defend a type of philosophical work that required sanctuary from political pressures. They did so by defending a university model that paralleled their philosophical views, that is, an institution free from political pressures yet concerned about the guidance of society. Partly because of their past isolation from partisan politics, they did not foresee the extent of the involvement of political parties in the university. Party politics proved to be more than they could handle. The philosophers' role in the university reform movement was thus confined to precipitating a crisis at their Faculty of Philosophy and Education, a crisis that nevertheless brought the entire university to its knees. Philosophers during this period confronted the real world of politics, but they all became losers in a struggle that came to be dominated by national political forces.

Philosophy would not be the same again in Chile after the university reform period. Philosophers struggled to find a meaningful philosophical activity in a society and an institution over which they now had little, if any, control. Some attempted to maintain their focus on the subjects characteristic of the happier, though brief and perhaps artificial, era of philosophical professionalism. Others attempted to comprehend politics by means of philosophy. But in both cases their efforts were overwhelmed by the politicization of higher education and the hostilities that brought Chilean institutions of higher education to the same level of political polarization affecting the rest of the country.

The period of military rule beginning in 1973 is open-ended, although some of the most characteristic features of philosophy during this time have already come to the fore. Philosophers began the period as a divided group, in many cases resentful of the past period of politicization and ambivalent about the military control of the universities. They would in time be isolated, persecuted, humiliated, and pushed aside by a newly created current of officialists who were willing, if not eager, to work with the military in restoring the perceived professionalism of the past. In this period, nonofficialist philosophers were forced to find new places of work, some in the provinces, some in academic centers out of the university, some in exile. In a few limited cases, they publicly came out in defense of the university, the discipline, and their colleagues, but by and large they have been hesitant, fearful, and silent during this trying period. Their philosophical thinking has also changed in unexpected ways; some have shifted their concerns from narrowly specialized to more social and politically relevant questions on violence and power. As a result of harassment and repression, professionalists and critics have come closer together. But they remain largely divided, if not estranged, and have little hopes for recovering the sense of collegiality and philosophical enthusiasm that characterized their formative years.

Through the examination of these six periods, this book attempts to show that Chilean philosophy, despite its polarization along professionalist and critical lines, has remained consistent in its concern for religion, higher education and politics. Philosophers have not confined themselves to the university; they have in fact taken strong political positions when they have felt their discipline threatened by forces within or outside the institution. The result has been a peculiar philosophical production that relates the aims of philosophy to those of the university, one that to this day struggles to decide whether philosophers should cast their lot among those seeking to relate the field to specific national problems or among those seeking to address the perennial problems of philosophy unmolested by national circumstances.

I

PHILOSOPHY, THE SECULARIZATION OF THOUGHT, AND HIGHER EDUCATION

1810–1865

The study of philosophy in Chile, just like in other areas of the Spanish empire in America during the colonial period, was a fundamentally academic pursuit. With the coming of independence in the early nineteenth century, philosophy demonstrated its potential for discussing issues of a political nature. Statesmen and intellectuals found the discipline useful for addressing the educational and cultural needs of a country just emerging from centuries of Catholic church dominance over these areas of national life. Partly because of this usefulness, philosophy attracted many of the most talented Chileans during the period and thus served as an excellent recruitment ground for high-level political positions. Other fields were equally useful, or ''functional,'' as Allen Woll has adeptly termed the historiography of the nineteenth century.[1] But philosophy led the way in addressing issues of religious and secular thought and in fostering the development of national education. Particularly because of Andrés Bello, philosophy proved its usefulness by helping him conceptualize and eventually found the country's principal university: the University of Chile (UCH), also known as La Casa de Bello.

The major problem facing philosophy during the nineteenth century was the changing relationship between church and state, and particularly the issue of religious tolerance. The constitutions of the postindependence period, especially the long lasting Constitution of 1833, all declared Chile a Catholic nation. This profession of faith presented several problems, particularly in connection with the desire and perceived need to attract immigrants, and the need to establish friendly relations with non-Catholic countries.

Historians agree that the first serious conflicts between church and state in Chile did not emerge until the 1850s, when ruling circles became deeply divided by their differences concerning the role of religion in society. The period preceding those years, however, was not lacking in confrontations and debates concerning religious tolerance. Some of the intellectuals who will be discussed in this chapter were not only aware of such debates, but often participants in them. This was the case of Juan Egaña, whose arguments for maintaining an official state religion during the 1820s were read and published beyond Chile, in countries where the problem of Catholic influence was also central.[2] Most discussions of religious tolerance took place in the press, but they also engulfed the Congress, which became the scene of repeated attempts to eliminate from the 1833 Constitution the article that proclaimed Chile a Catholic nation. By 1865, the Congress managed to reform this article so as to allow dissidents to practice their beliefs unmolested, thus inaugurating a series of decisive measures intended to secularize society.[3]

When philosophers were not directly involved in these political debates, they were still concerned with other aspects of religion. Much of their philosophical production was, in fact, in direct dialogue with the larger concern for the role of religion in the social life of the country. Philosophers were most cautious in their discussions of this issue, and in many instances they resisted the currents of secularization that swept the school and the nation. Overall, however, the discipline changed to reflect the larger secularization of education and society. Education, in particular, served as the point of contact between the discipline, practiced after all by only a handful of specialists, and the wider Chilean intellectual and political milieu.

Thousands of influential Chileans, those who could afford an education, spent their formative years in close contact with philosophers and their textbooks, learning from them the fundamentals of logic, ethics, and law.

PHILOSOPHICAL STUDIES IN CHILE AFTER INDEPENDENCE

The creation of the Instituto Nacional (IN) in 1813 was the most important educational achievement of the Patria Vieja (1810–1814), the brief period of Chilean history after the declaration of independence in 1810. Born out of the fusion of four colonial educational institutions, the Academia de San Luis, the Convictorio Carolino, the Seminario de Santiago, and the Universidad de San Felipe, the Instituto represented the first attempt at establishing a national system of education.[4]

The IN emerged from the closing of colonial religious institutions, but no real incompatibility existed between religion and the new state-run school, at least in the early years. The Instituto's creation was guided by the conviction of some leaders that education needed to be responsive to national needs, particularly in the area of economic development. Three of the most articulate spokesmen for this view of education, IN founders Juan Egaña, Manuel de Salas, and Camilo Henríquez, were all products of the strong current of Catholic Enlightenment developing in Chile at the end of the colonial period, and were also loyal to the cause of independence. Their religiosity, however, was brought to bear in the conception and curriculum of IN. Enlightened by early nineteenth-century standards, these men as well as others in charge of building the new republic were bound by tradition and a Catholic upbringing. The institutions they created often reflected some of their own loyalties to both revolution and tradition. The Instituto, for instance, continued to ordain ministers of the faith, but was new to the extent that it was conceived as a fundamentally national-oriented school. It was also run and staffed by clergymen, although in large measure this was out of necessity. Students and professors were required to attend mass daily and to give their confession periodically.[5]

The functioning of IN, bound up as it was with the destiny of the Chilean state, came to an abrupt halt with the Spanish *Recon-*

quista period of 1814–1818. As an expression of Chile's independence, the Instituto was quickly closed down by Spanish authorities, who reopened colonial institutions. However, after this hiatus the institute resumed functions along the lines that had inspired its creation in 1813. Still, securing independence from Spain militarily did not mean a sharp break with the past in educational matters. This can be seen clearly in the field of philosophy, which, perhaps more than any other, served the double role of providing an orientation for Chilean education as a whole and serving as a pillar of the curriculum.

During colonial times, the study of philosophy was central to higher education institutions. Along with Latin, philosophy was requisite for the training in and the practice of the religious and civil professions. The dominant philosophy, as in the rest of the colonies, was scholasticism, with Latin being the language of discussion.[6] The teaching of philosophy concentrated on the syllogism, and even though some scientific concerns were introduced in the curriculum during the late colonial period, most philosophical subjects such as psychology, metaphysics, ethics, and logic remained largely the same.[7]

Although this emphasis changed somewhat with the opening of IN, philosophy continued to occupy a preponderant place in the curriculum. It lost some of its influence as increasing emphasis was given to the teaching of scientific subjects. But many courses on such subjects could not be offered for lack of either students or faculty.[8] This left philosophy, just as in colonial times, as one of the dominant subjects including Latin, law, and theology. The teaching of philosophy was split into the courses of logic and metaphysics, and philosophy of law and moral philosophy. The course on logic and metaphysics was taught early, and students were considered ready for a choice of careers after successful completion of the moral philosophy requirements.[9] Philosophy, as the following 1819 examination report indicates, was largely concerned with religious themes:

> The student don Manuel Carrasco demonstrated the existence of God with moral, physical and metaphysical arguments; and the *manteísta* [nonboarding student] don Tomás Argomedo took charge of the demonstration of the general and supreme providence of God.[10]

IN founder Juan Egaña (1768–1826) was the most important philosophical figure during this time. His religious concerns informed both the creation of the Instituto as well as the philosophy courses, although generally he left the teaching to others, including his son Joaquín. Egaña's religiosity was not incompatible with revolutionary fervor. In fact, his credentials in this regard were impeccable: he had suffered persecution and deportation during the *Reconquista* and had served his newly independent country as congressman, senator, and author of the 1823 Constitution. And yet his philosophical stance remained closely linked to the Catholicism and scholasticism he had espoused as professor of Latin and rhetoric at the University of San Felipe during colonial times.[11]

Egaña's philosophical views, however, were neither exclusively scholastic nor purely guided by theological concerns. His strongest interest was in moral philosophy, a subject he viewed as the basis for the educational system. Egaña's emphasis on the practical usages of the field found a natural ally in education, as schools could instill important values in the new generations. He thought of philosophy, in particular, as a vehicle for inculcating not only morality but also a sense of nationalism among young Chileans.[12] This accounts for the emphasis on moral philosophy at IN as well as the religious character of the institution as a whole.

Winds of change began to sweep the Instituto as Chile consolidated its independence, particularly when the administrations of Bernardo O'Higgins and Ramón Freire moved to openly anticlerical positions during the first half of the 1820s. Clergymen had held the position of rector of the Instituto until a lay Frenchman, Charles Lozier, was appointed to the position in 1826. During his brief tenure, Lozier took decisive steps to secularize the teaching and administrative bodies of IN.[13] A mathematician by training, Lozier placed a strong emphasis on the teaching of mathematics and the natural sciences. But his influence also reached the philosophical field, as he brought to Chile numerous books and ideas by French intellectuals. In particular, he was conversant with the French school of Ideology, which he offered to teach while still looking for employment in Buenos Aires.[14] In Chile he had an opportunity to promote the teachings of this school: thirty-one copies of Condillac's works (Condillac was one of the major representatives of this school) were acquired during his rectorship.[15] Thanks to Lozier, young Chileans educated at the Instituto, many of whom later became professors themselves, were exposed to philosophical trends current in France at the time. Outstanding among them were Manuel Montt, later to become president of Chile, José Miguel Varas, and Ventura Marín, who would make substantial contributions to the teaching of philosophy.

Egaña's influence, however, was still strong during and after Lozier's tenure. He wrote the first philosophy textbook authored by a Chilean since independence, the *Tractatus de Re Logica, Metaphisica et Morali,* published in 1827.[16] This work has been severely criticized by subsequent liberal historians as a textbook "written in bad Latin and based on scholastic doctrines."[17] The text, however, served a useful purpose to the extent that it was primarily concerned with introducing and discussing elementary logical concepts. Furthermore, Egaña's work was not inspired by scholasticism alone, but in fact discussed such modern authors as Descartes, Hobbes, Locke, and Condillac. His acquaintance with Condillac suggests that Egaña was not only aware of the work of the French Idéologues, but that he also subscribed to the analytical method promoted by followers of that school.[18] More will be said about French Ideology below, but suffice it to say for the moment that this school of thought presented significant challenges to Catholic dogma in France during the early nineteenth century.[19] In Chile, it is true that Egaña did not use Ideology in this fashion and that his text was written in Latin. The language of the book would suggest a strong attachment to colonial styles, but there had not been much of a precedent for scholarly writing in Chile, let alone vernacular writing. In this sense, Egaña's textbook indicates that the boundaries between past and present during the immediate postindependence period were blurred enough to allow for the continuity of colonial cultural forms. However, Egaña's book demonstrates also that by 1827 modern philosophical ideas were appearing in writing in Chile.

This trend continued with the publication in 1828 of the *Lecciones elementales de moral* by José Miguel Varas (1807–1833), also a professor at the Instituto Nacional. There had been other professors of philosophy at IN prior to Varas, such as Domingo Amunátegui and Tomás Argomedo, but they moved to government positions before they could influence the development of the field in any substantial way. It was Varas who made important philosophical contributions after Egaña. His *Lecciones* was the first philosophy textbook written in Spanish in Chile. It passionately attacked scholasticism and it criticized the content of philosophical teaching at IN. Yet, as Spaniard José Joaquín de Mora, recently arrived from Buenos Aires, noted in *El Mercurio Chileno* the same year, Varas's book was a balanced, if not cautious, presentation of ethical subjects.[20] Largely inspired by Rousseau, Varas subscribed to those views of the French author that did not contradict Catholic doctrine.[21]

This avoidance of conflict with Catholicism, which characterized philosophical writings during the period, is understandable in light of the continuous tensions between church and state during the 1820s. The uneasy relationship between the two was also perceivable at IN, where Lozier antagonized the church with his secularization of the school in 1826. Due to this ongoing conflict, it is understandable that any philosophy textbook, and Varas's in particular, should have been cautious in its discussion of philosophical subjects, and most especially at a time when conservative clergyman Juan Francisco Meneses replaced Lozier as the director of the Instituto between 1826 and 1829.[22]

Despite such constraints, modern philosophical ideas continued to be pursued by Chilean intellectuals. Philosophers learned that religious subjects needed to be approached with caution, and in that sense Chilean philosophy was shaped by the realities of growing church-state tensions. However, this did not stop philosophy teachers from probing the field. In addition, there was an educational need to continue to produce philosophy textbooks, as attendance in philosophy classes kept increasing, not only at the Instituto but also at other secondary schools in Santiago.[23] Soon after the publication of Varas's *Lecciones,* a strong and productive relationship developed between him and another IN professor, Ventura Marín (1806–1877), which resulted in the coauthorship of a textbook titled *Elementos de ideología* in 1830.[24] As the title suggests, this text reveals the extent of the influence of Ideology in Chile. This is something of an anachronism, because this school was already in decline in Europe, particularly in France, during the 1820s. Still, France was a long way from Chile, and the authors found many useful points in Ideology that could be passed on to students.

The school of Ideology captured the attention of intellectuals in Chile, just as it did in Argentina, because of its emphasis on the acquisition of ideas.[25] It was a radical enough movement to be opposed to scholasticism and to suggest that knowledge derived from experience. This was fitting for the teaching of philosophy in a state-run educational institution. Yet it left enough room—at least Chileans managed to find it—for understanding consciousness, for instance, as something more than sensations and experience. This understanding, which made Ideology palatable in a Catholic country, had been in fact advanced by Laromiguière in France, who was known to Chileans in the late 1820s.[26]

Yet despite their agreement on Ideology generally, Varas and Marín had some differences on the subject of belief. They outlined such differences in separate comments at the end of their textbook. Their most fundamental disagreement concerned David Hume, whose skepticism Marín considered a threat to the notion of God.[27] Varas was not exactly an unbeliever, but he saw only idealism where Marín saw objectionable skepticism. Their disagreement did not transcend the walls of the Instituto, but as Marín recalled in 1834, they certainly harbored disquieting thoughts about the reception of their work. "Fortunately," Marín said, "our apprehensions were unfounded, for a prolongued silence of either indifference or approval left us in secure possession of the field."[28]

Whether Varas and Marín did in effect control the discipline is questionable, but they introduced significant modern philosophical approaches. Compared to 1819, philosophy examinations by 1830 had acquired a great deal of sophistication thanks to Varas and Marín. Students were examined on such subjects as the history of philosophy, grammar, logic, and on Ideology specifically. In all subjects, the focus on sense-experience as the basis of knowledge was apparent. In the program for the examinations, the authors made it clear that "it follows from the facts presented by the history of philosophy that the only true system is the system of experience."[29] And yet there was no overt rejection of, or even taking issue with, Catholic dogma. The field thus acquired a specialized flair that, although potentially antagonistic to religion, was by and large acceptable to Chileans at the time.

It was during this period and in this intellectual climate that two intellectuals who had a particular philosophical expertise arrived in Chile: the Spaniard José Joaquín de Mora (1783–1864) and the Venezuelan Andrés Bello (1781–1865). They would make significant contributions to the field, but they arrived in a deeply divided nation that demanded their immediate political commitments. Bello and Mora went to Chile to work as educators, but they found themselves caught up in the tumultuous politics of the time, and in opposite camps. The 1820s was a period when liberals and conservatives, also known as *pipiolos* and *pelucones,* respectively, struggled for control of the emerging national institutions.[30] In education, the struggle was over the control of IN, which during the twists and turns of the period was won by conservatives at a time of liberal political dominance.

The liberal administration of Francisco Antonio Pinto (1826–1829) attempted to bypass the conservative control of IN by creating the Liceo de Chile and appointing Mora as director. Conservatives, in turn, created the Colegio de Santiago to compete with the Liceo and asked first Juan Francisco Meneses and then Andrés Bello to serve as directors of the new school. In the inevitable struggle that ensued, Mora found himself besieged by the conservatives who won the revolution of 1830, and who cut the funding of the Liceo. As author of the liberal Constitution of 1828, Mora had excited the hatred of many *pelucones* who were in addition antagonized by the preferential treatment given to him by former president Pinto. Diego Portales, in particular, as the driving force behind the new *pelucón* government, demonstrated his pique at Mora by arresting him and deporting him to Peru.[31]

This was certainly not a good start for Andrés Bello, who found himself aligned with conservative forces that were all too eager to use him against Mora for their own political purposes. Liberals never forgave Bello for this, and generation after generation of them castigated the Venezuelan for his role in the expulsion of Mora and his alleged alliance with Diego Portales and the *pelucón* government.[32] Mora's own shortlived Chilean tenure was not any more auspicious. And yet both managed to influence Chilean education and philosophy in most enduring ways. Although the Liceo de Chile and the Colegio de Santiago did not last long, they proved to be viable alternatives to the Instituto Nacional. In philosophy, Bello and Mora brought themes, schools and authors that guided the subsequent development of the discipline in Chile. Both had spent a great number of years in England and were familiar with authors and philosophical approaches that would otherwise have taken much longer to become known in Chile, if they had become known at all.

Mora had extensive philosophical experience at the time of his arrival in Chile. He was knowledgeable about the authors of the Ideology school, and even though he was critical of it, he did use it for his teaching, as indicated by the Liceo's statutes.[33] However, he also included a discussion of philosophers of the Scottish school of Common Sense, which he introduced not only in Chile, but also in Bolivia and Peru.[34] He did not teach philosophy for long, and in fact he passed on the philosophy class to Juan Antonio Portés in 1829, who, as a student of Laromiguière in France, was also critical of the most extreme positions of the Idéologues. Mora's philosophical preferences were for the Scottish Common Sense philosophers whom he had studied in Spain but learned about with some depth during his stay in England between 1823 and 1826. A product of his interest in Scottish philosophy, and particularly in Dugald Stewart and Thomas Reid, is his *Cursos de lógica y ética según la escuela de Edimburgo.* Although he prepared this text in Chile and claims to have used it at the Liceo, he did not publish it until 1832, after his deportation to Peru.[35]

Mora's rationale for choosing the School of Edinburgh for his textbook was that in his view philosophers of the Scottish school situated themselves in the moderate middle between "metaphysics" and "physiology," that is, between the extremes of idealism and materialism. In addition, this school provided, in his view, easy access to the most complex subjects of philosophy by means of introspection. This concept was nothing short of revolutionary, for it assumed individuals could attain truth unaided by divine revelation. "What students must do," he explained to underline the advantages of the Scottish approach, "in order to understand what takes place in their own mental faculties as well as the means to direct them, is to study phenomena within the mind. To this effect, they are asked to move away from scholasticism and all the enigmas that pile up in philosophy courses."[36]

Mora revealed a clear awareness of philosophical developments in Europe, where "introspection" was used as a method by the Idéologues as well as by the schools that followed the main features of Scottish philosophy, particularly the Eclecticism that derived from Royer-Collard, Théodore Jouffroy, and Victor Cousin in France.[37] However, he stated in his text that he felt that Scottish influences had gone too far into the direction of idealism, particularly with

Victor Cousin.[38] These nuances reveal the extent of his philosophical knowledge, but the complexities of the field did not prevent him from presenting philosophical problems in an introductory fashion. Logic occupied most of the text, which represents by far the most complete treatment of the subject prior to Andrés Bello's *Filosofía del entendimiento.*

The significance of the introduction of Scottish philosophy in Chile is paramount. It charted the subsequent development of the discipline much as it did in France in the 1820s, when the Idéologues lost ground to the new currents emanating from Scotland. In Chile, the Scottish philosophers offered a modern philosophy which, despite some of its most radical positions, was still compatible with religious beliefs. This approach allowed philosophers to inquire about non-Catholic themes without offending Catholic doctrine, but it seems to have been more successful in Chile than elsewhere in this respect. In Lima, for instance, Mora was quickly accused by the press of promoting in his *Cursos* a form of materialism badly disguised under a thin veneer of religiosity, "because he knew all too well that without that cover he would have been stoned."[39]

However, Mora's correspondence with Bolivian strongman Andrés de Santa Cruz, to whom he offered his educational services, provides evidence that his beliefs were sincere. He stated, for instance, that "the philosophy of Edinburgh is one of the most effective methods of civilization known in our century," adding later that this school "predisposes the mind to religious ideas, and sets it apart from the spirit of unbelief that is as prevalent today as it is threatening to morality and political regeneration."[40] Mora was not antireligious, but his association with the liberals aroused the antagonism of Chilean conservatives. Like Andrés Bello, he was attracted to the moral aspects of Scottish thought. Mora's introduction of Scottish philosophy was to exert a lasting influence in Chilean circles.

Clearly, he could not have done it by himself. It was Andrés Bello who pursued the study of Scottish Common Sense in a more systematic fashion. However, Bello's master philosophical work, the *Filosofía del entendimiento,* appeared posthumously in 1881. Still, his philosophical influence began in earnest in the 1840s, when parts of his book appeared in several periodical publications, and, more importantly, when he was well positioned at the University of Chile to monitor the development of the discipline. During the 1830s, however, the field was in a state of flux: it suffered several serious setbacks such as the expulsion of Mora in 1831, the mental breakdown of Varas in 1830, and his tragic death in 1833. Some normalcy returned to the field when Ventura Marín took charge of the philosophy class in 1832, the year of a major reform at IN.

The 1832 reform, authored by Manuel Montt, Juan Godoy, and Ventura Marín, attempted to systematize secondary education at IN and separate it from higher and professional studies.[41] It established six sections, or *cursos,* for secondary education. The six year-long sections included humanities, law, medicine, mathematics, and theology. All sections were organized around three types of courses: "principal," "alternate," and "accessory." In the humanities section, the principal class for the first four years was Latin, followed by philosophy in the last two. During the fifth and sixth years, students concentrated on logic and ethics.[42]

It is in the context of the 1832 program, although parts of it remained on paper, that Marín prepared his *Elementos de la filosofía del espíritu humano,* the next philosophy textbook published in Chile following his own, which was coauthored with José Miguel Varas. It was published in two volumes in 1834 and 1835, and covered the two general areas required by the humanities curriculum. Although the work was dedicated to his friend Varas, Marín distanced himself from the philosophical assumptions that guided their previous book. He also distanced himself from the school of Ideology. He suggested that among his new philosophical mentors, who perhaps not too coincidentally had already been discussed by Mora and were well known to Bello, "I should especially include the works of Dugald Stewart, which introduced me to Scottish philosophy, Royer-Collard, who freed my opinions from the excess of sensualism that they acquired during my reading of Locke, Condillac and Destutt de Tracy; and finally, the celebrated Cousin, who assured me of the respect in which I always held the doctrines of the philosopher from Koenisberg [Kant], at least since I was capable of recognizing his great importance."[43] Thus, Marín's textbook signalled the end of the influence of the Idéologues as well as the beginnings of the French version of Scottish and German philosophy developed mainly by Victor Cousin in France.

The significance of Marín's work can be viewed in at least two important ways. First, it demonstrates that, even second hand, European philosophical influences had a fairly current impact on Chilean thought. True, this was aided by the arrival of several foreigners in the 1820s who introduced an important number of philosophical currents and authors, particularly from Great Britain and France. But still, Chilean intellectuals like Marín had to find their way through the European philosophical maze and choose paths and directions that were also being sought by their counterparts across the Atlantic. In Marín's case, he followed a French version of Scottish thinking developed by Victor Cousin. Second, it shows that Chilean philosophy was significantly expanding its incorporation of lay philosophical authors. While on the surface appearing more secular, however, philosophers were still cautiously developing the field within a framework of respect for Catholic doctrine. They felt compelled to do so in their writings. Marín, for example, just as he had done in 1830, once again castigated skepticism, an appropriate target for authors seeking to establish their philosophical credentials before a suspicious church.[44]

Andrés Bello, who was beginning to make his philosophical presence felt, reacted quickly and positively to the publication of Marín's two-volume work.[45] According to the Venezuelan thinker, Marín had not only "placed Chilean philosophical studies on a European level" but also, and more importantly, conciliated "liberal principles with religious respect for those great truths that are the foundations of social order."[46] Innovation within tradition was certainly the great issue of the period, and caution was the mark of the 1830s, particularly after the tumultuous 1820s in politics and education. Marín knew what to do in this respect, and Bello was emerging as the man who pointed the way and consistently defended moderation and balance in philosophical matters, a task at which he became particularly adept.

During the 1830s, Marín was clearly the preeminent philosophical figure, though not necessarily the most successful. When he attempted to designate a successor for his philosophy class at IN he failed to place either of his two favorite students: Antonio García Reyes and Ramón Briseño, who were to play important roles in the educational and intellectual life of the nation.[47] Both were deeply religious men who had graduated from the Seminary attached to the Instituto. Their religiosity, no doubt, played a role in their winning the favor of Marín, but it also influenced their not being chosen for the position. Future president Manuel Montt, who at the time of Marín's resignation in 1837 was rector of the Instituto, had different designs for both the school in general and philosophy in particular. In keeping with the slow but definitive trend of secularization of education, Montt managed to impose the appointment of the twenty-year-old Antonio Varas (1817–1886), the brother of José Miguel, to Marín's position.

Antonio Varas was an observant Catholic, though not as fervent as García and Briseño. Varas moved quickly up the ranks, successively becoming rector of the Instituto, congressman, and cabinet minister. His philosophical influence was therefore limited, but his appointment reveals that there was more to the field than mere philosophical expertise. Particularly because of the close connection between the Instituto Nacional and the state, which Montt saw clearly, the selection of professors was critically important. Montt, as Diego Portales before him, was determined to use the Instituto as a recruitment ground for the future leaders of an increasingly secular nation.[48]

The religious issue was sensitive enough to advise caution in all subjects related to educational and cultural change, particularly at a time when the state was increasing its role in these areas. The Seminary had been separated from the Instituto in 1834, and the colonial University of San Felipe was abolished in 1839, making the church understandably restless about its diminishing control of education. The role philosophers played in these developments was that of maintaining a degree of balance between the increasing secularization of society and the weight of a strong Catholic tradition. As Ventura Marín put it in 1834:

> I will not cease to tell my readers that these [philosophy] lessons are only essays and not a formal treatise. I am not publishing them as an expression of my philosophical beliefs, but rather as mere opinions. Of all the assertions contained in this book, I only consider as uncontestable truths those having to do with the spirituality, liberty, and immortality of the soul, and those referring to the existence of God and his principal attributes.[49]

By 1837, Marín was a troubled man who found it necessary to leave his teaching obligations at IN. In 1839, he was lost to insanity. He was only able to resume his philosophical work twenty years later.[50]

PHILOSOPHY AND THE UNIVERSITY OF CHILE

Philosophy textbooks up to Marín's departure from IN had been guided by the dual purpose of teaching the discipline to young students and of addressing the problems of lay thought in a Catholic environment. This continued to be the case with the next major philosophy textbook, written by Ramón Briseño (1814–1910) and published in two volumes in 1845 and 1846 under the title of *Curso de filosofía moderna.*[51] Previous philosophy texts had been guided by the authors' own assessment of the educationally useful and philosophically permissible. In contrast, Ramón Briseño's text appeared at a time when an entire apparatus had been devised to scrutinize and discuss textbooks for the discipline before their approval or rejection for teaching: the UCH and its Faculty of Philosophy and Humanities.[52]

The creation of the UCH came shortly after the closing of the one-century-old University of San Felipe in 1839. The decision was made as a result of a conflict between Manuel Montt, then rector of IN, and Juan Francisco Meneses, rector of the University of San Felipe, over the validity of examinations for graduation. According to an 1823 decree, only graduates of IN were eligible for university degrees. But the rector and the faculty of San Felipe University ignored the regulations and granted degrees to students of other educational establishments.[53] The conflict presented the government with a golden opportunity to close once and for all the colonial university and to create its own. The faculty of the University of San Felipe, all clergymen, staged a protest, but the church was unwilling to support them to the point of precipitating a conflict with the government. The recent victory in the war against the Peru-Bolivian Confederation (1837–39), which put the government in a strong political position, no doubt stymied the church's desire to pursue the issue.

The government commissioned Andrés Bello to write the statutes of the new institution and appointed him rector when the university opened in 1843. Much has been written about Bello's role in the conception and creation of the UCH that need not be repeated here. There is even a conventional wisdom which suggests that Bello modeled the university after the Imperial University in France, placing the institution under the strong aegis of the state.[54] However valid this perspective may be, significant dimensions have been overlooked, particularly the church-state conflict that led to the creation of the university and the philosophical underpinnings of Bello's conception of higher education. These two dimensions are interrelated, as Bello put to use his philosophical expertise to provide a rationale for soothing the wounds of minor, but continuous, skirmishes between church and state over educational issues.

Bello received his first philosophical training from Rafael Escalona at the University of Caracas, where he earned his bachelor's degree in philosophy in 1800. He expressed an early interest in British philosophy and even translated Locke's *Essay Concerning Human Understanding* into Spanish between 1802 and 1807.[55] His departure for England in 1810 provided him with an opportunity to travel "todos los caminos de la filosofía inglesa," as Mariano Picón Salas has put it.[56] In the following nineteen years, he developed his philosophical views under the influence of the leading Scottish philosophers of the period. Bello worked for James Mill in editing Jeremy Bentham's papers, but philosophically he stood closer to Thomas Reid, Dugald Stewart, and Thomas Brown. These central figures of Scottish philosophy saw no contradiction between their religiosity and their highly analytical approach to psychology, epistemology and metaphysics.[57] This may have drawn the devout Bello closer to Scottish Common Sense philosophy, but he followed Scottish philosophers closely in other areas as well, particularly in education.

As mentioned above, Bello's master philosophical work, the *Filosofía del entendimiento,* appeared posthumously. Parts of it, however, had been published in the 1840s.[58] He had also published earlier works that made his philosophical position known to his contemporaries.[59] But in his *Filosofía,* he treated more systematically the tenets of the Common Sense school if only to by and large agree with Reid, Stewart, and Brown on the most specialized elements of the discipline. Following these philosophers, he considered the study of the human mind to be of utmost importance and devoted more than half of his study to "Mental Psychology," that is, the focus on the mind that engaged much philosophical concern both in Scotland and France. He devoted the second half of the book to logic, a subject that in his view provided an effective guide for the mind. The very field of philosophy, for him, consisted in "the knowledge of the human mind and the adequate guidance of its actions."[60]

Bello's position in the context of European philosophy and the subjects that he believed to be most relevant for the discipline proved to be extremely influential in Chilean philosophical circles. This was due to the creation and character of the UCH, where Bello wielded enough power to regulate the development of the field. His preference for the Scottish school of Common Sense, which was after all one strand among many in the complex philosophical panorama of the period, reveals that Bello believed in the applicability of this school well beyond philosophy. He knew through his contacts in London, where he frequented the *Edinburgh Review* circle, that Scottish philosophical thinking devoted a great deal of attention to educational issues.[61]

The philosophers of the Scottish Enlightenment dominated church and university during the late eighteenth and early nineteenth century. They found in these institutions the best means for disseminating their own values of moderation.[62] Besides specific points of philosophical agreement with Reid, Stewart, and Brown, Bello followed their emphasis on the philosophical foundations of educational institutions.[63] He had no way of knowing that three decades after his arrival in London he would be entrusted with the creation of one such institution in Chile.

The creation of the UCH afforded Bello the opportunity to apply his philosophical ideas. In his carefully crafted inaugural speech before the university, he did not fail to give recognition to his Scottish mentors when he suggested that the cultivation of letters and sciences had a profound political and moral influence on society.[64] The very task of civilization rested, he said, on the dissemination of morality in society through education. And morality, he made it clear, could not be separated from religion. Bello knew from his Scottish models that the most advanced scientific and literary achievements need not be incompatible with religion.[65]

It may seem odd that Bello would place such strong emphasis on religion and morality in the creation of a government-sponsored, secular institution. Scottish universities did not have the same connection with the state that Bello's UCH had just established, and in that sense the two university systems were fundamentally different. Bello, however, was not interested in carbon-copying either Scottish or French institutions, but rather taking from both those elements he thought most appropriate for Chile: a national, centralized structure as in French institutions, guided by a strong moral orientation, like the Scottish ones. In this latter sense, Bello was adhering to one of the fundamental aspects of the Scottish Enlightenment; that is, the moralizing potential of higher education. In addition, he was sincerely, but also deliberately emphasizing such principles to repair the damage inflicted upon the church with the recent closing of the University of San Felipe. Philosophy served him well in this respect by providing him with a rationale for the marriage between science and religion. It also helped him to establish a parallel between the aims of the discipline and those of the university: the development of reason.

Bello thought it important to use philosophy to define the aims of the UCH. He was appealing in this way to the authority of a discipline that enjoyed significant prestige in the country. Many public officials listening to his inaugural speech, including cabinet minister Manuel Montt and congressman Antonio Varas, had not only been schooled in the discipline, but had also distinguished themselves as philosophy professors and students at IN.

Another element of particular relevance for understanding the subsequent development of both philosophy and the university was his defense of academic specialization. "The university," he said in his speech, "would not be worthy of a place among our social institutions if the cultivation of both sciences and letters could in any way be viewed as dangerous from a moral or a political standpoint."[66] Until his death in 1865, Bello made strenuous efforts to keep the university aloof from political and religious conflict. Bello was far from being an apolitical man, and in fact he distinguished himself for his long record of political service to the nation. But he understood his university mandate to be separate from political commitments. Still, he was criticized for turning the university into an arm of the state and for subjecting the institution to the political whims of the government.[67]

To aid him in the implementation of his views on higher education, Bello devised mechanisms that various scholars, as noted above, have correctly identified as French in origin. These include the University's supervision of the entire educational system and the division of the institution into five faculties charged with the development of their respective fields.[68] Indicative, however, of his own interest in balancing the learning of science and religion was the creation of a Faculty of Theology. He hired all the former professors of the University of San Felipe to staff this faculty. In addition, he gave particular importance to the Faculty of Philosophy and Humanities (FFH). He charged FFH with supervising primary education, monitoring the teaching of philosophy and humanities in the secondary schools, and examining textbooks.

It was in this context that Briseño's *Curso de filosofía moderna* appeared in the mid-1840s. Briseño had been, as mentioned above, a student of Marín as well as his substitute at IN. When Antonio Varas was appointed to Marín's chair, Briseño taught philosophy at other schools, such as the respected Colegio de Romo and the Colegio de Zapata. He was later hired, in 1840, as professor of ecclesiastical law at IN, and in 1845 he succeeded Antonio Varas as chair of the philosophy course. By the time of this latter appointment, Briseño was an experienced teacher and, soon, a member of the Faculty of Philosophy and Humanities of the UCH.

Philosophically, and as a student of Marín also trained at the Seminary, Briseño had a marked tendency to emphasize the most spiritual and theologically acceptable aspects of philosophy. The second volume of his *Curso,* for instance, was devoted to ethics and the philosophy of law, but was primarily concerned with God and the duties of man to him. In Briseño's view, the most important of those duties was religion because, "intimately connected as it is to the notion of God, the Lord of the universe, religion is both necessary and indispensable to the happiness of individuals, as well as to the life of society."[69] He saw no conflict between philosophical instruction and the advocacy of religious beliefs. On the contrary, he concluded with M. Rattier that "any philosophy that does not agree with Christianity is false and dangerous."[70] Not only in his philosophical writings but also in his autobiography, Briseño provided clear indications of the depth of his religiosity. Abdón Cifuentes, who was one of his students at the Instituto, described him as a calm man "who would never allow himself to show any irritation toward or before his students."[71]He could, however, become combative when defending and advancing his religious beliefs.[72]

The tremendous philosophical stature of Andrés Bello forced Briseño to make certain concessions. Additionally, the regulations of FFH served to place checks on the militant advocacy of beliefs, be they religious or political.[73] Bello had already proven that he could speak authoritatively on philosophical subjects and reacted soon after

Briseño's text came out with an impressively erudite review. Published in the official paper *El Araucano,* Bello's review contained a major critique of Briseño's discussion of logic.[74] Bello emphasized that logic was for him one of the most important subjects of the discipline and stated that "not all the necessary attention has been given to this part [of philosophy] in our schools, even though this is perhaps one of the very few areas in which philosophical thinking has made an enduring contribution, in addition to providing useful and necessary guides that are destined to last as long as human reason itself."[75]

Briseño, in all fairness, did treat many subjects of logic, but not the kind that Bello advocated. Briseño relied perhaps too heavily on the syllogism, a method of thinking based on deduction. Bello argued that reasoning could also be inductive, particulary scientific reasoning, and expected Briseño to bring his logical exposition up to date. What was clearly in Bello's mind was the relationship between the syllogism, deductive thinking, and scholasticism. He regarded the latter school as "narrow enough to use the syllogism as its only instrument, and lost in abstractions with application to neither the natural nor the social sciences, nor the arts."[76] Bello knew that much progress was being made in scientific methodology thanks to logic and objected to Briseño's reduction of the field to the ancient exercise in deduction.

Even in these arcane areas one can see a reflection of larger differences related to secular versus religious thinking. Briseño's emphasis on deduction demonstrated his adherence to logical procedures that were not only compatible with but also instrumental to Catholic doctrine.[77] Bello was not prepared to criticize Briseño on these grounds, partly because he was a believer himself and partly because it was against his own approach to scholarly criticism. He placed himself in a more detached position, that of an academic, to criticize the work. Still, his criticism was strong. Publicly, in his quinquennial report to the university in 1848, Bello said that Briseño's textbook deserved much credit but that he expected the philosophy professor to give logic its due importance in a second edition. "In the first edition," he stated, "logic does not have the extensive treatment that it deserves. I give great importance to logical studies, and particularly to the inductive method that is so appropriate for the experimental sciences."[78]

Briseño's text and teaching at IN were also criticized later by the son of the rector, Juan Bello, himself a member of the Faculty of Philosophy and Humanities. He found Briseño's book to be inferior to the *Elementos de filosofía* by his predecessor and mentor, Ventura Marín. He even stated that not only the text, but also the philosophy course, "which more than any other should influence the mental development, moral orientation, and punishment of the young is the most sterile and worst directed of all in this respect."[79] Still, it was in the nature of the newly founded University of Chile to provide a platform for such criticisms without threatening the target of the critiques. In fact, the *Curso de filosofía moderna* was approved by FFH and went through several subsequent editions. Briseño, who taught philosophy for more than thirty years, until he also became a victim of a "congestión cerebral," exerted a powerful influence in the development of philosophical studies in spite of the critiques of the no less influential Bellos.

Briseño's philosophical authority was well established by 1848. At that time, he won a substantial victory in a discussion over another philosophy text at FFH. The faculty asked Briseño to translate and evaluate a French textbook by Rattier.[80] José Vicente Bustillos, a member of the Faculty of Physical and Mathematical Sciences, submitted his own translation of the textbook and sought approval for his version. His translation was literal and therefore contained a section on "physiology"; that is, the more empirical study of the mind. Briseño's version eliminated that section and expanded the one on ethics. Bustillos argued forcefully, albeit not convincingly, about the need to provide an empirical basis for teaching philosophy to secondary school students.

Clearly, given the choice between a scientific and a moral educational emphasis, the faculty did not hesitate to take the latter. Approval went to Briseño's version and soon after he was commissioned to prepare a program for philosophy teaching and examinations. In the 1848 proposal, Briseño included the subjects of psychology, logic, ethics, history of philosophy, and the philosophy of law, which had all been covered, albeit under a different arrangement, in the philosophy course since the 1830s. But he added a section on theodicy that extended the already religiously oriented section on ethics.[81] Again, Briseño's proposal was approved by both the faculty and Bello himself, and his program was recommended for adoption in all the schools of the republic.[82] Henceforth, Briseño's name appeared consistently in every major discussion concerning philosophy at FFH, his word being among the most authoritative, if not final.

However influential in the teaching and practice of the discipline in Chile, Briseño's philosophical stature was dimmed by Andrés Bello's. As noted by Feliú Cruz, Briseño was not a philosopher, but rather "a practitioner of the teaching of philosophy."[83] Due to his remarkable longevity (he lived to be ninety-six), he was a member of FFH for sixty-four years and served for thirty-seven as secretary of the institution. This presence and continuity gave him tremendous leverage when discussions turned to philosophy, his preferred field. At times, his views ran counter to Bello's, particularly in regard to the place of religion in philosophy. Nevertheless, Bello ultimately set the pace of philosophical developments through his quinquennial reports, his reviews, his students, his erudite writings, and, not the least, the influence of his office over fundamental decisions on the teaching of philosophy.[84] In the end, Bello's philosophical views and educational designs were dominant because he enjoyed the strong support of the government. His rationale for integrating secular and religious views without conflict was agreeable to a government that was cautious in its dealings with the Catholic church. By advancing a philosophy that was not antagonistic, but rather conciliatory, Bello established the basis of and gave credibility to an institution that paid respect to Catholicism and yet secured strong government control over education.

CHILE'S ENGAGÉ PHILOSOPHERS

Ramón Briseño knew how to play the rules of the newly established UCH and used the institution's influence on secondary education to promote a view of the discipline that was friendly to Catholicism. This ability made Briseño an important opponent to Bello's more moderate philosophical approach. He was not alone, as a number of other intellectuals during the 1840s and 1850s put forth views of the discipline that also challenged Bello's academic approach in fundamental ways.

These intellectuals no longer felt the need, as their predecessors had, to address delicate religious matters with oblique philosophical language. They attempted to give a more political character to philosophy partly as a response to the creation of the UCH, which gave increasing emphasis to specialization. In particular, they shunned philosophical specialization in order to refer more explicitly to the religious issue. During the 1840s, the government of Manuel Bulnes accelerated the pace of secularization of society. To the dismay of the Catholic hierarchy, the government allowed Protestant services to be held in the city of Valparaíso, despite the fact that the Constitution of 1833 prohibited it. Catholics founded the *Revista Católica* in 1843 in order to present their position on political matters and defend the church against the critiques of liberals who took advantage of the more tolerant political climate of the Bulnes administration. Because of the polarization that resulted, an unusual amount of intellectual activity focused specifically on religious questions.

Two intellectuals who achieved prominence in this regard were José Victorino Lastarria (1817–1888) and Francisco Bilbao (1823–1865), both former students of Andrés Bello but heirs of a Chilean liberal tradition that was antagonistic to Catholicism and to Bello himself. The work of Lastarria and Bilbao cuts across a wide range of disciplines, but it is in the context of philosophical developments that their famous critique of Catholicism in the 1840s can be best understood; namely, as a reaction to the increasing specialization of the discipline and as an attempt to put philosophy in the service of political positions.[85]

Neither Lastarria nor Bilbao were professors of philosophy, let alone philosophers, but their interest in the field as well as their writings reveal a clear sense of what they expected from the discipline. Both wanted it to help, if not precipitate, the transformation of Chilean society, whose ills they identified as stemming from centuries of Catholic domination. Lastarria had enough prestige and influence to carry his views to the full academic body of the University of Chile, criticizing Catholicism in the name of a "philosophical history" which he expounded in an essay titled "Investigaciones sobre la influencia social de la conquista y del sistema colonial de los españoles en Chile."[86] This presentation prompted a quick response from Andrés Bello, who handled the matter in a way that is indicative of the usefulness of the UCH for avoiding conflict over the sensitive religious issue. He criticized Lastarria's presentation as contrary to the university statutes, which required the promotion of research based on primary sources rather than interpretation, much less philosophical interpretation, of historical events. This permitted Bello to sidestep the issues raised by Lastarria, and focus instead on less sensitive procedural matters.[87]

Bilbao's own attack on Catholicism, also made in the name of philosophy, caused more damage to his own credibility than to the conception of philosophy emerging from the UCH. Accused of blasphemy and expelled from the Instituto Nacional as a result of his publishing the *Sociabilidad chilena* in 1844, the tragic Bilbao began a wandering life between Latin America and Europe, particularly France, where he became a disciple of the ultramontane Félicité de Lamennais. Although Bilbao achieved some intellectual prominence, he did not manage to influence philosophical developments in an enduring way except to the extent that he represented a current of thinking that claimed a philosophical basis and which was clearly opposed to Bello's.[88]

The same can be said of two outstanding Argentine intellectuals living in Chile in the 1840s and 1850s: Domingo Faustino Sarmiento (1811–1888) and Juan Bautista Alberdi (1810–1884). Their work by no means focused on philosophy alone, yet they emerged from a liberal philosophical tradition and used philosophical arguments to criticize Catholicism and to legitimize their political views. Alberdi, more than Sarmiento, demonstrated a relatively sophisticated philosophical background, and was particularly sensitive to the discipline's potential for advancing political ideas. In his "Ideas para presidir la confección del curso de filosofía contemporánea" (1842), he revealed a keen perception of philosophical developments well beyond Chile. He identified Scottish philosophy as having a significant presence in the continent, but suggested that there was "nothing less appropriate to initiate the tender intelligences of South America in the problems of philosophy than the Northern European spirit and forms of thought."[89] He found them too abstract, and advocated instead a philosophy that not only addressed but also advanced national cultural, social, and political interests.

Alberdi's attitude of bringing philosophical views into politics was characteristic of the engagé philosophers, and many did indeed achieve prominent political positions. Alberdi became the architect of the 1853 Constitution that ruled Argentina for almost a century. Lastarria was a leader of the Liberal party, a congressman, diplomat and cabinet minister. Sarmiento was also a diplomat and later president of Argentina. Even Bilbao attained some political prominence through his involvement in the *Sociedad de la Igualdad* during the ill-fated upheaval of 1851 in Chile. What characterized these men was their view of the discipline as essentially political and their determination to use it for practical purposes such as countering the social influence of the Catholic church. This view did not enjoy much favor among members of the emerging philosophical profession in Chile's schools, but it was significant enough to be espoused by many of the country's leading intellectuals, and also to produce some substantive pieces of writing that stood in sharp contrast to those of their more academically inclined counterparts.

It should be kept in mind that the conflict between differing philosophical views was not as belligerent as it may seem on the surface. It took place within a small elite of intellectuals who had much in common, including family ties, and who were in addition colleagues in the same educational institution or functionaries of the same government. Lastarria and Sarmiento were both members of the Faculty of Philosophy and Humanities, and sat together with Andrés Bello and Ramón Briseño in numerous policy-making meetings. Alberdi was a graduate of the UCH and a friend of Bello. Even the radical and passionate Bilbao exchanged affectionate letters with Bello, who, in spite of critiques against his political views, was widely recognized as the leading intellectual figure of the period.

Still, their fundamental philosophical positions remained unchanged, and their points of contention were to recur subsequently, as will be seen in the following chapters. The UCH allowed representatives of conflicting views to coexist, and cultivated a brand of philosophical activity that was neither overtly political nor overtly religious. It did so by keeping tight control, closely supervised by Bello, over the adoption of philosophy textbooks and the philosophy curriculum for secondary schools. The one tendency that Bello could not and would not oppose forcefully was the religiously inclined. This accounts for the influence of Briseño, whose philosophy program and *Curso* were in use for much of the nineteenth century. Still, Andrés Bello made certain that Briseño's, or anyone else's, textbook maintained a level of academic rigor which in this case meant a greater emphasis on logical matters.

Andrés Bello's view of philosophy was the most successful, but his success cannot be explained on philosophical grounds alone. He kept not only the discipline of philosophy but also the University of Chile away from partisan politics, and in this endeavor he received the strong and continued endorsement of the state. For as long as he was at the helm of the institution, his contenders had no choice but to recognize, although they did so willingly, that Bello had devised the most effective mechanism for guiding the development of the discipline in an apolitical direction.

The mechanism consisted of placing philosophical discussions under the control of the FFH, whose members had previously pledged to honor the academic inspiration of the institution and who guarded the university from conflict with the Catholic church.[90] They could espouse whatever positions they wished, and indeed they did so quite vocally outside the UCH. But when they came together as a group within the institution, there existed a fundamental consensus on the procedures for the conduct of academic pursuits. Highly symbolic in this regard is the nomination in 1860 of Ventura Marín, now recovered from his mental breakdown, as a member of the Faculty of Philosophy and Humanities. Representatives of such diverse views as Lastarria, Briseño, and Bello all paid tribute to this pioneer of Chilean philosophy and unanimously voted for his incorporation as a member of FFH.[91] In this fashion they recognized the UCH as the true home of philosophical studies and agreed on its most distinguished representatives. Bello himself made certain concessions for the sake of cultivating a university-based Chilean philosophical tradition, such as accepting the incorporation of José Joaquín de Mora, the mentor of many liberals and his opponent in the 1820s, as honorary member of the faculty in 1860.[92] He also allowed a certain degree of religious advocacy in philosophical matters through his blessing of the work of Briseño and Marín. But by this time philosophy was already established as an academic field at the UCH, it was safe from overt political and religious conflict, and the Faculty of Philosophy and Humanities maintained effective control over the cultivation and teaching of the discipline throughout the nation.

The academic view of philosophy prevailed over the political and religious due to the increasing importance of the UCH. Had it not been for the strong government support for this institution, intellectual discussions, especially philosophical ones, would have been primarily the province of political groups. Bello succeeded in creating an institution of higher learning that was above political squabbles to the extent possible under strong governmental supervision. The consolidation of the institution entailed the depoliticization of the academic disciplines. Philosophy became the locus, and perhaps even the proof, that such depoliticization was indeed possible. Andrés Bello, who devoted substantial attention to philosophical studies, proved this with his highly specialized *Filosofía del entendimiento*.

The philosophers of the political orientation responded to this type of academic specialization with a view of the discipline that advocated a direct connection between philosophical pursuits and politics. The more radical among them were less interested in making an impact on academe than they were in influencing society, and therefore renounced control over Chile's burgeoning higher education institution. Bello thus dominated the field as well as the many other disciplines in which he was equally competent. But his control was closely related to the government's determination, particularly during the administrations of Manuel Bulnes and Manuel Montt, to make the UCH the premier higher education institution in the country. Even so, Bello found mighty opponents among the engagé philosophers and the more confessionally inclined. Politically inspired philosophy, it became clear, represented a strong current of thought in Chile. It was not seen, however, as an academic endeavor at a time when academic credibility was rapidly becoming a standard for the discipline. Chilean intellectual life had, in this regard, changed dramatically because of the creation and consolidation of the University of Chile.

II

THE ERA OF POSITIVISM

1870–1920

The University of Chile concentrated a great deal of talent as well as influence over the country's culture, education, and politics. Intellectual life in Chile, however, also thrived beyond the university. This was particularly the case with the arrival of positivist ideas, which provided intellectuals with a new set of arguments to, on the one hand, oppose the cultural influence of the Catholic church and, on the other, promote the secularization of society in more radical ways than attempted thus far.

Although positivism initially thrived in small but nevertheless influential intellectual circles outside the university, it was not long before the movement penetrated the University of Chile. This was mainly due to Valentín Letelier, perhaps the most important Chilean positivist, but the success of this school of thought could not have been possible without the efforts of the tireless José Victorino Lastarria, who disseminated the rudiments of positivist ideas with the enthusiasm of a new convert. He was not alone, as many younger intellectuals echoed his ideas and discussed them in such newly founded intellectual circles as the Círculo de Amigos de las Letras, and the Academia de Bellas Letras.

As in other countries in Latin America, particularly Mexico and Brazil, positivism made a strong impact on education and politics. In Cuba, Enrique José Varona revamped the educational system along positivistic lines. Although there are significant national differences in the extent and depth of positivistic influence, this school of thought managed to establish roots in the region mainly because it provided a rationale for attempting to solve some of the key problems confronting society and its intellectuals. In Chile positivism quickly became a part of the ongoing debate on the nature of education, which was in turn an expression of a larger debate on the role of the Catholic church in national life.

THE INTRODUCTION OF POSITIVISM IN CHILE

José Victorino Lastarria was the first Chilean intellectual to publicly acknowledge his adherence to positivism and to disseminate it in liberal circles. He had not managed to influence the University of Chile and its educational bias as much as he wished. The university was firmly established by then and in addition controlled much of the intellectual life and education in the country. It had effectively stripped intellectual activity, at least that which took place within the institution, of overt political positions. Lastarria himself seems to have been partly content with his role at the university, and while he criticized the institution in his writings, he still accepted the position of dean of the Faculty of Philosophy and Humanities (FFH) in 1860. He took part in the regular meetings of the faculty and was active in one of the most important activities of FFH: the supervision of primary education. But he felt limited in his university position and was anxious to use positivism to advance anticlerical positions, something he knew he could not do from an arm of the state such as the UCH.

At the time, there was a sense of urgency in Chilean society concerning the religious question. During the 1870s, the conflict between church and state was no longer a muted one. It had in fact seriously fragmented Chilean politics and society. Liberals had gained ascendancy in government circles, and several measures curtailing the influence of the church had been enacted since the 1840s. In response, the Catholic church became more ideological and intolerant of liberal currents condemned by Pious IX in the *Syllabus of Errors* (1864). The Chilean clergy adhered unconditionally to this and other encyclicals condemning liberal positions and encouraged the creation of militant Catholic circles like the Sociedad de Amigos del País (1865) led by Abdón Cifuentes. Positivism arrived at this time of increasing ideological conflict and added fuel to the fire by espousing anticlerical, antitheological positions.[1]

In his *Recuerdos literarios,* Lastarria mentions that his interest in positivism began when he happened across Comte's work in

1868.[2] He was particularly impressed by the key positivistic notion of "progress," which for Comte means the successive development of society through three kinds of stages: theological, metaphysical, and scientific.[3] Lastarria's use of positivism was at best selective, for while he adhered to the positivist view that the passage from stage to stage of social development was inevitable, he still remained a liberal who defended individual, laissez-faire liberalism. As Thomas Bader has pointed out, this gave way to the awkward combination of "absolutist" positivism, that is, the belief in the necessity of reforming society to reflect "social laws," and the staunch defense of individual liberties characteristic of laissez-faire liberalism.[4] Lastarria was not very concerned about the consistency of his views. Instead, he was satisfied with the ammunition positivism provided him to attack the influence of religion in society. For instance, positivism helped him to conclude that "religious beliefs are no longer dominant; they are now weakened. The traditions that conform the old regime are contrary to social justice because they obstruct the work of freedom and progress, which are the laws of humanity."[5]

The terms "freedom" and "progress" represent Lastarria's adaptation of positivism's "order and progress" and reveal his adherence to liberal principles. He was not an orthodox Comtean by any means, but positivism, used selectively, allowed him to discuss ideas of relevance to the society of his day. Lastarria presented his positivistic views at the foundation of the Círculo de Amigos de las Letras in 1869 and the Academia de Bellas Letras in 1873, where he delivered the inaugural speeches. The Academia, in particular, immediately attracted much attention and was joined by many of the leading and most promising intellectuals and politicians of the time, including future president José Manuel Balmaceda, Guillermo and Manuel Antonio Matta, Gabriel René Moreno, and historians Diego Barros Arana, Benjamín Vicuña Mackenna, and Miguel Luis Amunátegui, among others.[6]

Positivism was certainly an exciting new intellectual import, but the reasons for the Academia's success went beyond mere intellectual curiosity. The year before, education became the locus of mounting tensions between church, state, and the parties that supported them. This happened when the government of Federico Errázuriz Zañartu (1871–1875) appointed Abdón Cifuentes, a staunch Catholic conservative, as minister of education in order to appease conservatives already antagonized by liberal influence on education.

One of Cifuentes's first measures was to force prominent historian Diego Barros Arana out of his position as rector of the Instituto Nacional, on the grounds that Barros Arana was unable to maintain discipline and morality within IN.[7] Clearly, ideological differences and contending conceptions of education were at work. On the one hand, students and friends of Barros Arana believed that the rector had been forced out of his position because of his role in promoting a secular and increasingly scientifically oriented education in the leading secondary school of the nation. On the other hand, Cifuentes was determined to reform the already strong tradition of the *Estado docente,* or government control of national education mainly because that control had fallen into the hands of anticlericals. He issued a law that in effect destroyed the government monopoly over education by allowing private schools, which in Chile meant primarily Catholic schools, to grant degrees recognized by the state. The law eventually led to such confusion and proliferation of degrees that the government was forced to rescind it and remove Cifuentes from his post.[8] Conservatives withdrew from the Errázuriz administration shortly after these events.

At the time of the foundation of the Academia in 1873 there was a great deal of apprehension with respect to the future of the secular, government-controlled education advocated by the liberals. Lastarria and his positivistic views struck a receptive chord in an audience that found anticlericalism supported not only by a distinguished French school of thought but also justified on an allegedly scientific basis. Positivism, as presented by Lastarria, offered not just a forum for the discussion of current national educational problems, but a school of thought that offered a radical departure from the religious thinking that liberals believed to be still powerful in Chile.

Thus, the introduction of positivism in Chile bears the mark of very specific political and educational problems in the late 1860s and early 1870s. Positivism also bears the mark of Lastarria, who found in this school a critical philosophical instrument to attack Catholicism and an appealing notion of "progress" that provided him and others with a forward-looking philosophy that related directly to society. While such social concerns provided Chilean philosophy with an alternative to the more specialized type of philosophical work promoted by the UCH, the notion of "progress" was still abstract and probably unappealing to the larger society that such Chilean positivists as Lastarria intended to serve. There had been, during the second half of the nineteenth century, an impressive increase of railroad tracks, telegraph lines, international trade, and other quantifiable results of industrialization and economic growth. Lastarria's notion of "progress," however, was fundamentally a hypothetical societal development whose main appeal was the elimination of the theological stage in Catholic Chile.

Members of the Faculty of Theology at UCH were also clear that anticlericalism was behind the introduction of positivistic ideas. Catholic thinkers like Guillermo Juan Cárter (1842–1906) were still attacking liberalism in 1878 as an ideology bent on destroying the church. However, they knew that the propounders of positivism were the same liberals of yesteryear. By equating liberalism and freemasonry, the secretive organization to which many Chilean positivists belonged, Cárter sent the message that regardless of their names, Catholics considered liberals and their heirs "una misma cosa."[9] It is significant that these attacks against liberalism were made through and published by the UCH, that is, the institution that best exemplified the state control of education. The government was not threatened by vocal Catholic manifestations against the liberalism that characterized its educational policy, but it was astute enough not to appear as censoring Catholic doctrine. In the climate of the late 1870s, when the government had re-established firm control of the educational system, Catholic protests were symptoms of retreat rather than ascendancy. By 1883, Joaquín Larraín Gandarillas (1822–1897), dean of the Faculty of Theology at UCH, was clearly upset by the growing influence of positivism in the classrooms of the republic and labeled this school as "that sad philosophy that preaches materialism and atheism."[10]

The reason for the Catholic reaction lies as much in the substantial growth of positivistic influence in the country as in the fact that positivists made an effort to transform the curriculum in Chilean schools. Education was the one area that positivists concentrated on the most because, on the one hand, many of their most distinguished followers occupied positions of influence in the educational system, and, on the other, they shared with Catholics the belief that whoever controlled the educational system had a significant say in shaping the values and character of Chilean society.[11]

The positivists' interest in educational matters was consistent with the desire of liberals to advance their anticlerical views and recover some of the ground lost to conservative-clerical forces in the early 1870s. This happened quite soon, as a number of intellectuals who had a specific concern for public education and who were cognizant of positivistic ideas attained positions of influence in the mid-1870s. Miguel Luis Amunátegui, for instance, in his position of Minister of Public Instruction in the Aníbal Pinto administration (1876–1881) gave strong emphasis to the teaching of scientific subjects in secondary schools. Diego Barros Arana, who had already done so during the 1860s at the Instituto Nacional, collaborated closely with Amunátegui in the drawing of the Law of Secondary and Higher Education in 1879, a law which institutionalized the teaching of science.[12] There were many other important educational reforms in the 1879 law, but the emphasis on science was key to the positivists who sought to balance, if not eliminate, the remnants of religious educational content in the Chilean secondary schools.[13]

Initially, positivists used the philosophy of Comte to attack clericalism. Increasingly, however, they turned their attention to education because they thought that what positivism had to contribute in this area would help them in both their short-term interests of attacking the Catholic church politically and in their longer-term interest of reforming society. One indication of strong positivist concern for educational issues came from Juan Enrique Lagarrigue (1852–1927), who declared in 1878 that the best way to diminish the church's influence on society was to develop curricula that would allow Chileans to think for themselves, unaided by Catholic practices. The curriculum he proposed was based fundamentally on the six sciences recommended by Comte, namely, mathematics, astronomy, physics, chemistry, biology and sociology. Only the teaching of science, in his view, could accomplish the unity of ideas that would lead to the progress of society.[14]

As important as the teaching of science for Lagarrigue was the teaching of women. He thought that for as long as women remained the "slaves of religion" the problems of divisiveness in society would continue. "Our school for women teachers today is run by nuns," he stated, "who only know how to preach and pray. These nuns educate our teachers, and the teachers in turn educate the girls who are the future mothers of the new generations. What a pity for progress! What a pity for our country!"[15] Lagarrigue's arguments in this regard were a reflection of steps already being taken by minister Miguel Luis Amunátegui that allowed women to obtain professional degrees and attend technological institutes.[16] The motivation for the reforms, at least initially, was to further undermine the church's influence via the secular education of women.

The Catholic church did not remain impassive before anticlerical attacks. However, its interest in educational issues was stymied by the pressing problems resulting from the death of Archbishop Rafael Valentín Valdivieso in 1878. Exercising colonial *patronato* rights, the government of Aníbal Pinto nominated Francisco de Paula Taforó for the position, who was unacceptable to both Chilean conservatives and members of the clergy. As a result, and despite lobbying from both sides before the Pope, the archbishopric remained vacant until 1887, severely straining the already tense relations between church and state. When Mariano Casanova was finally appointed in 1887, the church was in a position to devote concentrated attention to education. The first moves included the creation of the Pontifical Catholic University in 1888 and the appointment of Joaquín Larraín Gandarillas as rector.

The stated purposes for the establishment of the Catholic University included the integration of the Catholic faith into the educational process and the defense of religious studies from the attacks of state institutions.[17] As Daniel C. Levy has pointed out, the creation of the Catholic University in Chile represented a Catholic alternative to the UCH, the first such challenge to state control over higher education in Latin America.[18] The fledgling university could not compete with the scope, funding, and prestige of the older UCH, although it would in time, so that its initial role was largely symbolic, and even an indication of church defeat in the competition for control of education.[19]

The positivists themselves did not focus exclusively on education, for they viewed positivism in different ways. Juan Enrique Lagarrigue's brother Jorge, for instance, developed an interest in Comte's Religion of Humanity. A trip to Paris in 1876 and acquaintance with followers of the two major positivist currents led by heterodox Emile Littré and orthodox Pierre Laffitte convinced Jorge Lagarrigue (1854–1894) that Comte's Religion of Humanity was not the brainchild of a senile man, as he had come to believe, but was indeed the culmination of his philosophy. Lagarrigue, just as Lastarria and most Chilean positivists, had learned about Comte through Littré, who had repudiated his mentor's religious views. Both Lagarrigue and Lastarria absorbed Littré's condemnation of Comte's later views. Jorge Lagarrigue, in fact, declared in 1875 that Comte had betrayed his own "objective" method and had made the very serious mistake of reversing to "subjectivity," meaning religion, in his last works.[20]

During the course of his stay in Paris, however, Jorge Lagarrigue had a change of heart. In his "Una conversión a la religión de la humanidad" (1879), he declared that he had been deceived by Littré, who prevented him from understanding fully the views of Comte in his later period.[21] It was now his belief that Comte's Religion of Humanity represented the social and political application of the cardinal concepts of the *Cours de Philosophie Positive*. The Religion of Humanity was the climax of Comte's philosophy, in Lagarrigue's view, and not an unwelcome turn. By integrating science and belief, Comte had accomplished a synthesis that could effectively replace theology in general and Catholicism in particular. As he put it, "no religion has ever been able to accomplish the unity [of ideas] as fully as the Religion of Humanity does. This is because no religion can, like [Comte's] integrate into its principal foundation our three main faculties: feelings, intelligence, and action."[22]

Another important reason for Lagarrigue's conversion was his view that religious positivism transcended the merely critical phase and had something to offer in the way of beliefs. He suggested that, despite critiques against it, Catholicism was still strong and would continue to be so for as long as there was no alternative to replace it with, such as a system of beliefs based on science that also provided for the moral well-being of mankind.[23] Some pragmatism may have been at work in Lagarrigue, interested as he was in social order, but there is no doubt that he felt deeply about this. In recounting his formative years at the Instituto Nacional, he recalled that he absorbed many scientific subjects that demolished his belief in Catholicism, "but put nothing in its place." He added that "I was left without certainties, without goals, and without a conception of either the world or humanity."[24] His confidence in positivism was restored through his contact with the Parisian orthodox positivists. Their support and his reading of Comte's later work led him to conclude that without the Religion of Humanity, "there can be nothing stable in our society."[25]

Ironically, the religion Jorge Lagarrigue wanted for all humanity found only a few adherents in Chile. His own brother Juan Enrique joined him in this new belief only after much travail in 1881.[26] Both wrote extensively and could have had a larger influence in the country had it not been for their support of the beleaguered José Manuel Balmaceda administration (1886–1891). Balmaceda was a strong advocate of many of the reforms desired by the positivists, such as secularization of society and state control of education. He was in addition conversant with the doctrine, which he learned at the Academia de Bellas Letras. As president of the republic, and particularly during the latter part of his administration, Balmaceda allegedly acted without much concern for congressional opinion. The Lagarrigue brothers, who condemned parliamentarism and approved of Comte's authoritarian tendencies, cast their lot with the embattled Balmaceda at a time when the president was being opposed for abusing the prerogatives of the executive branch.[27]

The more eclectic positivists like Valentín Letelier became upset by Balmaceda's disregard for congress and his concentration of executive power. Balmaceda's authoritarianism reminded them of Comte's support for Louis Napoleon, which they rejected as strongly as the philosopher's Religion of Humanity. Although certainly advocates of strong government, these Chilean positivists had no stomach for strong individual rulers. Valentín Letelier thus sided with the congressional forces that defeated Balmaceda in the 1891 civil war.[28]

The division among positivists was one of ideas. Ultimately, however, it was their political affiliations and their sides in the civil war that decided which current would carry the day. In this case, it was the positivism of Valentín Letelier that exerted the most powerful influence in the decades to come.

VALENTÍN LETELIER'S POSITIVISM AND GERMANIC INFLUENCES

It is in this general political and intellectual context that Valentín Letelier (1852–1919) developed his thinking and achieved a position of influence that was to leave an impressive mark on Chilean education generally and on philosophy in particular. Letelier studied at the

Instituto Nacional between 1867 and 1871, where Diego Barros Arana took a personal interest in him. As a student of law at the UCH between 1872 and 1875, Letelier witnessed the removal of his mentor from the rectorship of the Instituto by minister Abdón Cifuentes. It was this event as well as the introduction of positivism in the Academia that shaped many of his convictions about public education and philosophy in the future.[29]

After a brief career as a professor of philosophy in the northern mining city of Copiapó, the cradle of the Radical party, Letelier returned to Santiago in 1878 to become a member of congress. He returned at a time when positivists where still debating whether to follow orthodox or heterodox positivism. But they all shared a strong anticlerical commitment as well as an interest in educational reform. The reform of 1879, in particular, represented a major victory for positivist-inclined educators, who managed to institutionalize the teaching of science, and who made religious courses no longer compulsory.[30] Letelier joined the ranks of intellectuals interested in furthering educational change upon his return to Santiago, although at a time of serious confrontations between Chile and its northern neighbors.

Chile became engulfed in the War of the Pacific between 1879 and 1883. The hardships of war delayed the implementation of reforms but did not prevent positivists like Letelier from studying national educational problems and reflecting on the tenets of positivism. By 1882 it was clear that Letelier had chosen to follow heterodox positivism. He and Jorge Lagarrigue were friends who attended the meetings of the Sociedad de la Ilustración, a version of the Academia de Bellas Letras for younger members. Letelier, however, resisted Lagarrigue's invitation to join the Religion of Humanity. An exasperated Lagarrigue reported that he and Letelier met to discuss positivism in Paris in 1882. After a lengthy and disappointing discussion, Lagarrigue concluded that "the revolutionary hydra, plus pride and vanity, have given Letelier a shield of personal infallibility which prevents his conversion."[31]

Letelier's refusal to convert to orthodox positivism did not mean that he rejected the doctrine in its totality. He particularly agreed with the law of the three stages, and believed that education constituted the vehicle for achieving the third and final scientific stage. In 1882 he embarked on a brief foreign service career that took him to

Prussia, where he closely studied the educational system and became an admirer of educational practices in that country. In particular, he viewed with approval the freedom from religious interference that schools enjoyed. For three years he was able to examine the functioning of education at all levels, and he returned convinced that similar practices could be introduced in Chile, particularly in regard to the separation of church and state on educational matters, as well as what he viewed as an integral education, that is, a combination of intellectual and practical elements at all educational levels. Additionally, he thought that teacher training was an important German emphasis that could be brought to Chile. He became a strong advocate of pedagogical training in the country, for he thought that if teachers were provided with positivist values, profound transformations could be brought about in society.[32]

Upon returning to Chile in 1885, the creation of a pedagogical institute became his major concern. He found a receptive audience in the personnel of the newly installed Balmaceda administration. He discussed the project with the minister of public instruction, Pedro Montt, who made Letelier's arguments his own. Despite a favorable reception of the project on the part of influential members of the administration, implementation was delayed by the constant cabinet crises that plagued the Balmaceda government. It was not until 1888 that Minister Federico Puga Borne, a friend of Letelier's, approved the plan and charged the Chilean ambassador in Berlin with the hiring of six German professors to form the teaching corps of the Instituto Pedagógico. Puga himself resigned after a cabinet crisis, but Letelier was lucky and persistent enough to secure the support of yet another minister, Julio Bañados Espinosa. It was Bañados who eventually founded the Instituto Pedagógico (IP) on April 29, 1889.[33]

The IP combined French and German characteristics. It was French to the extent that its students were selected on the basis of merit and provided with scholarships; it was German to the extent that it viewed teaching as a science and was staffed by German professors. Letelier was aware of his use of foreign models and defended his actions by saying that "we did not hire German professors out of any special inclination for the Germanic race, but rather because Germany is the nation that trains the best teachers, and also the nation that is better prepared to respond to our demand for services."[34] He pointed out that French educators had themselves sung the virtues of German pedagogy, and that using the best a country had to offer was not only wise, but also "the only way to take advantage of all cultures."[35]

National realities also influenced the conception of IP, for Letelier was aware that innovation was not always acceptable to older institutions. He was particularly concerned about the Instituto Nacional and the University of Chile, and sought to establish the new school, at least during the early stages, independently from these two institutions. In fact, the strongest opposition to the creation of the Instituto came not from clerical circles, which were at the time occupied with the creation of the Catholic University (1888), but from the Faculty of Philosophy and Humanities at UCH. The faculty questioned the legality of IP, and even though it was its mandate to comment on and approve of the plan of studies, it sat on the proposed curriculum for a year. When it finally turned out its report, the faculty demanded restoration of the teaching of metaphysics and theodicy, subjects that had been ignored in the initial proposal. Much to the regret of IP supporters, they had no choice but to comply.[36]

The reasons for the antagonism of FFH included, according to Letelier, the distrust with which many initiatives of the Balmaceda administration were being received at the time as well as the novelty of IP.[37] Ironically, Letelier was a strong opponent of Balmaceda, but he separated his political convictions from his interest in the establishment of IP, which he knew could not come about without government support. To members of FFH, the Pedagogical Institute was more than a political problem: they felt their fields encroached upon by educators who elevated pedagogy to the category of a science. They were also aware that many teachers felt threatened by the nature and purposes of education at IP, which made no secret of the intentions to revamp secondary school teaching. In time, many Chileans felt unfairly displaced by foreigners whose credentials some deemed questionable.[38]

The government, however, lent strong support to IP and even gave it a university recognition that made its professors full members of FFH. The Institute offered the degree of Profesor de Estado, mainly a certification for secondary school teaching, in different disciplines such as philosophy, mathematics, chemistry, and others. Having attended a government-sponsored educational enterprise, IP graduates were rapidly placed in the national educational system.

This gave important influence to the secular and scientifically inspired graduates whom Letelier hoped would render religious education obsolete in the country. With strong government backing and growth from a handful of students in 1889 to more than a thousand by 1921, the Institute became a complete success.[39] This was no doubt aided by the fact that Letelier, the architect of IP, occupied several key educational positions, including that of rector of the UCH between 1906 and 1911, and was in addition closely associated with other key political figures, including Pedro Montt, president of the republic.

Although political connections certainly helped, the radical educational transformations that took place in the last quarter of the nineteenth century were in large measure due to the influence of positivism and the willingness of Letelier to translate a speculative endeavor such as positivism into a series of measures that placed a strong emphasis on a scientifically inspired and secular education. Positivists put their doctrine to use in guiding educational developments in the country. Letelier, in particular, went beyond that to produce the most detailed account of the influence of positivism on Latin American educational thought with his *Filosofía de la educación,* first written during a prison term in 1891, and substantially expanded by 1912.[40]

In his *Filosofía,* Letelier applied Comte's three-stage theory of historical evolution to education. He structured his work on the basis of a discussion of theological, metaphysical, and scientific models of education, just as Comte had done in relation to society in general. Comte had understood the progress of humanity as successively going through a theological stage, a metaphysical stage, and finally a scientific stage that was the culmination of the process—the stage Comte urged his contemporaries to help bring about. Comte believed that this progress was inevitable and that each stage superseded the other in an ever-increasing degree of universality and rationality.

This Comtean model for understanding society and history could not but appeal to Letelier, who was very aware of the civil confrontations that had torn the country apart in 1830, 1851, 1859, and again in 1891. He thought that the scientific stage, as defined by Comte, provided the foundations for the orderly progress of society in such a way that political conflicts of this nature would not come about. To Letelier, the realization of the scientific stage became a priority, even if in purely intellectual terms. The appeal that this scientific stage had for him was that it rendered obsolete the previous stages in the evolution of humanity, particularly the theological. Traces of this stage were conspicuous, in his view, in the repeated conservative attempts to control the Chilean educational system. Since conservative and clerical forces had already been opposed by liberals with alleged little success, Letelier believed that the adoption of a scientific stage would do by means of reason and education what had not been accomplished by means of political and even armed confrontations.

However anticlerical, Letelier was not any kinder to the liberals. In an effort to fit Chilean reality to his positivistic beliefs, Letelier viewed Chilean liberalism as an expression of the metaphysical stage described by Comte, mainly characterized by anarchy, and guided by abstract and ineffective concepts of liberty. Much of the development of Chilean history after independence from Spain seemed to him to confirm this, particularly in light of the disarray he saw in education and politics.

Since for Letelier these theological and metaphysical forces struggled to prevail on political as well as educational levels, he concentrated on education to launch his positivistic proposals for a reorganization of the educational system. Underlying his interest in education was the belief that this endeavor was essentially social in nature and that it reflected the norms and values of society. The times, which in his judgment badly needed order and progress, demanded an educational program guided by a comprehensive philosophy. Should the educational system be structured by a scientific philosophy, Letelier believed, students would effectively contribute to the development of society.[41]

Science, Letelier thought, could help Chilean society achieve the order and progress that he saw missing in his day. Adhering to the positivistic arrangement of societal stages, Letelier suggested that theology had never accomplished what was most needed at the time: the unity of beliefs. He pointed out that theological truths had failed to appeal to all men and, in addition, that they introduced conflicts of an unresolvable nature in society. Metaphysics, the second stage in Comte's scheme, was equally fallible in Letelier's application to Chile. He indicated that the metaphysical concerns that characterized liberalism produced an eclecticism—meaning a variety of doctrines rather than the specific French school of thought—in educational matters that only confused the minds of the young and introduced rebelliousness and anarchy into the political life of the country.[42]

Only science, he suggested, could bring about much-needed unity to society and provide the basis for the orderly progress of humanity. He pointed out that scientific truths were of such nature that they did not leave much room for the type of debates and controversies on whose basis anarchy thrived. Only science could bring about order due to its ability to resolve problems beyond political and religious discussions.[43]

The concern for "order" was not alien to other Latin American countries, especially Mexico, where Gabino Barreda also envisioned positivism as a doctrine that could bring order to society by first informing the reorganization of the educational system. This concern for social order was key to positivists everywhere in the region who looked for solutions to endemic internecine warfare and economic vulnerability. Despite variances from nation to nation, positivism appealed to intellectuals generally because of the promise of orderly, rational development.[44]

Chile's brand of positivism concentrated on education informed by science as a means for achieving social order. Letelier used this concept of education to attack the educational models that he accused of being inspired by theological and metaphysical beliefs. To demonstrate that science could develop knowledge and enhance national education better than any other system, he relied on Comte's classification of the sciences and suggested that any system of education should follow a process of learning ranging from the "simplest" to the most "complex" sciences.[45] Letelier believed that this Comtean classification of the sciences should be applied to the Chilean educational system, and it did in fact inform his proposal for the implementation of a "concentric" plan of studies that was officially sanctioned in 1889 and put into practice in 1893.[46] Neither theology nor metaphysics, he claimed, could guide education as thoroughly as science could.[47]

Letelier's notion of science was more general than what one would expect from this notion today. The reason for this lies in the form of the scientific stage of humanity as defined by Comte. Science was more of a philosophy than anything else in Comte's system, and Letelier was quite clear about this when he advanced his own proposals for a scientific system of education. He used the term *science* as a guiding philosophy not only in a Comtean sense, but also in a way that approximated Andrés Bello's own usage: a general system that integrated and advanced all branches of human knowledge.

Science served a useful purpose to positivists who believed scientific truths to be uncontestable. Their use of the concept of science was ideological and anticlerical. It was politics, in the end, and not the pristine world of science, that resolved educational issues in favor of the positivists. The reforms of 1879, the establishment of the Instituto Pedagógico in 1889, and the implementation of the "concentric" system for secondary schools in 1893 all succeeded because of strong state support as well as the backing of Liberal and Radical political forces. Valentín Letelier was more than an articulate intellectual in this regard. He was also an influential member of Congress as well as a leader of the Radical party. Moreover, he enjoyed the support and friendship of such powerful political figures as President Pedro Montt. Letelier, to be sure, was not without influential enemies, including the church hierarchy. But ultimately, it was his political support, and in the long run students like future presidents Arturo Alessandri and Pedro Aguirre Cerda, who applied Letelier's educational ideas and made Chilean public education free, obligatory, and secular.

THE IMPACT OF POSITIVISM ON PHILOSOPHICAL STUDIES

It was via education that Letelier was to leave a profound mark on Chilean philosophy. On a theoretical level, his familiarity with positivism as well as his writings on the philosophy of education make him one of the principal philosophers in Latin America during the period. He was also a practical man whose educational reforms had a concrete impact on the teaching and practice of philosophy in the country. Prior to his decisive influence, Chilean philosophy, particularly as taught at the Instituto Nacional, seemed to confirm Letelier's description of the theological stage. Philosophy, especially in the early positivist period, was dominated by the Catholic influence of Ramón Briseño. The discipline, however, soon became engulfed in the conflict between secular and religious views that polarized the society at large.

During the early positivist period, philosophy teaching maintained the traditional emphasis on the subjects of psychology, logic, theodicy, and ethics. Briseño's *Curso de filosofía moderna* was still in use at the time, although in a different format. The two-volume *Curso* was consolidated into one volume in 1854, when philosophy teaching had been reduced by an 1853 decree to one year at the Instituto Nacional. Briseño was very unhappy about the reduction of philosophical studies in the secondary schools, and argued in 1857 that "if there is any area of human knowledge that deserves to be studied in some detail, that is philosophy, for this is a fundamental and abstract science that requires much reflection. More important, because philosophy has a great influence in the course and direction of all our ideas."[48] He was once again successful in his recommendations for the study of the discipline, such as the reinstatement of the two-year curriculum. In 1864, Briseño also edited a new volume of the *Curso* which included the history of philosophy and the philosophy of law.[49]

Despite the changes in both the duration of philosophical studies and the content of the volumes of the *Curso,* Briseño's religious emphasis remained the same. Briseño used direct translations for some sections of his textbooks, but even there he made certain that the authors selected conformed to Catholic doctrine. For instance, the section on the history of philosophy that became part of his 1866 edition of the *Curso* was extracted from a French philosophy manual by Esteban Géruzez. In 1869 Briseño also translated a textbook titled *Nociones de filosofía* by French professor Charles Jourdain for use at the Instituto Nacional. This textbook covered the traditional areas of psychology, logic, ethics, and theodicy, and included a section on the history of philosophy. It was also a Catholic text, but Briseño had no qualms about changing or rebutting those parts that did not conform exactly to Catholic doctrine as he interpreted it. Jourdain defined philosophy as "the science whose object is the rational knowledge of man and God, as well as the means to direct the human spirit to the following supreme ends: truth, beauty and goodness."[50] Briseño could agree with such general statements, especially when affirming God, but was ready to take issue with more minute points such as Jourdain's reference to the notion of divinity as an "innate idea."

> There is no need to resort to the erroneus theory of *innate ideas* to assert that the idea of God comes from God himself. It is a dogma of Catholicism that there was a primitive revelation made to our first parents, and through them, to humanity as a whole. In this revelation God manifested Himself as Author and Supreme Legislator of the Universe . . . This revelation is a *fact,* as Moses shows in the Genesis, and no philosopher can ignore the facts.[51]

Briseño's version of Jourdain's textbook went through a second and a third edition in 1870 and 1882. In his post of secretary of the Faculty of Philosophy and Humanities, Briseño was also in a position to determine the content of the philosophy examinations for the schools of the republic. In 1882 FFH consulted the French philosophy program for secondary schools, which included roughly the same areas of psychology, logic, ethics, theodicy, and history of philosophy, but added political economy.[52] Briseño's program, tailored to reflect the contents of his translation of Jourdain but more pointedly to maintain philosophical concern for religious issues, prevailed and was still in use in 1884.[53]

Briseño was not alone in advancing a religious version of the discipline at a time of positivist ascendancy. In 1872, that is, in the midst of the religious versus secular conflict over education, Ventura Marín published his third edition of the *Elementos de filosofía.* Marín had recovered from his long illness and now felt it necessary to revise his views of 1834 in order to respond to the problems of the day: "to this effect," he wrote, "I have subjected the old textbook to a rigorous revision, purging it of everything that can offend correct thinking and the just devotion of the Catholic reader."[54] He continued to believe in the importance of philosophy, particularly when used to understand religion better, but was upset by the abuses committed in its name: "this reason alone is sufficient for the good Catholic to appreciate the study [of philosophy], and to initiate himself in it with the saintly and commendable purpose of keeping his faith. He may not be able to silence or humble the audacity of the free thinkers, but he will at least manage to keep them at bay."[55] Both Marín and Briseño used philosophy during this time as an ideological weapon to defend Catholicism.

Briseño's model of philosophical studies was firmly entrenched but required defense and support to an extent proportional to the growth of positivist influence. In the 1880s, Joaquín Larraín Gandarillas came out in defense of the traditional division of the field when he suggested that "psychology teaches the young the nature of both the soul and its noblest faculties; logic teaches them to use these faculties righteously and to think correctly in order to achieve knowledge of truth; theodicy tells them what reason knows about God and his attributes; ontology offers them knowledge about the fundamental truths; ethics the rules of behavior; and the history of philosophy presents them with a view of the philosophical schools and systems that have fought for predominance through the centuries."[56] Larraín also defended the connection between religion and philosophy, saying that one could not be taught without the other. The study of philosophy without religion was "not only without much interest and benefit, but also harmful if not lethal."[57]

During the 1880s, Catholic thinkers also concentrated on defending the subordination of philosophy to religion. In a review of Francisco Ginebra's *Elementos de filosofía,* a textbook that refuted positivism, Guillermo Cox Méndez, a Catholic historian and lawyer, argued strongly that "philosophy is . . . nothing but the rational confirmation of theology; the philosophy that is based on this principle is the only true philosophy."[58] Cox thus attempted to respond to positivist currents in Chile while also reflecting some of the new concerns of international Catholicism. During the papacy of Leo XIII (1878–1903), the philosophy of Saint Thomas Aquinas was actively promoted. The encyclical Aeterni Patris (1879) encouraged philosophical investigation guided by Thomistic views.[59] Francisco Ginebra (1839–1907), a Jesuit who taught at the Colegio San Ignacio in Santiago between 1874 and 1899, echoed the papal call by stating that the scholasticism of Thomas Aquinas "is the only doctrine that brings harmony between science and faith, as well as between reason and revelation." More important, the scholastic method "is the best for teaching the young the right habits of disquisition."[60] Similarly, Rafael Fernández Concha (1832–1912), a UCH theology professor, congressman, and later bishop, advanced Thomistic doctrine in his writings on the philosophy of law. His *Filosofía del derecho o derecho natural,* in particular, went through several editions and was used by law students at the Catholic University for several decades.[61]

Positivists, however, were gaining considerable ground on the contents and methods of teaching. An early positivist critique of the model of philosophical teaching came from Juan Enrique Lagarrigue in 1878, when he wrote about the current secondary school philosophy program and stated that "various philosophical systems since Thales' time are reviewed, but they are judged according to a totally superficial criterion. The notions of psychology, logic and ethics that are taught are completely erroneous. Nothing is said about the true philosophy, nor about its history, nor about the effective progress of the human spirit."[62] The alleged lack of connection among subjects of the discipline as well as its lack of concern for science provided the grounds for positivist critiques and action. In 1886, the year that Ramón Briseño retired from his lengthy tenure as philosophy professor at IN, provisions where made for the teaching of scientific subjects under the rubric of "natural philosophy."[63]

Valentín Letelier delivered the most devastating blows against the religiously motivated study of philosophy in Chilean secondary schools. In his *Filosofía de la educación,* Letelier devoted ample attention to the twin and interrelated subjects of the rejection of metaphysics and the cultivation of logic. He rejected metaphysics primarily because "its most precious achievements are mere collections of disputes and either conventional or obscure definitions of unknowable matters whose very existence is a subject of additional doubts and denials."[64] His basic contention with metaphysics was related to the view, which he shared with Comte, that metaphysics and science were incompatible, and that anything worth knowing could be known scientifically. The teaching of both theodicy and metaphysics, he suggested, were "less able to unite than to disperse the human spirit and less able to discipline than bring anarchy to it."[65] This in turn had, in his view, important implications for society, as a metaphysically based education was sure to bring confusion to the mind, and confusion was unlikely to provide a strong foundation for social order.

Logic was for him the most important philosophical subject. "Logic constitutes," he stated, "the complement of all other studies because it is a science designed to perfect, relate, and systematize them."[66] Logic became part of the curriculum for secondary education that he proposed in 1889, replacing the philosophy course that was part of the curriculum introduced by the 1879 reform. By the time of the adoption of the plan in 1893, the title of the course was changed back to philosophy, but was primarily for the teaching of logical topics.[67]

The introduction of an increased logical emphasis, as suggested by Letelier in his *Filosofía,* was not an easy task. In effect, he recalled that in 1888, "when the Council on Public Instruction [of the Ministry of Education] discussed the concentric plan of studies, it was necessary to wage a battle between those of us who argued that the philosophy course should concentrate on logic, that is, the philosophy of science, and those who wanted, because of an instinctive and superstitious distrust, to maintain the old amalgam."[68]

The "old amalgam" that he referred to was the division of philosophy prevalent in Chile since the early part of the century, that is, psychology, logic, ethics, theodicy, and the history of philosophy. Letelier felt that although there were some useful aspects to this division, such as the study of psychology and logic, he did not think very highly of the others, and suggested that the diversity of branches in the teaching of philosophy was a sorry reflection of the general state of knowledge in Chile. Calling Chilean philosophy "an unwelcome French transplant," Letelier suggested that the field was "a contrived amalgam of unconnected disciplines. Metaphysics, psychology, ethics, logic, theodicy, and the history of philosophy are lumped together despite their having no more of a connection among themselves than they have with heraldry or numismatics. To fulfill his duties, the teacher must change subjects four or five times a year, and students are forced to do likewise."[69]

It was nothing short of a victory when, in 1893, Letelier managed to restructure the teaching of philosophy to give increased emphasis to logic and successfully recommended the adoption of a textbook on logic by Alexander Bain, a Scott who followed John Stuart Mill and who was a skeptic in religious matters.[70] It was at this time, when secondary education had been reformed and the Instituto Pedagógico had been strongly established, that positivism reached the peak of its influence: philosophy was taught at IP with a scientific character not just for the sake of cultivating knowledge, but to prepare secondary school teachers, who rapidly found jobs in the national educational system and who were invariably committed to advancing the cause of a national, secular education with a heavy practical and scientific emphasis. Additionally, IP faculty members sat at the regular meetings of FFH and therefore had an important say in the design of philosophical teaching in the schools of the republic.

Positivist influence was not confined to Santiago. In Copiapó, where Valentín Letelier started his career as philosophy professor, Juan Serapio Lois (1844–1913) became an influential positivist educator who founded the Augusto Comte School and the paper *El positivista.* Lois had studied at the Instituto Nacional in Santiago in the 1860s and received the influence and support of Diego Barros Arana. A physician by training, Lois chose to devote his life to the teaching of philosophy, and positivism in particular, in Copiapó. It was he who authored the most complete treatise on logic published to date in 1889. His *Elementos de filosofía positiva,* which was approved as a philosophy textbook, contained a massive exposition of Comte's views and application to logic. In addition to a presentation of formal logic, Lois fulfilled Andrés Bello's call for the application of logic to scientific methodology. Bello had done so with respect to physics in his *Filosofía del entendimiento.*[71] Lois extended his analysis to include mathematics, chemistry, and biology and treated sociology and history as social sciences subject to the rules of logic.[72]

Lois's interest in logic and the methodology of sciences was not entirely disinterested. A formidable polemicist and a celebrated anticlerical,[73] Lois immersed himself in logical and scientific studies to demonstrate the shortcomings of theology and metaphysics and also to show that the primary purpose of the field was the coordination and advancement of scientific knowledge.[74] In the context of the 1880s and 1890s, such emphasis on science was explicitly anticlerical. However political the inspiration, Lois's logical endeavors produced a monumental study of logic, the most complete known in Chile and perhaps the continent.

Whether because he was in a distant province or because German professors already in Chile were being favored to occupy university positions, Lois did not achieve the position that some thought he deserved. Fanor Velasco, who was commissioned by the government to investigate charges against Lois for his alleged anticlerical propaganda, paid a surprise visit to his philosophy class in 1902. Velasco was so impressed by Lois's erudition that he declared upon his return that Lois deserved a chair (*cátedra*) in Santiago.[75] Lois did not attain such a position and in effect retired in Copiapó a few years later.

The Instituto Pedagógico became the major locus of the new philosophical tendencies approved by Letelier and the positivists. At IP the German professor in charge of teaching philosophy and pedagogy was Jorge Enrique Schneider (1846–1904). As a former student of biologist Ernest Haeckel and psychologist Wilhelm Wundt, Schneider gave a strong scientific character to the field of philosophy at IP, an emphasis that accorded well with positivism and Letelier's own interest in the discipline.[76] He also emphasized logic, and successfully recommended to the FFH the use of books by Alexander Bain, John Stuart Mill, and Wilhelm Wundt.[77] The philosophy program he designed for secondary schools, which concentrated almost exclusively on logic and the philosophy of science, received official approval in 1893.[78]

Under Schneider's influence, the field of philosophy was brought into the twentieth century deprived of theological and metaphysical contents. Julio Montebruno, one of Schneider's students and later dean of FFH, reported that in the philosophy class the German professor "displayed an impressive knowledge derived from observation and experience. The theories and doctrines of Darwin and Haeckel and the methods of Wundt informed his lectures. Evolution, for him, was not only the key for understanding the universe, but also the norm for guiding human activity. Hence, he indicated that progress and perfection were the objects of life. And to guide us through the philosophical labyrinth, he used experimental psychology as a lantern."[79]

Others did not think that Schneider and the German professors in general were as learned or even as qualified as IP supporters claimed. Eduardo de la Barra (1893–1900), for instance, wrote a powerful critique of the "Germanization" of Chile as well as an exposé of the German professors whom he described as arrogant and contemptuous of things Chilean.[80] A member of the Radical party, De la Barra was not exactly an enemy of public education, nor a conservative defending the church's educational philosophy. On the contrary, De la Barra enjoyed significant prestige as a liberal educator who had taught at the Instituto Nacional and the Liceo de Valparaíso and had written defenses of Francisco Bilbao and the secularization of cemeteries.[81] Regarding the Germanic reforms, however, he felt strongly that they were unnecessary and too expensive for a country like Chile.

De la Barra considered Schneider to be the most respectable of the Germans but suggested that his contributions to pedagogy and philosophy were modest. On the one hand, he indicated, Schneider's pedagogical efforts were not new in Chile, where concern for teacher training went back to the 1840s. On the other hand, Schneider's philosophy consisted basically of a reduction of the discipline to experimental psychology. "In Schneider's sensualistic philosophy," he wrote, "everything comes down to responses of the nervous system to stimuli." As a result, "the fragments of philosophy that students absorb [at IP] will only lead them into a sea of confusion."[82]

Despite the critiques of De la Barra, experimental psychology remained the main focus of philosophy work at IP even beyond Schneider's death in 1904, when he was succeeded by another German, Wilhelm Mann (1874–1948). A full-fledged laboratory of experimental psychology was established at the UCH in 1908, and Mann devoted a great deal of his time to measuring and testing the cognitive capabilities of children. Later, however, Mann developed an interest in philosophy along the nonpositivist lines that heralded the changes that would come about in the field during his own tenure, which spanned through 1918. He criticized positivism, for instance, as he felt that this school reduced human knowledge to pure experience. He suggested that men generally, and Chileans in particular, strived for knowledge beyond the merely material in search for more intangible but no less significant absolute truths. On this account, he thought that the study of metaphysics was justified, particularly if subordinated to the subfields of logic and psychology, and he even taught a course on the German philosopher Fichte in 1917.[83]

Still, the field of philosophy during the positivist era was dominated by the scientific and educational character given to the discipline by influential reformers like Valentín Letelier. Philosophy, particularly after the 1893 reforms and the creation of IP, did not distinguish itself for its creativity, as practitioners of the field devoted their efforts almost exclusively to teaching or applied research. Letelier's own philosophical talents were displaced by an active career in politics, education, and law. But this did not mean that philosophy faded away. On the contrary, it achieved a strong position at the university that allowed its faculty to not only regulate the development of the field through the supervisory means instituted by the UCH but also to actively participate in the training, guided by positivist ideals, of secondary school teachers. Logic and philosophy of science flourished at the time, as did the emphasis on the experimental psychology cultivated by Schneider and Mann. But the neglect of metaphysics eventually helped bring about a new era of philosophical concerns. Theology, to use the positivists' terminology, lost a great deal of influence on national education mainly because of the successful secularization of society, but metaphysics still had an important appeal to Chileans who were not convinced that positivism had the final word on either the field or on education.

From its early beginnings in the 1860s until its demise in the 1910s, Chilean positivism was guided by a strong anticlerical inspiration. Positivists first used the doctrine of Auguste Comte to attack the church, but soon concentrated their efforts on establishing a foothold in the educational system. Their success in this area was impressive, although the Catholic church and its intellectuals defended themselves eloquently and eventually established the Pontifical Catholic University to compete with the UCH.

Chilean positivists were selective in their adoption of Comtean views, their main source of inspiration. The orthodox branch of positivism received some attention from outstanding intellectuals but, partly for political reasons, it did not acquire the stature of heterodox positivism. Because of the changing circumstances of church and state relations, Chilean intellectuals required a doctrine that allowed them the flexibility to pick and choose the thinkers and views that served them well at any particular moment. As a result, Chilean positivism was never a coherent body of ideas, although the issues of anticlericalism, education, and science remained central throughout its period of influence.

Compared to other countries in Latin America, Chilean positivism revolved around Comte more than any other thinker. The evolutionism that came to be so closely associated with positivism elsewhere was rarely discussed in Chile. This is so because during the last quarter of the nineteenth century Chile was almost completely absorbed by the struggles of church and state. Similarly, Chilean positivism was not as closely related to authoritarian government as in Mexico. Quite to the contrary, it served as an instrument to attack the strong executive power established by Diego Portales. Surely, and particularly in connection with education, positivism became a rationale for social order and control, yet not to the point of advocating the strong rule of any particular individual. With the exception of the ill-fated effort of the Lagarrigues, mainstream Chilean positivism did not attempt to furnish a justification for authoritarian government.

Just as during the previous liberal era, proponents of positivism and Catholicism fought openly in the Chilean press and in the specialized clubs, societies, and periodicals of Santiago and other urban centers. They also fought within the schools through philosophy textbooks and curriculum changes. Philosophy textbooks, however specialized and sophisticated, sought to address, if not take sides with, the competing intellectual currents of Catholicism and positivism. This competition provided philosophy with a privileged position, for intellectuals came to recognize the field's reservoir of arguments, historical lessons, and potential for appealing to the mind of the young. With two years of obligatory philosophy courses in the secondary schools, the young were an appealing captive audience indeed. Intellectuals also used philosophy to advocate educational and even social models. Positivism, with its rejection of religion and metaphysics and advocacy of science, succeeded in revamping the educational system and expected society to follow suit. Philosophy, however, was not exclusively functional: it allowed for the development of specialized knowledge, particularly in the area of logic.

The decline of positivism was ultimately due to the declining urgency of the religious question. At the turn of the century, secularly inclined educators were firmly in control, and the state had established an equally firm foothold in areas of traditional church dominance. With their own Catholic University to look after, conservatives and clergy became less active except for occasional outbursts directed against individuals. As a result, the positivist philosophy that dominated the UCH and philosophers in general were lacking the sort of central national issue that they had become accustomed to discussing. The field stagnated, a victim of its own success in the long and often painful struggle for secularization.

III

THE FOUNDERS OF CHILEAN PHILOSOPHY

1920–1950

Positivism was the most pervasive philosophical movement in Latin America during the last quarter of the nineteenth century and the first two decades of the twentieth. By virtue of this extended influence over the entire region, the response against it was also of continental scope. Latin American intellectuals became aware of French critiques against positivism and particularly of the work of Henri Bergson. They also became disappointed with the movement's largely unfulfilled agenda for progress. But it was the degree to which positivism became imbedded in national political affairs that accounts for the strong reaction against it that characterized countries like Mexico. Based on these multiple factors, the intellectuals who led the antipositivist reaction ushered in a new era of philosophical activity, and have thus received the name of founders (*fundadores*) of Latin American philosophy.[1]

In Chile, philosophers also reacted against positivism but in a fashion that was similar to the reaction that took place in Argentina. Across the Andes, the positivist movement was appreciated for its educational contributions, and positivists themselves encouraged the discussion of nonpositivist currents.[2] With the exception of ever more infrequent Catholic attacks, Chile, like Argentina, was devoid of strident condemnations of positivist thought, although intellectuals distanced themselves from the doctrine just the same. Due to the decline of church-state ideological disputes, Chilean intellectuals directed their attention to other schools of thought and examined more closely the principles of positivism itself. The result was a gradual abandonment of interest in the doctrine, encouraged in many instances by those who had propounded it in the past. Officials of the UCH opened the doors of the institution to the discussion of non-, and even anti-positivist currents. The cradle of positivistic influence, the Instituto Pedagógico (IP), graduated intellectuals who criticized the doctrine while recognizing its major contributions to the country.

This mild, by continental standards, rebellion against positivism took place in an educational context. It was also formulated from within the state-controlled UCH. The reaction thus took the form of a philosophical as well as an educational critique. Philosophy became the vehicle for such a critique because many believed that educational policy was based on philosophical premises. As a result, new educational models were advanced, particularly for higher education, not surprisingly by philosophers who had inherited from the positivists the conviction that there should be a guiding philosophy for the entire educational system. Unlike the positivists, they denied that such a philosophy should be inspired by science and in fact criticized what they perceived to be the stifling effects of scientism.[3]

Perhaps not as a result of, but certainly in conjunction with, the demise of positivism, philosophers during the period effected a significant development that took philosophy beyond the classroom. For most of the nineteenth century as well as early parts of the twentieth, philosophers limited their philosophical production to the writing of textbooks for secondary school use. There were exceptions, of course, such as Bello's *Filosofía del entendimiento* and Letelier's *Filosofía de la educación*. But the twentieth-century philosopher began to write books that, despite their speculative nature, were intended for a wider audience. To some extent this was due to the very nature of the antipositivist reaction, which moved emphasis away from the specialized concerns of logic and philosophy of science to the more accessible subjects of man, values, freedom, and creativity. But to an even larger extent, the transition from textbook- to essay-oriented writing was due to the philosophers' preoccupation with politics. Their interest in politics did not necessarily entail social or partisan commitments. Rather, they understood that politics allowed them to find a place in society without involving themselves in the often convoluted workings of Chilean democracy. They had inherited from positivism a strong and sincere concern for education, which was one of the most controversial political issues of the nineteenth century. But they had greater ambitions in the twentieth: they saw themselves as the mentors of a new Chilean society, one that was at once more spiritual and whose culture would be informed by philosophical sources. Their vehicle became the essay of ideas, a vehicle that allowed them to keep a distance between their thought and the mundane affairs of their nation. It was also a vehicle that allowed them the freedom to take philosophical thinking to heights of unprecedented abstraction.

THE DEFENSE OF SPIRITUALITY

The most outstanding among the philosophers who led the Chilean rebellion against positivism was Enrique Molina (1871–1964). Molina was the founder of Chile's first private secular university, the Universidad de Concepción, and later became minister of education.[4] As a member of the first class to graduate from the Instituto Pedagógico in 1892, Molina was initially a positivist who shared the ideals of secular education as promoted by the Instituto, defending them while principal at the Liceo de Talca. Here he was frequently attacked by Catholics on the grounds that he allowed the teaching of Darwinism.[5] Historian Ricardo Donoso, who was a Liceo student at the turn of the century, has reported how Molina and Alejandro Venegas (also an IP graduate) motivated his classmates' commitment to advancing the education of Chileans.[6]

Molina inherited IP's stress on education as a means to reform society but did not entirely agree with its scientific emphasis. Nor could he agree with the church's orientation towards education. Instead, he geared his intellectual efforts towards defining educational aims that were still secular, but not necessarily scientific. In the process, Molina introduced philosophical ideas that precipitated the demise of positivism and consolidated the importance of this school's nemesis: metaphysics.

Early in the twentieth century, it was Molina's concern for education that demonstrated the degree to which he shared in the positivist ideals of the time. Speaking before the Chilean Federation of Students (FECH) on the occasion of Argentina's independence centennial, Molina availed himself of the opportunity to express his educational views:

> Let us salute the Argentine Republic, the premier democracy of Spanish America. This is a democracy that offers free, secular, and compulsory primary education. Let us salute Argentina by adopting its [educational features]. In effect, the elementary education of the Argentine Republic, which is for children aged six to fourteen, is completely secular. There is no religious education offered unless the students and the parents request it explicitly. And in that case such courses are offered to them only after regular school hours. In this way, the Argentine Republic has reduced illiteracy to approximately thirty per cent while we [in Chile] maintain nearly a seventy per cent rate of illiteracy. These are the lethal results of a concept of freedom, still powerful among us, which resists making obligatory the indispensable education of the citizen. A freedom thus understood is nothing more than an erroneus, individualistic, feudal, and anarchical lack of organization.[7]

Molina's fledgling philosophical views similarly expressed a strong attachment to the positivist ideals acquired during his formative years. Like other Latin American philosophers who led the reaction against positivism, Molina's early philosophical concerns centered on the concept of freedom. But in contrast to such thinkers as the Uruguayan Carlos Vaz Ferreira and the Peruvian Alejandro Deústua, who used the concept to attack positivism,[8] Molina defended deterministic views associated with the movement. His rationale was that the idea of freedom as an absolute was indefensible, just as the view of freedom as the ability to follow the dictates of the will was self-defeating. Both presupposed, in his view, a degree of independence from social and individual constraints that was unrealistic. For Molina determinism was not necessarily a bad word. On the contrary, he thought of determinism as a necessary understanding of social and individual limitations that allowed man to pursue his ideals in a realistic and more effective fashion. As he put it, "determinism helps to cultivate the personality and to form individualities that are rich in possibilities for action and thought; they in turn help to enhance the only possible freedoms that humanity as a whole can enjoy."[9]

As his speech to students regarding education indicates, Molina was well aware that freedom, particularly freedom of education, had been used by Catholics as an ideological tool to attack the Chilean *Estado docente*, or state-controlled educational system. As a result, he was not easily charmed by the appeal of the notion of freedom. National experiences had led him to believe that freedom should not be taken literally, let alone absolutely. In addition, he had worked with positivists whom he perceived as liberating the country from illiteracy. Thus his philosophical concern for the notion of freedom, while echoing the concerns of antipositivists elsewhere in the continent, did not in his case become the basis for his critique of positivism. At the same time, the concerns that animated him went beyond positivism, at least narrowly understood, to the extent that he addressed issues of moral responsibility, individual will, and freedom itself.

Still, he was critical of Chilean positivism. Without rejecting it entirely, he sought to go beyond the two major ideological camps that in his view characterized the turn of the century in Chile: Catholic doctrines of a conservative character and the liberal currents embodied in positivism and scientism.[10] To his dismay, the reactions against positivism taking place in Europe were unknown in Chile, thus adding to the lack of intellectual vitality that he associated with positivist and Catholic currents. He attempted, then, to introduce ideas that departed from the dominant ideological division in Chilean society.

One effort in this direction was Molina's paper on the ideas of William James.[11] He submitted it to the Pan American Scientific Congress then meeting in Santiago in 1908, but could not present the paper there. He tried the University of Chile. Engineer Domingo Victor Santa María, then acting rector of UCH, accompanied his permission to lecture on the subject with a patronizing comment. "I cannot believe there are still people talking about such things," Santa María said in reference to philosophical activity. Molina later described this reaction as a mere reflection of the times, dominated by men whose philosophical outlook was narrow, if not antagonistic, towards schools other than positivism. "He ignores, of course," thought Molina as he walked out the door, "the existence of James, Bergson, and Eucken, and has no idea that metaphysics, condemned by positivism to perpetual oblivion, is springing anew in the concerns of the spirit."[12]

Molina's chagrin was quickly cured when he travelled to Germany in 1912, meeting with Georg Simmel of the University of Berlin. Simmel confirmed his belief that philosophy was moving drastically away from positivism. He also assured Molina that in his view Henri Bergson was "the greatest philosopher of the age," and Molina, upon returning to Chile, set out to study the Frenchman's ideas. Significantly, it was the presumably positivist-dominated UCH that invited him to give a series of lectures on Bergson in 1914.[13]

Molina's reading of Bergson bears the mark of his ambivalent attitude towards both positivism and the new currents of European philosophical thought. He was an eager student of those currents, yet he remained faithful to the convictions acquired during his positivistic years. The concept of freedom, for instance, was one of his greatest concerns but he resisted the notion that freedom should be related to an individual's free will. In his characterization of Bergson, freedom was the product of the impulses of the self. He rejected this notion on the grounds that "the Bergsonian free will is like a spontaneous act: good or bad, noble or wretched depending upon the personality involved, it is beyond any ethical, juridical, or social constraints."[14]

It was the concept of freedom that led Molina, unlike counterparts elsewhere in the region, to reject the philosophy of Bergson. He claimed that the freedom defended by the French philosopher fell within the realm of feeling and was therefore elusive, if not inexplicable. Furthermore, such a view of freedom "has nothing to do with the empirical and practical freedoms that are of interest to man."[15] And yet Molina was clearly attracted to the French author. He appreciated Bergson's concern for the complexities of the human personality but was disturbed by his "severing of all ties with positivism, Spencerian evolutionism, and science." In Molina's view, Bergson's philosophy was "an immersion into the mysteries of the being well beyond the limits where science can reach." He was convinced, however, that Bergson represented "a very modern philosophical position."[16]

Despite Molina's distance from Bergson, he was willing to explore new philosophical avenues, even if to the detriment of his earlier positivistic views. Gradually, but nonetheless surely, he severed his own ties with positivism. By the time of the publication of his *De lo espiritual en la vida humana* (1937), perhaps the most elaborate expression of his philosophical thought, Molina had come to believe that the subjects of philosophical importance were closely related to human spirituality. After a long journey through the themes of positivism as well as the new currents of European philosophy, Molina was convinced that the ultimate basis for human life and culture was spirituality. He also came to the conclusion that metaphysics was not only a necessary branch of philosophy but indeed the center of the discipline. Thus he undertook the complex task of subsuming positivism under a new philosophical conception that both rescued some of the concerns of positivism and went beyond it in order to relate human spirituality to metaphysics, culture, and philosophy itself.

His examination of the concept of "progress" provides evidence of his dual purpose of addressing positivistic concerns and advancing newer, and hopefully better, philosophical conceptions. In his *De lo espiritual en la vida humana*, he stated that not only positivists but also utilitarians and pragmatists had appropriated the notion of progress and reduced it to its narrowest technological connotations. But technology, he argued, had done little to increase human happiness. Too many instances of the evil usages of science and technology rendered, in his view, the notion of progress based on materialistic criteria suspect at best. Progress, for him, should be found in man and his ability to realize his spiritual life. "The enhancement of the spirit," he wrote, "should be the apex and supreme finality of any notion of progress."[17]

Molina's attack against the positivistic notion of progress was an attempt to introduce a humanistic philosophy that placed a premium on spiritual values over materialism. In this sense, he was reacting not only against positivism but also against the Marxist doctrines that were acquiring significant strength in Chile during the first third of the century. He found both positivism and Marxism to be too deterministic and materialistic in their views of man and history, reducing man to economic factors and questioning his spirituality.[18] As will be seen below, Molina presented his views about Marxism at about the same time of the publication of his *De lo espiritual en la vida humana*.

Molina divided human activity into two major areas: material and spiritual. He made it clear that spiritual aspects were the highest expressions of humanity and suggested that progress could only be understood as the achievement of ideas, concepts, and values that served to enhance human happiness. Certainly there was room for progress in the material area, but only to the extent that technology served to facilitate human aims. Man and spiritual life, for him, were "ends," while industry, science, and technology were only "means" to achieve those ends. There was some level of interaction between the two, he suggested, as it was likely that the material area would deteriorate in case any harm occurred in the spiritual area.[19]

Molina believed that material progress was necessary but should only be seen as the very bottom level of a hierarchy of values at whose top was man's spirituality. On this subject, he adhered to the hierarchy established by Nicolai Hartmann, a German phenomenologist, for the values of man and society: spiritual aims were in a higher position than those belonging to the "organic" or material areas.

The implications of this ordering of values proved to be consequential for Chilean philosophy. Molina intended to make spirituality the ultimate goal of philosophical activity, and he succeeded to a great extent. To this effect, metaphysics was used as the most important vehicle for the study and advancement of spiritual values. Other specialized areas of the discipline, particularly those that had been preferentially cultivated by positivism, were also viewed by Molina in the context of the hierarchy of values. Hence, logic and philosophy of science were viewed by him as "instruments" to be subordinated to the more essential spiritual philosophical concerns. Molina never worked on logical subjects except to criticize them when he felt that philosophers gave logic too much importance. Perhaps as a result of Molina's rationale, the field was by and large neglected during the first half of the twentieth century. Politics, also, was confined to the lower echelons of the hierarchy of important subjects of philosophical concern.

With his *De lo espiritual en la vida humana*, Molina successfully detached himself from positivism. His thinking became more spiritual, and significantly more personal. This became apparent with the publication of his *Confesión filosófica* (1942), where he advanced a defense of metaphysics that argued that science could never answer the questions that mattered most to man. He was responding to the phenomenological views of Edmund Husserl, who conceived of philosophy as a rigorous science.[20] If man was to seek answers for his concerns, he could not use a philosophy defined as a science: he needed a philosophy that recognized the complexities of the human spirit. "Clearly, a philosophy worth the name must rest on a solid critical base; but it is not always possible to avoid, during the course of speculation, the imprecisions and the personal character that goes with the complexity of both the subject and the intuitive method which is the only means to approach [philosophical questions].''[21]

Perhaps aware that he had gone far beyond his initial commitment to address the needs and concerns of all human beings, which he had made in both his discussion of the concept of freedom and his critique of Bergson, Molina emphasized that the spirit was not immaterial, and that it could not be found apart from living human beings.[22] And yet spiritual life was hardly an easy state to achieve. ''We do not know [the spirit],'' he stated, ''except through the experiences of our inner life, and that includes our intuitions of values and essences.''[23] Moreover, not all were qualified to achieve such a state, least of all the politicians.[24] His review of the spiritual accomplishments of humanity made it clear that those accomplishments belonged to the select few through history.

In praising spirituality as the highest expression of human life and asserting the inability of any discipline to precisely determine the complexities of the spirit, Molina had reached a point of no return. Philosophy, now separated from the less consequential exercise in logic and the methodology of science, became an anguished search for ever more elusive spiritual certainties. In a 1942 account of his philosophical trajectory, at the age of seventy-one, Molina indicated that the ultimate goals of the spirit could not be ascertained, and here resided the tragedy of spiritual life. ''Tyrants and bad leaders are the enemies of the spirit, and bring much pain to it. But even when these obstacles [to spiritual life] are surmounted, there still remains the biggest of them all: the mystery, or mysteries if you will, of Being and life. This is the essential and the greatest tragedy of the spirit, and sometimes, the cause of its desolation.''[25]

Molina thus crowned a philosophical evolution that took him from positivism to the discussion of various philosophical currents, including phenomenology and existentialism. He did not develop an original philosophy, nor did he claim to adhere to any particular school. Yet he effectively brought Chilean philosophical thinking to a new stage. By emphasizing the primacy of spiritual life, he shifted the focus of philosophical activity from educational concerns to providing guidance for the entire culture, not only for Chile, but for humanity as a whole. As a widely travelled man who had the rare chance of visiting several countries and meeting with numerous scholars around the world, Molina was comfortable in producing sweeping statements about the nature of Being and humanity. He was less comfortable about the encroachments of materialism and politics on Chilean culture and thus devised a conception of the field that confined them to the lower levels of a scale of values. His philosophy was not devoid of social content, but he made it clear that it was the discipline, and not society, that should dictate what was best for humanity, in Chile and elsewhere.

Enrique Molina, by virtue of his experience and extensive writings, established himself as the leader of the Chilean antipositivist reaction. But the rejection of positivism, perhaps not surprisingly, also came from Catholic thinkers such as Clarence Finlayson (1913–1954).[26] Like Molina, Finlayson was a graduate of the Instituto Pedagógico, but he was hired soon after graduation by the Catholic University in 1936. He spent most of his career, however, in other countries in the region. In fact, he achieved a reputation that took him to teaching positions at Notre Dame, Swarthmore, and Harvard in the United States and to several Latin American universities in Mexico, Colombia, and Panama. His return to Chile in 1954 was tragically followed by an untimely death.

Early in his career, Finlayson observed with dismay that "unfortunately, positivism has officially dominated education in Brazil and Chile throughout the nineteenth century and during the first part of the twentieth. Few things have had the stifling effects of Comte's and Spencer's positivism on the mentality of these nations. Positivism has limited their intellectual ingenuity and put iron bars around their imagination. It is only lately that we are beginning to see promising new directions and projections in the spiritual realm."[27] It was not just any influence, however, that he considered promising. Indeed, he criticized several new currents of thought such as existentialism and phenomenology because he found them to be confined to "the area of mere phenomena."[28] In his view, the essence of philosophy was metaphysics, and therefore it was to be mainly concerned with spiritual matters.

In the context of Latin American philosophy, Finlayson's thought is part of the broader neo-scholastic movement that acquired significant strength in Latin America during the first half of the twentieth century. Neo-scholasticism was inspired to a great extent by Jacques Maritain and claimed such adherents as Octavio Derisi of Argentina, Oswaldo Robles of Mexico, and Alceu Amoroso Lima of Brazil.[29] The major significance of this movement in Latin America resides in the effort to call attention to the universal and eternal essence of man.[30] Such an effort was consistent with the desire to eradicate positivist conceptions of man based on phenomena rather than on essences. Thus the movement was initially part of a larger antipositivist reaction, but once positivism lost its influence, neo-scholastics concentrated on the theological issues that characterized their neo-Thomistic philosophy.

Although Finlayson was part of this neo-scholastic movement, he claimed independence from its alleged lack of vitality. "As a scholasticist," he stated, "I must assert my profound conviction in the value of scholastic philosophy. However, I must also point out that the attitudes and positions of the modern scholastic philosophers, especially in ecclesiastical circles, represent an obstacle [because they] are out of step [with the times]. Their studies concentrate only on the times of Saint Thomas Aquinas and his contemporary commentators." He felt that neo-scholasticism needed to take stock of the current social and cultural situation and to elaborate new solutions to new problems. "Evidently," he concluded, "it is a good thing to know how Aquinas refuted Averroes. But [for scholars] to remain studying that particular problem is simply incomprehensible."[31]

Just as Enrique Molina had previously pointed out, Finlayson agreed that some of the most pressing problems were the problems of society. Finlayson's solution to these problems was also similar: to uncover and emphasize the spiritual character of human life and civilization. He indicated that while contemporary society had seen tremendous scientific advances, such progress was confined to the material realm. He thought about the contemporary world as one dominated by machinery and lacking in spiritual concerns. In contrast, he said, "the greatest and most creative times in history have been metaphysical. These were epochs that stayed away from the material structures of technology."[32] He called for a reemphasis of spiritual values so that man, society, and ultimately civilization would abandon their dangerous course. As did Molina, Finlayson showed tremendous optimism in the spirit's ability to inspire and lead social phenomena.

Despite his interest in society, just as in Molina's case Finlayson's thought was highly personal. He was consistently preoccupied with such matters as existence, destiny, and death. Finlayson did not elaborate fully on many of his concerns, but his view of philosophy was distinct from that of other Chilean philosophers, and particularly from Enrique Molina's. Finlayson viewed the discipline as only an instrument, and an imperfect one at that, to deal with human issues. But beyond them, he thought, philosophy was at a loss. On the matter of death, for instance, he stated that "it cannot be resolved by either metaphysics or any philosophical system. The theories that attempt to explain it inevitably base themselves on religious dogma."[33] Regarding human suffering, Finlayson went on to say that "suffering presents problems that go beyond philosophy. There is no rational answer . . . and it is perhaps this inability that gives credence to the religious-historical explanation of the original sin."[34] In the end, it was theology, or the belief in God, that gave satisfactory answers to the fundamental problems of man.

Regardless of whether or not such ultimate answers came from either philosophy or religion, it is the emphasis on human spirituality that emerges as the most significant feature of Finlayson's thought. Intellectuals concentrated on the spirit in part as a reaction against positivism. In Finlayson's case, one must add the interest of the neoscholastic movement in the supposed eternal essence of man. But it was his own personal inclination and religiosity that led him to the themes of human spirituality. In the Chile of the 1920s through the 1940s, philosophers had managed to reorient the fundamental concerns of the discipline and even attach a personal character to it.

Jorge Millas (1917–1982), Finlayson's junior by four years, also elaborated a conception of philosophy that was comprehensive, personal, and fundamentally oriented to the defense of human spirituality. He called his philosophy *personalismo* in order to distinguish it from individualism in a liberal, nineteenth-century sense. His *personalismo* concerned the defense of individual freedom understood as the spirit's ability to act solely on the basis of individual consciousness, free from social and political coercion.

Millas, who started writing in the 1930s, had no direct experience of positivist philosophical predominance, but he shared with the critics of positivism the concern for freedom and spirituality. While his concept of freedom was not completely different from Molina's and Finlayson's, Millas's owed less to the former's antipositivist views and to the latter's neo-Thomist stands. He elaborated a conception of freedom that viewed the individual as the ultimate basis for understanding the notion. As he put it in his *Idea de la individualidad* (1943), "This is where the nature of freedom lies: the individual feels free, and is free in fact, because there is nothing in him that comes from beyond his own act of decision. The Being is fully present in this act of decision; one *is* when one decides; man would not be free were he to be something other than his own actions. We would then have to talk about him as being determined by external forces."[35]

This concept of freedom was fundamental for Millas's view of spiritual life. Man was free to the extent that he was an individual, and he was an individual to the extent that he followed the dictates of his own spirit without interference from such external forces as politics, society, and the state. "Only the individual," he stated, "has an effective reality. Everything else has a purely symbolic character. Family, nation, state, citizenship, and society are all symbolic entities which may be instrumental for the fulfillment of practical needs. But in them one suspends the true, real, and authentic diversity of individual types."[36] Enrique Molina, who commented on Millas's work in 1953, stated that his younger colleague's view of individuality had "more than a touch of existentialism."[37] Millas, however, thought that his defense of individuality had a basis beyond whatever philosophical creed he might have adhered to. "What matters to me," he said, "is the metaphysical essence of the human being. My view is that man, at all times, projects himself to the objective world, which appears to him as a system of images in which he is at the center."[38] The entire matter of existence, he stated, "makes no sense except as a task and drama of the individual."[39]

Related to his concept of the individual was Millas's view of philosophy, which he understood as more than an intellectual exercise. The rational knowledge of the world was the subject of science. Philosophy, in his view, had larger, although not contradictory, aims. For instance, it not only consisted in "turning science into spiritual power" and "comprehending, not just knowing, the world," but it also represented "a higher stage where the spirit presents itself with all its forms."[40] Hence, philosophy could be "the highest expression of thought," but it was still related to the individual and the spirit that gave him his individuality. Thus philosophy "must be founded on spiritual freedom and on man's capacity to make history through his daily and non-transcendental living and suffering."[41]

Like Molina and Finlayson, Millas took philosophy to the realm of the spirit, and thus became concerned with metaphysical questions regarding existence, spiritual freedom, and individuality. Although each of these intellectuals made some efforts to relate philosophy to their nation, their themes became universal and increasingly detached from the specifics of their culture. They referred to Chile when discussing philosophical matters, but generally to indicate that their country was too involved in materialistic political events and often deaf to a spiritual or philosophical calling. They all retained the faith that by cultivating philosophy they would make a contribution to Chile's cultural and even social and political, life. But Millas in particular agonized over the question of relating to his country and continent while also addressing the themes of a supposedly universal culture.

In an open letter to José Ortega y Gasset in 1937, the then twenty-year-old Millas observed that his country and continent were beginning to put forth expressions of a "cultural Americanism." He felt uneasy about this because in his view such expressions contradicted the "increasing universalization of values" and the "ecumenical spirit" that he believed characterized the times. He pleaded with Ortega for an answer as to whether his judgment was correct in that he should follow the trend toward "universalization" of values as opposed to the "new" values of Latin America. "Please consider for a moment," he asked Ortega, "that on your answer depends nothing less than the adherence to, or rejection of, the destiny of a continent."[42]

With the publication of his *Idea de la individualidad*, Millas answered his own question by fashioning a view of philosophy in Latin America that was responsive to universal themes. "I believe that [Latin] America is the appropriate place for the constitution of a philosophy of man which is founded on the metaphysical, ethical, and historical exaltation of the individual, who is perhaps the only means to realize the ideal of a free and ethically superior humanity.''[43] Millas's ambivalence was gone. As he wished, many important Chilean philosophers exalted man's spirituality. And they did so to an extent proportionate to their scorn for politics.

THE SPIRIT AND POLITICS

The period between 1920 and 1950, that is, the period between the administrations of Arturo Alessandri Palma (1920–1924) and Gabriel González Videla (1946–1952), was one of fundamental political change in the nation. The election of Arturo Alessandri in 1920 signaled the end of the parliamentary regime inaugurated at the close of the 1891 civil war. It also signaled Chile's populist response to the social and economic problems brought about by the end of the First World War. Most importantly, the period between 1920 and 1950 saw the dramatic growth of the Chilean left, which came to share a political arena traditionally divided between liberals and conservatives.

The left was a new political actor, though not the only one responding to the concerns of labor as well as Chile's economic woes. The military became heavily involved in politics and pursued reformist as well as corporatist goals during the period. An array of other parties and groups, including the Falange (which would later become the Christian Democratic Party) and the Nazi National Socialist Movement (MNS) were born during these decades. Chile became politically more diverse, but its economy grew more dependent on the export of copper after the collapse of the nitrate industry. The country thus became more vulnerable to both international economic changes and internal demands for the distribution of income. Import substitution industrialization, the expansion of the public sector, Chile's insertion into a new world political and economic order, and new political actors all substantially altered the precarious status quo developed during the parliamentary era. Chile had changed, but in a manner that many people, particularly intellectuals, did not like. And what they liked least was the introduction of materialistic concerns, the politicking and rhetoric that burst into the open with Arturo Alessandri's first presidency.

Alessandri, a former student of Valentín Letelier's, ran an antioligarchic campaign that gave him much popularity, particularly in the northern provinces, and ultimately victory in the electoral contest of 1920. However, when faced with an obstructionist congress, a restless military, and an antagonistic right wing, Alessandri compromised on many of his promised reforms and turned against labor. Alessandri also encountered a new political phenomenon consisting of increasing leftist activity, an activity which all subsequent governments during the period would have to confront with varying degrees of success.

The left in the 1920s consisted of only a few groups that included communists and anarcho-syndicalists who were mainly active in the provinces. The left acquired significant strength, including electoral strength, throughout the country after the Great Depression. After the turmoil that followed the fall of General Carlos Ibáñez del Campo in 1931, there was even a short-lived "Socialist Republic" that lasted one hundred days. The Socialist party was created in 1933, and soon the social issues pressed by the left became central to the politics of the country.

The second administration of Arturo Alessandri (1932–1938) unleashed further repression against labor movements and the growing militancy of leftists. But the left, and Marxism, had come to the country to stay. Encouraged by the Comintern, the Communist party participated in electoral politics and entered into negotiations with centrist parties such as the Radical party. The left's first major participation in government came with a Popular Front coalition of radicals, communists, and socialists which led Pedro Aguirre Cerda to the presidency in 1938.

The participation of the left in government, as one observer has indicated, helped to tone down the militancy of Marxist groups.[44] But the rapid entrance of the left in the political arena, its electoral strength, and especially its involvement in rural unionization, sent shock waves through right wing parties and a citizenry unaccustomed to the rhetoric and tactics of these new actors. The Radical party, which represented a large and growing middle class, realized that it could not govern without leftist support. Indeed, such support was essential for the governments of Pedro Aguirre Cerda (1938–1941), Juan Antonio Ríos (1941–1946), and Gabriel González Videla (1946–1952) to be elected and viable.[45] And yet these governments found it necessary at different points in their administration to turn against the left to satisfy the apprehensions of the right, particularly regarding rural labor activity. Liberal and conservative politicians, who were no longer divided over the religious issue, were likely to be landowners whose loyalty to the democratic system depended on the maintainance of the status quo in the countryside. Through the Sociedad Nacional de Agricultura (SNA), they became powerful lobbyists against leftist activity. Often, they forced governments to make concessions to the detriment of rural unionization.[46]

It was with the government of González Videla that the successful growth of the left met its biggest challenge. Pressured by the right wing in Congress as well as by the United States, González eliminated leftists from his cabinet, enacted legislation that dealt harshly with labor unrest, and eventually promulgated a "Law for the Defense of Democracy" that banned the Communist party in 1948.

The issue of communism had been agitated earlier by right wing circles, particularly during the Spanish Civil War. Chilean newspapers such as *El Mercurio* and *El Diario Ilustrado* blamed the bloodshed in Spain on the participation of communists in the government. On the eve of the 1938 presidential elections, the example of Spain was used to suggest that the formation of the Popular Front and communist participation in it would lead the nation to civil war.[47] Parties of the left were not oblivious to events in the peninsula, and struck a conciliatory note in the form of support to the mild reformism of Aguirre Cerda. But their continued support for labor, particularly in rural areas, did little to assure the confidence of liberals and conservatives in Congress. Growing distrust on the part of Chilean politicians, plus increasing pressure from the United States, which made economic aid for development plans conditional on the elimination of Marxists from government positions, culminated in the massive repression of the left in the late 1940s.[48] Yet Marxism had succeeded not only in gaining impressive electoral strength, but in changing the political landscape of the nation.

Philosophers who between 1920 and 1950 were writing about the spirit were not unaware of political developments in the nation. They even attempted to explain such developments, although generally they eschewed politics and called instead for increased attention to spirituality in national culture. They believed that politics had the potential for the realization of spiritual values but that Chilean politicians had failed to inform their actions with a philosophical vision. The philosophers' emphasis on spirituality and metaphysics, as indicated above, was a response to positivism. But their defense of the spirit also represents their view of how politics should be conducted, and for what aims.

Chilean philosophers felt that their views on the spirit and politics had the support of influential European intellectuals such as the Spanish philosopher José Ortega y Gasset. They believed that Chileans had come to support such views when Ortega, who was a metaphysics professor at the University of Madrid, was invited to address the Chilean Congress in 1928. Ortega was greeted by an audience that included two cabinet ministers and more congressmen than the chamber had seen in a long time. On this occasion, Ortega produced a rationale, if not for the subordination of politics to ideas, at least for the strengthening of the role of intellectual life in the country. He told his audience:

> Do not have any illusions about it: intelligence is the enemy of politics; both have different functions, and if they are faithful to their respective missions, it is only natural that they collide. However, it depends on you to make certain that in these [Latin American] countries there be an epicenter of serene intellectual life balancing politics; also, that you create institutions and make every sacrifice needed so that an exemplary minority emerges from them which can in turn lead, encourage, and correct you. I ask, aspire, wish, and expect that in the future you Chilean politicians favor, encourage, and confirm intellectual life.[49]

Chilean philosophers like Enrique Molina, who through metaphysics had already discovered the value of placing spiritual life and politics on opposite ends of a hierarchy, echoed Ortega's ideas. He further agreed with the Spanish philosopher on the necessity of institutions that advanced the interests of the spirit in a climate of serenity. With similar interests in mind, Molina had created the private secular University of Concepción, in the south of Chile, in 1919. He gave the university the motto, "for the free development of the spirit," thus linking higher education, philosophy, and spiritual life. In 1934,

Molina underscored this link by stating that, like philosophy, "the university is the mansion of spiritual serenity. Social and political unrest have no place in it"; he added that "the spirit of the university must exist in an ethical and philosophical environment."[50] For philosophy to be a model for the university, which would in turn be a model for society, it was first necessary to define the field as spiritually oriented and apolitical, an effort in which he was particularly successful.

The confinement of politics to the lower levels of a hierarchy of values, if not its complete separation from the new philosophical concerns, was indeed Molina's most consequential legacy to the field. Molina was by no means an apolitical man, and in fact did not miss the opportunity to attack Marxism, then referred to as *maximalismo*, during the growth of leftist influence in the 1930s. He later accepted political appointments such as the ministry of education in 1947. But he managed, perhaps more successfully than his predecessors in the nineteenth century, to impress upon the field the view that spiritual concerns and politics did not mix except to the extent that the latter was subordinate to the former. "Philosophy," he stated, "frees the spirit from the lowly sentiments and places it under the influence of higher values, which are essences related to man and the human personality."[51]

Subordinating politics, and particularly Marxism, to the interests of spiritual life was one of Molina's major efforts in the 1930s. In 1934, he published his *La revolución rusa y la dictadura bolchevista* ostensibly to provide an account of the Russian revolution, but actually to criticize the abuses and the failures of the bolshevik regime. Most important, he wrote his account in order to demonstrate why, in his view, communism would not work in Latin America and in Chile.

The study was based on secondary sources, many of which were written for political purposes to either condemn or defend the regime. He excused himself for not writing an account that was based on his own experience—he had previously written a report on his extensive travels through the United States—but he justified this by saying that in the Soviet Union one could not rely on the monitored visits allowed by the state. In any event, he thought it important to summarize his reading of the sources in order to provide an account of the revolution that would be of interest to Chilean readers. Although describing events in distant Russia, Molina was writing for a Chilean audience in the hope of demonstrating that revolution was the wrong answer to the problems of the country. Most pointedly, he was articulating the views of a Chilean middle class that abhorred radical political solutions.

Molina described the bolshevik regime as brutal, immoral, and inefficient. He formed this negative assessment after examining accounts of communist activity prior to the 1917 revolution and then under the Lenin and Stalin regimes. He concluded that communists were blinded by their political goals and ready to sacrifice generations of Russians for the sake of uncertain socialist ends. They had no respect for individual liberties nor any regard for spiritual values. Molina was careful not to embrace monarchical solutions, but he characterized the assassination of the royal family as a tragedy of epic proportions. His criticisms, rather, were made on the basis of a conception of democracy which, not surprisingly, he found lacking in the history of the Soviet Union.

Russians, he believed, embraced such dictatorial solutions as bolshevism due to an excess of oriental influence and a proportionate lack of European experience. "A country," he stated, "that did not receive the solid framework of Roman juridical culture nor enjoy the splendid influence of the Renaissance, and for which the English and French revolutions—the educators of people—have been for the most part nonexistent, has had to confront its national problems with [several disadvantages]: a great vacuum as far as its concept of the law, no knowledge of respect for human individuality, and almost no political education."[52]

In the case of Chile, which did have democratic traditions and a fundamentally European experience, social change could come about through other means, particularly education. Thus, in Molina's view, communist solutions in Chile were impractical because of the different historical traditions. And yet there were many in Chile who were "naive" or "ambitious" enough to advocate revolution when a "profound educational reconstruction" could be realized through legitimate government and without destroying the "institutional framework of the Republic."[53]

Molina was in effect articulating a nineteenth-century belief in the power of education to transform society. But in the context of the 1930s, when the problems of society were approached by leftists from perspectives other than the gradualistic, evolutionary means of liberals and positivists, Molina attempted to show that revolutionary solutions could not work where democratic traditions existed. But he was advancing a belief more than drawing a conclusion from the successes of Chilean education. It was the philosopher who was speaking, and one who rejected Marxism on the basis of what he believed to be an incompatibility between communism and human spirituality.

In order to dispel any doubts about his motivations for criticizing the Russian revolution and to reaffirm his commitment to democracy, he recalled how Vicente Huidobro, the famed Chilean poet, burst into the room where Molina was lecturing about the subject in 1933. Huidobro, who sympathized with the communists, questioned the evidence that Molina quoted to criticize the revolution. "And so," explained Molina, "there was the paradoxical situation where on the one hand an aristocrat, the son of a millionaire who had never worked for a living, presented himself as the defender of the working classes. And there was I, on the other, who appeared as their enemy because of my defense of democracy but who had never owned estates or factories, and who had worked my entire life as an educator."[54]

Molina had in fact spent his life as an educator, but this did not prevent him from discussing political issues and even participating actively in politics. In 1947, for instance, he accepted the position of minister of education in the cabinet of President Gabriel González Videla. It was during that year that González Videla asked the Congress for extraordinary powers to crush leftist activism. Molina attended the session of Congress and spoke in support of the government crackdown. Socialist senator Salvador Allende, the future president of Chile, confronted Molina on the connection between his defense of spirituality and the character of the extraordinary measures:

> The *señor ministro* is rector of a southern university which carries the motto 'for the free development of the spirit.' Don't these extraordinary faculties that are asked from us deny freedom, suffocate the free development of the spirit and, consequently, inflict a mutilation on culture? How does the *señor ministro* reconcile the libertarian norm of his university with the oppressive attitude of the government that he is a member of?[55]

Molina explained how the two points mentioned by Allende were not incompatible. He stated first that the motto of the university was not to be confused with unbridled freedom. He then stated that the extraordinary powers were intended to restore social discipline and order, and concluded that "the requested extraordinary faculties are simply for the purpose of furnishing the means for the republic to have an environment conducive to work. Therefore, the project is enhanced by a spiritual and moral value. In its articles, there is no specter of tyranny nor is there any threat to the constitutional rights of the citizens."[56] The response further alienated a communist member of the senate who reproached Molina for providing a repressive policy with a spiritual façade.

Molina resigned his post as minister of education in July 1948, just prior to the promulgation of the Law for the Defense of Democracy in September of that year. During his tenure as minister he was convinced of the validity of the measures and of their compatibility with his own political and philosophical thinking. He was willing to lend his prestige as an intellectual to the antileftist politics of the government not because of naivité regarding the specifics of repression, but because of a consistent conviction that politics, and particularly the politics of the left, got in the way of the spiritual achievements that governments should aim for.

Clarence Finlayson and Jorge Millas were less specific about Marxism, but they were just as concerned as Molina about politics. They judged it on the basis of their respective views on philosophy and coincided in their negative assessments. Finlayson, for instance, found that "the most important and urgent task for philosophers today is in the realm of ethics and politics, and that is to undertake a moralizing endeavor. Politics is completely divorced from the moral order, and it is thus necessary to insist on the personal values of man."[57] Millas, having already determined what was essential to man, that is, individuality, viewed politics as an external factor at best that detracted from the most fundamental pursuits of the spirit. At worst, it constituted an "impersonal force" that "continuously attacks individuality, and sometimes harms, though never extinguishes, its profound reality."[58]

Millas was less antagonistic than Molina towards the Russian revolution. He even believed that in the long run socialism would "redeem" individuality.[59] Millas was also a student leader, a member of the Socialist party, and in 1938 became president of the FECH. Along with other Chilean intellectuals, he supported the embattled Republicans during the Spanish Civil War. But these were all youthful options that the maturing philosopher would cast aside because of a stronger commitment to individuality and spirituality. His concern for politics became a concern for the factors impeding the development of the individual.

> It is only occasionally that our personality, that which is ours, intervenes in politics. By ours I mean all that expresses the singular fact of our own existence. What we do in politics is to project our action on a state level, that is, on a level which is relative and in the periphery, not part of the internal individual drama.[60]

Finlayson and Millas, just like Molina, arrived at a conception of the spirit that was concerned with, but antagonistic to, politics. In the case of Molina, his critique of politics led him to the critique of Marxism, but not to the entire rejection of political activity. Finlayson and Millas viewed the spirit and politics in antithetical terms. Millas, in particular, would make this theme his major philosophical concern in subsequent writings.

While these three major philosophers of the period attempted to distance the spirit from politics, or at least to subordinate the latter to the former, there was one important attempt to conciliate the two. This was the case of Eduardo Frei Montalva (1911–1982), then a professor of philosophy of law at Catholic University, and later president of Chile (1964–1970). In his book *La política y el espíritu* (1940), Frei criticized Marxism on grounds similar to Molina's arguments, that this doctrine was materialistic to the point of reducing man to real, but inferior, levels.[61] He also criticized capitalism and indeed any social form that did not take man and his values as its most fundamental basis. "The person, by virtue of his immortal soul, precedes and is superior to the state; he has inalienable and natural rights that guarantee the realization of his personal and superior finality."[62] Frei thus embraced the views of the neo-Thomists regarding the eternal essence of man but went one step further in seeking to define political formulas that would advance spiritual interests.

Frei's major inspiration came from Jacques Maritain and the papal encyclicals *Rerum Novarum* (1891) and *Quadragessimo Anno*

(1931). His interests were not purely philosophical, and indeed he would soon launch a political career that would lead him to the presidency of the nation in 1964.[63] But in the context of the 1930s and 1940s, Frei's *La política y el espíritu* responded to what had become a dominant concern on the part of philosophers on the subject of the spirit. The tendency among philosophers was to effect the independence of spiritual life and values from politics, partly because they had become discouraged with politics, and also because their new conception of philosophy was centered on metaphysics and spirituality. Frei, who was part of this intellectual climate and himself a professor of philosophy, parted the company of his colleagues in that he believed in the realization of spirituality through political action. As he put it, "ideas are effective only when they develop their own style. That is why . . . we must seek a new way. It is in that immense human reservoir of those who suffer and live in obscurity that hope may rise, a hope that is founded on the spirit, and from which a new social structure may emerge. Because the point is not to preach only a philosophy, but to create a new regime."[64]

The spirit was strongly established as a dominant concern among philosophers during the period. Intellectuals struggled to immerse themselves in the study of spirituality, but the political realities of the time forced them to pay attention to politics. And they did so by elaborating conceptions of the spirit that were, not surprisingly, antagonistic to politics. They had achieved freedom from the religious constraints of the nineteenth century. They had furthermore achieved greater independence from the scientific and educational concerns of positivism. But politics now presented them with new challenges and opportunities—challenges to the extent that they were forced to refer their speculations to political realities in Chile and elsewhere, and opportunities to the extent that politics had replaced religion as the central issue of the period. They could seize the opportunity, and indeed they did, to establish their position in society as commentators, if not guides, on subjects of social importance. This time, however, they approached the subject with greater freedom from the educational constraints of the past century. Philosophy was no longer solely the philosophy of classrooms and textbooks. And yet this is also the period when philosophy developed a strong institutional base at Chilean universities.

THE IMPACT ON PHILOSOPHICAL STUDIES

Perhaps no other philosopher besides Andrés Bello has had Molina's influence on both the field of philosophy and higher education in Chile. The above-mentioned Universidad de Concepción, situated far from Santiago, came close to Molina's ideal of a serene environment devoted to the higher pursuits of knowledge until the student activism of the 1960s shattered the ideal. During the thirty-seven years of his rectorship, Molina turned that institution into one of Chile's leading universities.[65] Molina's remarkable success at forming and running institutions was mirrored in his disciplinary activities, as he devised mechanisms that helped promote his view of philosophy as a specialized and professional endeavor. Among these was the journal *Atenea*, which he founded and edited in 1924 and which served as a vehicle for the dissemination of diverse nonpositivist philosophical views. Moreover, while minister of education in 1948, Molina played a pivotal role in the creation of the *Sociedad Chilena de Filosofía* and its journal *Revista de Filosofía*.

Molina was certainly not alone in his effort to turn the discipline into an institutional and professional pursuit. During the early part of the century, philosophy had been taught at the UCH by Jorge Enrique Schneider. His successor Wilhelm Mann was influential in sustaining the teaching of philosophy at the Instituto Pedagógico, often departing from the heavy emphasis on experimental psychology. In 1907 Mann was responsible for the introduction of the subjects of ethics and history of philosophical systems into the IP curriculum.[66] Additionally, he paid important attention to the teaching of philosophy at secondary schools. He found the teaching of the field to be necessary to rescue youth from "vulgar propaganda," "materialistic theories," and "spiritualism."[67] Most importantly, he viewed philosophy as a field which could "unify the multiple forms of knowledge that the student acquires in the course of studying different subjects."[68] This view of the unifying role of philosophy extended beyond the intellect to also include matters of daily conduct, morality, and values.[69]

The importance of Mann's view of the teaching of philosophy resides in the fact that he departed from the positivist emphasis on logic not by eliminating it but by subsuming it under a more comprehensive conceptualization of the field. A few decades earlier, positivists had turned the study of philosophy into the study of logic and even changed the title of the philosophy course to "logic." Mann recognized the centrality of logical subjects but placed more importance on the field of philosophy as a whole. Likewise, he viewed psychology as an important yet subordinate branch of the discipline. Psychology for Mann was as necessary to the discipline as logic, "but this does not mean that it is a substitute for philosophy."[70] At least for the purposes of secondary school teaching, philosophy needed also to include some elements of social philosophy.[71] Although he considered metaphysics and theory of knowledge to be central philosophical subjects, he was less enthusiastic about their teaching in secondary schools. He thought that the comprehension of these subjects was beyond the reach of secondary school students, and that "no other subjects are as susceptible as these to the danger of doctrinaire struggles, because they are so closely connected with the religious institutions of our culture. Under such circumstances it is most difficult to avoid that the classes on these subjects become instruments of sectarian propaganda; it is not feasible to tell teachers which opposing doctrine to choose and defend before the students."[72]

In 1915, the memory of conflicts between religious and secular education was too recent for Mann to ignore. In any case, he thought that many of the fundamental problems of metaphysics and theory of knowledge could be introduced via psychology and logic.[73] The problems of ethics and aesthetics could also be included in the teaching of psychology. He was thus making an effort to avoid an excessive fragmentation of the discipline while broadening the scope and importance of logic and psychology, particularly the latter. In the context of Chilean secondary education, where the teaching of philosophy consisted of only two hours a week in the last two years of secondary school, he felt that "it really is enough to study the two principal subjects of logic and psychology, because it is possible to treat all the matters of ethics, social philosophy, theory of knowledge and history of philosophy that are important to discuss in secondary schools as mere extensions of logic and psychology."[74]

Wilhelm Mann left his position as professor of philosophy and pedagogy in 1918. By that time he had achieved for philosophy the recognition that a variety of the themes that were anathema to the positivists were indeed essential to the discipline. His successor, Pedro León Loyola (1889–1978), could thus build upon the work of Mann so as to further broaden the scope of the discipline. Yet both retained the focus on secondary school education that characterized the philosophical concerns of the positivists.

Pedro León Loyola took Mann's position in 1918, after years of close collaboration with his German mentor. He encountered more favorable conditions for the teaching of philosophy, as pedagogy and philosophy became separate in 1919. Loyola and Darío Salas, also an IP graduate, shared the responsibilities of Mann, with Salas taking pedagogy and Loyola the introduction to philosophy, psychology, logic, philosophy of science, and history of philosophy. In 1923, Loyola was further relieved of the teaching of psychology, so that under his tenure the field began to shed some of the heavy pedagogical orientation acquired during the first three decades of the IP. In 1921, Loyola created the first Center for Philosophical Studies which, although in existence only until 1929, provided the basis for the subsequent institutionalization of philosophical studies at the UCH.[75] On his recommendation, the university opened a special training course for philosophy teachers in 1935. The special course included several novelties. Only students who had achieved distinction at the end of the third year at IP were eligible for admission. It was also a demanding course that included the philosophy of mathematics, physics and biology, the theory of knowledge, and metaphysics. Additionally, a score of professors, including Roberto Munizaga, Eugenio González, Marcos Flores, and Mariano Picón Salas, among others, taught the diverse areas within the program.[76] Thus the bases for a full-fledged department of philosophy were laid by the special Curso, which demonstrated the viability of a complex philosophy curriculum taught by a group of faculty.

The increasing emphasis on the specialization of philosophy was partly the result of the efforts of professors like Mann, Loyola, and the students that they educated. There was also a philosophical tradition in the country that ensured the continuity of philosophical interest. But the emphasis on specialization was also the product of wider changes in Chilean higher education. In 1931 a massive reform of the UCH significantly challenged the highly centralized structure that had characterized Chilean higher education for nearly a century. The reform provided for the emergence of strong individual faculties already demanding more autonomy from the central administration. The central apparatus of the UCH continued to be quite large, but beginning in 1931 the faculties achieved a substantially higher degree of independence in deciding on their internal organization and academic thrust. One of those faculties was the Faculty of Philosophy and Education (FFE), which fused the Faculty of Philosophy, Humanities, and Fine Arts with the newer Instituto Pedagógico, thus overcoming the initial tension between the two institutions and diluting the heavily scientific and professional emphasis given to the different fields at IP.[77] Yet the fusion brought new problems, as coordination between the two emphases was not always easy, and the new generation of philosophy professors and students showed more interest in philosophical research than in secondary education.

One of the important features of the 1931 reform was the end of the traditional UCH supervision over secondary education.[78] The Instituto Pedagógico, now part of FFE, retained its responsibility over the training of philosophy Profesores de Estado, or secondary school teachers, but a direct line of communication between higher and secondary education no longer existed. Surely, philosophy professors maintained an interest in and influence on secondary school teaching and the philosophy of secondary education. This is the case of Roberto Munizaga (b. 1906), a student of Pedro León Loyola's, who devoted his *Filosofía de la educación secundaria* (1947) to the subject of secondary education. While his colleagues ventured into metaphysical realms, Munizaga issued strong calls for maintaining the continuity of philosophical work in Chile as he understood it, that is, philosophical work that related directly to education and to the efforts of Andrés Bello and Valentín Letelier. As a professor of philosophy and history of education at IP, Munizaga defended a philosophical focus on secondary education not so much in order "to advance new, attractive, or spectacular views, as to extract from both the good traditions of the past and the renovating impulses of the present a body of simple, consistent, and especially, clear, ideas." In the present, he regretted, there was only a "sweeping high tide of ideas," a great deal of confusion and improvisation, and above all, a threat to the continuity of sensible philosophical work in Chile.[79] He was as skeptical about the new philosophical currents as he was alone in a scholarly community that sought independence from the constraints of secondary education.

The very statutes of 1931 conspired against Munizaga's view of philosophical work. The 1931 reform provided the basis for the pursuit of academic concerns beyond the professional educational emphasis of the positivist era. For philosophers the reform meant more freedom to pursue philosophical interests not directly connected with education, but also the beginning of a new and uncertain period of national philosophical history. Philosophers experimented, as discussed in the previous section, with new avenues of philosophical concern. But the overwhelming response was to institutionalize philosophical studies, although this time with a mixed legacy of interest in secondary education and a growing interest in the most specialized aspects of the discipline.

It was Pedro León Loyola's task to set up the institutional basis for the specialized study of philosophy in the aftermath of the positivist era. He was by no means as productive as Molina or Finlayson, but his works were highly significant. Among his few published works was his *Lógica formal* (1927), a textbook for use at the Instituto Nacional and the Liceo de Aplicación, where he was also a philosophy teacher.[80] The *Lógica* by Loyola represents a major development in the field of logic in Chile. Compared to Lois's sections on the subject in the *Elementos de filosofía positiva*, Loyola's work treated a wider variety of mostly French authors, although he also incorporated the views of the British neo-Hegelians, particularly Bernard Bosanquet. Most important, he went further than Mann in emphasizing the link between logic and metaphysics that the positivists denied.[81] Thus Loyola brought the study of logic in Chile to a more sophisticated level through his scholarly treatment of contemporary logical works, especially with his view about the fundamental, rather than instrumental, character of the field in relation to philosophy as a whole.

Loyola shared with his colleagues during the period an interest in spiritual matters. In presenting his *Lógica*, for instance, he took the opportunity to defend the study of philosophy, which he found most necessary during the difficult times of his day. "The current problems of man," he stated, "are problems in his soul: I wish the reformers of the present would not forget this axiom! . . . How can those problems be cured if not through the elevation of the soul? Let us then exalt the life of the spirit, especially among the young, for they are the future of our country.''[82]

Loyola also shared with his colleagues an antipathy towards politics, and most specifically Marxism. As he put it in his autobiography, ''On social, moral and political matters my ideas are totally opposed, in doctrine as well as in methods, to Marxism.''[83] Like Molina, however, he did not rule out periodic interventions in politics. In the 1910s, for instance, he was first vice president and then president of the Chilean Federation of Students (FECH) created during the rectorship of Valentín Letelier. His major contribution in this period was the foundation of a night school for workers. Loyola coincided with radicals and positivists in the belief that education, particularly the education of workers, could bring about social change without violent revolution.[84] He later founded, in 1918, the Universidad Popular Lastarria, also intended for the education of workers, and taught philosophy until its closing by the first administration of Carlos Ibáñez del Campo.[85] Once Ibáñez fell, in large measure due to student activism in 1931, Pedro León Loyola became rector of the UCH for a brief period under the presidency of Juan Esteban Montero.[86]

Generally, however, Loyola was a reluctant actor in the politics of the period. Already in 1919 he expressed unhappiness about the FECH's shift to the left.[87] He eventually resigned his university position due to student activism in 1944. He later returned, in 1956, to the Instituto Pedagógico to occupy the *cátedra* of metaphysics, but he retained a sense of bitterness towards politics generally and student politics in particular. ''It was the lack of discipline among the students,'' he stated when he again left the university in 1961, ''that led me to leave teaching. The students had taken over the school and prevented the faculty from carrying out their duties.''[88] He felt compelled, however, to express himself politically in 1964, on the eve of the presidential elections, to help prevent the repetition in Chile of ''the success of red totalitarianism in Cuba.''[89]

Although Loyola's participation in and commentary on the politics of his lifetime as well as his contributions to the fields of logic and the philosophy of science were all substantial, his fundamental legacy to the field was in the area of education.[90] Loyola became one of the few Chilean philosophers to be accorded the title of *mae-*

stro (mentor) on account of his dedication to students.[91] Additionally, he trained many of the people who would advance the professionalization of the field, such as Roberto Munizaga, Luis Oyarzún, and Jorge Millas. Ironically, his emphasis on French authors in the fields of logic and the philosophy of science was not pursued by his students, who tended to concentrate more on German philosophy and the work of José Ortega y Gasset. Luis Oyarzún (1920–1972), for instance, has mentioned that his friend Jorge Millas, an IP student in the 1930s, was reading and briefing him and others on the works of José Ortega y Gasset, Sigmund Freud, Oswald Spengler, Georg Simmel, and the contributors to the Spanish *Revista de Occidente*.[92]

Although the subjects of philosophical interest were different, there was a parallel institutionalization of philosophical studies at the Catholic University (UC) during the rectorship of Carlos Casanueva (1920–1952). The UC established a Curso Superior de Filosofía in 1922, an Academy of Philosophy in 1923, and a School of Pedagogy in 1943. At the Curso, the level of philosophical activity was restricted to three years of learning such subjects as logic, ontology, theodicy, and ethics. After successful completion of the Curso, students could obtain the degrees of Bachiller and Licenciado. With the creation of the School of Pedagogy, however, the study of philosophy acquired significant complexity. To obtain a teaching credential, students took philosophy courses distributed across a four-year curriculum by 1944, extended to five years in 1950. The courses now included epistemology, metaphysics, aesthetics, Latin, and Greek, all taught by a variety of professors, but mainly clerics.[93]

The UC was openly competing with the UCH during this period. Part of the reason for establishing a School of Pedagogy was for the training of Catholic professors who could teach in private schools and hence provide an alternative to the influence of Pedagógico graduates in public schools. The content of philosophy courses at UC was also distinct from the secular-oriented UCH. Thomistic philosophy predominated, and specific courses were designed to refute evolutionism, pantheism, socialism, and communism, and to demonstrate the existence of God.[94] And yet philosophy at both universities coincided in the critique of positivism and, most significantly, in the drive to institutionalize the teaching of philosophy. By 1950 both schools had major departments of philosophy, and their respective faculty members interacted as colleagues in such organizations as the Sociedad Chilena de Filosofía.

The new climate of philosophical concerns mirrored similar developments throughout Latin America. Almost everywhere in the region, philosophers were involved in similar intellectual and institutional developments that drastically departed from positivism and helped establish the systematic study of their discipline. Intellectually, Latin American authors coincided in their interest in Henri Bergson and José Ortega y Gasset, who had been influential in Latin America since as early as the 1910s. Indeed, the philosophers' familiarity with such authors as Max Scheler, Nicolai Hartmann, and Martin Heidegger was due to Ortega's influence through the *Revista de Occidente*.

Institutionally, in the process of learning and discussing the major European philosophical currents of existentialism and phenomenology, departments and faculties of philosophy mushroomed throughout the continent.[95] In 1939, the *Handbook of Latin American Studies* edited in Washington, D.C., considered it necessary to open a section on Latin American philosophy in order to cover the ever-increasing philosophical production in the continent. The respected Argentine philosopher Risieri Frondizi, then teaching at the Universidad Nacional de Tucumán, covered a decade of dazzling growth of professional philosophy in Latin America for the *Handbook*.

Philosophical developments in Latin America at large had a strong impact in Chile. These developments are meaningful because they provided each national philosophical community with a sense of professional identity that transcended geographical boundaries. These communities and their members could look upon their peers elsewhere in the Americas as participants and potential audiences for the increasingly specialized nature of their philosophical work. This sense of continental community also permitted some general trends of philosophical thought to take root simultaneously throughout the area. During his tenure as editor of the philosophy section in the *Handbook*, for instance, Frondizi pointed out that German phenomenological thought was by far the dominant philosophical current, thanks to Ortega's influence. He also gave much praise to the fact that journals of philosophy as well as inter-American congresses of philosophy were proliferating. He indicated in 1944 that the latter were particularly important "at a time when Western culture has almost perished under the totalitarian ideologies that dominate a great part of Europe."[96]

The Second World War period was indeed the background for much of the interest in promoting inter-American activities. Also important was the impact of the Spanish Civil War. It meant the arrival in Chile of Spanish philosophers—few in number but very competent—who brought a style of philosophical work that fit well with the process of professionalization of the discipline already underway. As José Luis Abellán has suggested, Spanish émigrés understandably avoided political involvement in their host Latin American countries and in addition gave a strong impulse to the professionalization of the discipline as they extended their withdrawal from politics to their philosophical work.[97]

In Chile, Spanish philosophers such as José Ferrater Mora contributed to the already remarkable growth of philosophical specialization through his writings and students.[98] Gastón Gómez Lasa, who was a student at IP in the 1940s, expressed pleasant surprise when he found himself the only student of five European professors, including Ferrater Mora, Marcelo Neuschlosz, and Bogumil Jasinowski.[99] Other European philosophers fleeing the war in Europe brought their philosophical expertise and educational experience to the country. It was their contacts with a network of scattered, but most accomplished, philosophers throughout the region and their experience with European universities that contributed greatly to reinforcing the tendency toward the specialization of Chilean philosophy.

Many factors account for the institutionalization and increasing professionalization of Chilean philosophy between 1920 and 1950, but none was as influential as the separation of philosophy and politics accomplished by several philosophers during the period. There had certainly been attempts at separating the two throughout the nineteenth century, but it was only after the demise of positivism that a specialized and by and large depoliticized version of the discipline laid roots in Chile. Positivism had been used by intellectuals responding to the allegedly narrow and inconsequential character of the philosophy advocated by Andrés Bello. It had also been used as an instrument to advance the perceived need for the secularization of society. But later positivists, especially Valentín Letelier, showed an inclination towards philosophical specialization and a determination to establish positivism academically at the UCH, if not throughout the entire educational system. The positivist emphasis on science as well as the movement's lingering attempt to promote an antimetaphysical bias led to a rebellion whose outcome proved how intimately connected philosophy and higher education were in Chile.

The tension between specialization and political commitments was clearly not confined to philosophy, as it was a theme of great concern at the UCH. But philosophy led the way, perhaps because individual thinkers were freer to speculate on the nature and limits of specialization and politics. Once philosophers became convinced of the advantages of specialization, they lost little time in attempting to extrapolate their philosophical views to involve higher education generally. But their view of specialization was most certainly not that of the positivists. It was a type of specialization that fit well with their spiritual concerns and that allowed them to be political while rejecting overt political activity. In short, philosophers were political to the extent needed to keep both the university and the discipline free from social and political pressures.

IV

THE INSTITUTIONALIZATION AND CRITIQUE OF PHILOSOPHICAL PROFESSIONALISM

1950–1968

The independence of the discipline from a century-old concern with the sensitive religious issue provided philosophers with an opportunity to seek further independence from politics, particularly from the Marxist ideologies that they believed sought to politicize not only the field but also the university and society in general. Philosophers such as Enrique Molina were highly political themselves, for they did not hesitate to take issue with Marxism or accept high-level political appointments. But they developed an apparently apolitical rationale that served them well to defend both the university and the discipline from political encroachments. This rationale consisted of a view of the university and philosophy—which they argued were intimately connected—as a haven for the free development of reason and as a guide for society at large. To achieve such a status, neither the university nor philosophy could afford to be involved in the political debates that agitated society. After the achievement of independence from the secular-religious conflicts of the past, philosophers were not willing to become engulfed in new conflicts emerging from the growing influence of the left.

As suggested in the previous chapter, the philosophy resulting from the reaction against positivism was characterized by a concern for spiritual values—as opposed to materialistic politics—and by an emphasis on specialization aided by both international influences and internal institutional developments that gave professors and faculties autonomy to decide the content of their academic interests. This combination of factors spurred a genuine enthusiasm on the part of the philosophical community to probe into philosophical areas, particularly metaphysics, that they felt had been neglected by the previous involvement in politics. As philosophical production along these lines grew, philosophers sought to institutionalize the new orientation of the discipline. The successful product of that effort was a level of philosophical professionalism that produced a new generation of thinkers who effectively broke their ties with the past, and who led the field to a level of specialization that eventually elicited a strong revolt against the alleged social and political detachment of the discipline and its practitioners.

THE SOCIEDAD CHILENA DE FILOSOFÍA

In the late 1940s, the tendency towards augmenting the institutional presence of philosophical studies was in full swing. The climate for such institutionalization was particularly favorable at that time. A strong indication of this was the creation of the Sociedad Chilena de Filosofía (SCF). Chilean philosophers seized on the opportunity to establish a philosophical society when Enrique Molina occupied the ministry of education in 1948. Molina hardly needed any convincing when Pedro León Loyola, Luis Oyarzún, Roberto Munizaga, Santiago Vidal, Mario Ciudad, and many others approached him with the idea. Molina was so enthused with the project that, after a series of meetings, he accepted the presidency of the society.[1]

Philosophers felt that the establishment of SCF was necessary to attain the following aims: the pursuit of philosophical studies with "methodological rigor, honesty and tolerance"; the contribution of philosophical studies to the understanding of Chilean culture; and the dissemination of philosophical knowledge. These aims became in fact part of the statutes of SCF, and philosophers also agreed on the means to achieve them: holding periodical meetings, conferences and congresses both nationally and internationally; creating courses, publication series, libraries and archives; and establishing relations with similar institutions within Chile and abroad.[2]

Underlying these aims and procedures was the effort to coordinate philosophical activity beyond the mere supervision of philosophical teaching in secondary schools. During the 1940s members of the Chilean philosophical community were exposed to international congresses and the arrival of competent foreign professors. The time had come, they felt, to further institutionalize the growing sense of philosophical professionalism among scholars. SCF was only the culmination of a series of steps which turned Chilean philosophy into a field regulated by a growing consensus on the academic nature of the discipline.

SCF became the point of encounter for philosophers, Catholic and secular, nationally and abroad. The roster of members grew rapidly, including foreign honorary members such as Francisco Romero and Risieri Frondizi. A number of visitors attending the National Congress of Philosophy in Mendoza in 1949, including José Vasconcelos and Francisco Miró Quesada, visited Chile and delivered a series of lectures cosponsored by SCF and UCH. They encountered an enthusiastic community of professionals who hailed them with banquets and addresses which underscored the Chilean philosophical community's own sense of international respectability. Additionally, shortly after its foundation, SCF was recognized by the Inter-American Federation of Philosophical Societies, the Institut International de Philosophie, and the Fedération International des Sociétés de Philosophie. In Chile, the rector of the Universidad de Chile, Juvenal Hernández, welcomed the creation of SCF and arranged a substantial grant to support both the Society and the creation of a journal of philosophy.[3]

The first issue of the *Revista de Filosofía* was published in 1949 and presented to Rector Juvenal Hernández at the first annual meeting of SCF. Edited by the secretary of publications of the Society, Mario Ciudad, the first issue of the *Revista* featured articles, reviews, and a section on institutional affairs. Jorge Millas and Luis

Oyarzún, among others, published essays on topics that ranged from philosophical methodology to contemporary French philosophical trends.

The *Revista* sought to facilitate acquaintance with European philosophy. Under the editorship of Mario Ciudad between 1949 and 1956, eight issues were published containing a total of forty-two articles and twenty-seven reviews. Most of the articles dealt with European philosophical figures; they included seven on Descartes, six on Goethe, five on Kierkegaard, and seven direct translations of works by Edmund Husserl, Max Scheler, and Martin Heidegger. The remaining essays by such foreigners as José Ferrater Mora, Alberto Wagner de Reyna, and Francisco Romero dealt with general methodological problems. Belying the aims stated in the statutes of SCF, there was only one article on Chilean thought published during Ciudad's tenure.[4] European philosophy, mainly German and French, dominated the contents of the official journal of SCF.

The deaths in 1948 and 1949 of Wilhelm Mann and Luis Lagarrigue, both heirs of the positivist tradition, marked the launching of the new era of philosophical studies initiated by Enrique Molina and Pedro León Loyola. Their passing was treated with solemnity, and other philosophical landmarks, such as the three-hundredth anniversary of Descartes' death and the bicentennial of Goethe's birthday were commemorated with lectures, conferences, and publications. To boost the philosophical community's sense of professional pride, a branch of SCF was founded in Valparaíso, and the UCH Department of Philosophy welcomed the arrival of the Italian Ernesto Grassi, who was hired to teach metaphysics. Grassi encouraged the study of the classics in their original language and employed a method of textual analysis that enriched the nature of philosophical studies at the department.[5]

Despite consensus on the need and desire to institutionalize philosophical activity, members of the SCF had their differences of opinion. Such differences concerned the limitations, if any, that should be placed on membership to the society. Pedro León Loyola was of the opinion that membership should be restricted to scholars, while Enrique Molina was of the view that a Chilean society of philosophy should be broader in nature. In one of the annual luncheons of the society, an animated exchange took place between Loyola and Molina on the subject. José Echeverría, who was present at the meeting, recalled that Loyola punctuated his argument by stating that Molina's principal role and contribution was as rector of the University of Concepción, implying that on matters philosophical his judgment was not as authoritative.[6] Juan Rivano, who attended a lecture by Jorge Millas, also recalls how Loyola stated his opinion that the only valuable work in Chilean philosophy was Millas's *Idea de la individualidad*, leaving Molina, also present at the lecture, pointedly out.[7]

Underlying these personality clashes and differences of opinion were conflicting views on the extent and depth of the professionalization of philosophical studies. Enrique Molina, who had played a pioneering role in defining the areas of philosophical concern after the demise of positivism, was by the 1950s no longer the leading voice for the increasingly specialized concerns of the philosophical community. In fact, when a number of intellectuals, including several national and international figures, paid homage to Enrique Molina in 1957, there were no philosophy specialists among them.[8] Even Pedro León Loyola had become somewhat passé by the 1950s, but he had the advantage over Molina of having educated many of the new breed of specialists. To be sure, both Molina and Loyola taught philosophy courses and wrote philosophical pieces in the 1950s, but the baton of philosophical leadership had been passed on to a new generation of professionals which included foreign professors but also Chilean scholars such as Jorge Millas.

By 1954 the faculty at the UCH Department of Philosophy had designed a program of philosophical studies that offered courses on aesthetics and the theory of knowledge, in addition to courses on the traditional fields of history of philosophy, logic, ethics, psychology, and metaphysics. Most important, they created a system of seminars and "monographic" courses, or courses devoted to the examination of specific themes, that allowed specialization to thrive. In 1956, for instance, monographic courses were offered on Aristotle, Plato's *Meno*, mathematical logic, Max Scheler's philosophy of values, and existentialism.[9]

The celebration of the First Congress of the Inter-American Society of Philosophy in Santiago in 1956 was the pinnacle of a rapid succession of achievements of the Chilean philosophical community. In the context of inter-American cooperation during the Second World War, several philosophical congresses had been celebrated, but Latin American philosophers proved that they could continue to run their meetings well beyond the initial inspiration of the international meetings. Several had been held in a host of Latin American countries through the 1940s and early 1950s. At those meetings, the idea of creating an Inter-American Society of Philosophy was discussed and finally came to fruition at the 1954 meeting convening in Brazil.[10] At this last meeting, it was decided that Chile would be the host of the first congress of the Society.

The organization of the congress was the greatest challenge encountered thus far by the Chilean philosophical community. Both SCF and UCH played an important role in organizing the meeting, whose arrangements rested on Jorge Millas and various UCH philosophy professors. Jorge Millas had already emerged as one of the leading Chilean philosophers of the period because of his writings, his teaching experience in the United States and Puerto Rico, and his acquaintance with Latin American philosophers through his active participation in previous philosophical meetings.[11] He and the other members of the organizing committee, which included Mario Ciudad, Félix Schwartzmann, Juan de Dios Vial Larraín, and others, secured the international sponsorship of UNESCO, the OAS, and the International Federation of Philosophical Societies. In Chile, the Ministry of Education, the Superintendency of Education, and the Universities of Chile, Católica, Concepción, Austral, Técnica del Estado, and Federico Santa María, also sponsored the event.[12]

The congress was a resounding success. Chileans participated in all of the major panels, discussing philosophical themes with such well-known figures as Miguel Reale, Eduardo Nicol, Risieri Frondizi, Francisco Romero, José Gaos, and José Ferrater Mora.[13] But more than providing professional satisfaction to the individual philosophers, the congress represented the climax of a longstanding effort to develop the field professionally. Chileans had worked hard creating their department, their society, and their journal of philosophy. They had succeeded in attracting the support and recognition of learned societies around the globe and internally in Chile. But above all, Chileans met the rewards of specialization in the form of a major international congress that gave recognition to their efforts. The way to achieve an international philosophical reputation, it became clear to them, was to become specialists in a field that knew no borders.

Similar developments took place at the Catholic University. During the rectorship of Carlos Casanueva, philosophy at both major universities was distinct, if not competing. But under the rectorship of Alfredo Silva Santiago (1953–1967), UC philosophers broke the ice that had existed between secular and Catholic philosophers for over a century. Surely, this rapproachment had a great deal to do with the muting of the old church-state conflict, particularly when the government of Carlos Ibáñez del Campo began subsidizing private education in 1954. This financing of private and public institutions, as Daniel C. Levy has noted, made Chilean higher education exceptionally homogeneous by Latin American standards.[14] But homogeneity was not confined to public funding; faculty members at both universities now shared similar intellectual and institutional interests.

In the field of philosophy, faculty members at UC showed the same penchant for publications, conferences, and visiting lectureships. The journal *Finis Terrae*, for instance, published more than eighty philosophy-related essays between 1954 and 1967. UC also hosted a luncheon for the participants to the 1956 congress of philosophy and invited European scholars such as Etienne Gilson, M. F. Sciacca, and Paul Henry to lecture during the 1950s.[15]

The philosophy curriculum itself now differed little from UCH's except for an understandable emphasis on theodicy and Latin. The most important difference resided in the fact that UC not only had Thomism as its official philosophy but also made it a part of the department's charter. But then again, article ten of the charter indicated that "this [official philosophy] does not prevent professors with different ideas from being invited by the faculty, as presenters, to expound a philosophical topic."[16]

Without the barriers that separated them in the past, philosophers from both universities published in each other's journals and shared membership in the same national philosophical association. Yet UC faculty retained an interest in theological questions and only rarely ventured into the subjects that concerned their secular counterparts, particularly logic and philosophical anthropology. But they all became part of a community that viewed its role as one of advancing, or at least disseminating, specialized philosophical concerns. This agreement between formerly antagonistic groups of thinkers proved that philosophical professionalism could provide a common set of principles and practices for philosophers to agree on. Professionalism meant a consensus on the procedures for philosophical activity. It worked in uniting Catholic and secular intellectuals in large measure because the conflict between the two no longer polarized the society as a whole. But professionalism remained hostile to politics in general, and Marxism in particular, because professionalists felt that both politics and Marxism were only concerned with materialistic subjects and not really with the life of the spirit. Thus professionalism adhered to a rationale that appeared to be open and undisturbed by philosophical differences of opinion, but was in fact antipolitical and anti-Marxist.

THE REACTION AGAINST ACADEMIC PHILOSOPHY

An important aspect of philosophical professionalism was the emphasis on specialized academic concerns, often originating in Europe and the United States. Still, some scholars retained a philosophical approach that sought to address social and cultural issues of relevance to the nation. The most significant effort in this regard was by Félix Schwartzmann (b. 1913), who published *El sentimiento de lo humano en América* in two volumes in 1950 and 1953. Schwartzmann himself became a professional philosopher who succeeded Mario Ciudad in the editorship of the *Revista de Filosofía*, taught the course in history and philosophy of science, and produced specialized philosophical pieces that matched those of his colleagues.[17] But in his *El sentimiento de lo humano*, Schwartzmann undertook the characterization of man in Latin America, although more specifically in Chile. The study utilized as sources a wide range of cultural forms, such as poetry, literature, and the essay. He identified the influence of nature, solitude, and the lack of expressive abilities as some of the keys for understanding man in the region. An extensive usage of sociological and philosophical literature made his work both a scholarly piece and an essay in its own right. No such interpretive work of this scope had ever been produced by a philosopher in the nation.[18]

Schwartzmann was not a philosopher by training. In fact, he had been appointed University Professor of Sociology in 1949. Sociology had been introduced in Chile by positivists who, following Comte, felt that this field was the highest expression of positivist philosophy. Chilean sociology evolved by and large as a philosophical offshot that concerned itself primarily with social and cultural issues. It was only in the 1950s, as Edmundo Fuenzalida has shown, that sociology became a specialized and university-based field of study, producing a sharp break with the essay-oriented production of the past.[19] Schwartzmann wrote perhaps the last of the encompassing works concerned with culture and society on the eve of the professionalization of both sociology and philosophy. His willingness to adapt to the specialized demands of the UCH Department of Philosophy, as *catedrático* of history and philosophy of science, underscores the tremendous influence of the nascent philosophical professionalism emerging at Chilean universities.

Yet despite the growth and specialization of the Chilean philosophical community, various young scholars felt uneasy about the new model of philosophical studies. Some, in fact, were motivated to study philosophy for reasons having little to do with the impulse to institutionalize academic specialization. Gastón Gómez Lasa (b. 1926), who was a philosophy student in the late 1940s, entered the discipline after several trials in other fields. None gave him satisfactory answers to concerns that only vaguely did he know to be philosophical. Additionally, he found the study of philosophy at UCH to be narrowly oriented towards pedagogy. It was only when he was assured by FFE Dean Juan Gómez Millas, later rector of UCH, that he could pursue an academic, as opposed to a professional, degree that Gómez Lasa decided to pursue a program of philosophical studies under the direction of Ferrater Mora, Bogumil Jasinowski, and other local and European professors. But his original motivation for entering the field was highly personal and did not conform to a structured philosophical curriculum.[20]

Similarly, Humberto Giannini (b. 1927), who became a philosophy student in the early 1950s, was motivated to study philosophy by personal experiences going back to his adolescence. He had been a secondary school dropout who had gone to sea to join the merchant marine and went back to night school with a vague and romantic interest in the discipline. At the university, he was influenced by Bogumil Jasinowski and Jorge Millas, but generally he felt estranged from the abstract character of philosophical studies. "The department during those years," he recalled, "was essentially concerned with a 'pure' philosophy . . . there were also some fads that I disliked very much. [Nicolai] Hartmann was in fashion at the time. He was everywhere. There was also some emphasis on the theory of values and on a very limited positivism. But the climate of ideas was not very original."[21]

Juan Rivano (b. 1926), who was also a student at the time, found the study of philosophy to be not only shallow, but also removed. "At the university," he said, "we studied philosophy by looking at both the history of the field and the philosophical disciplines. There was no emphasis on how to encourage philosophical habits in the students. I never found myself, my classmates or my professors in the position of being the subjects of philosophical examination. It was as if it would have been in bad taste to descend from generalities in order to test [the validity] of philosophical notions in our concrete selves."[22] Rivano, like Giannini, developed his philosophical interests prior to his formal university training, enduring the hardships of working by day in a variety of menial jobs and studying by night.

Another young scholar who developed philosophical interests outside academe was Marco Antonio Allendes (b. 1925). He was motivated to the study of philosophy by his uncle Jorge de la Cuadra, the author of *Filosofía de la realidad* (1949). Allendes, like Gómez Lasa, studied law for one year and then dropped out of school. He then accidentally met Ricardo Gálvez, a Spanish anarchist who would talk about Indian philosophy to anyone willing to listen in the Parque Forestal along the Mapocho River. Allendes was so impressed by Gálvez that he studied with him for eight years, until Gálvez's death. It was only then that he completed his formal philosophy studies. By that time, his interest in philosophy was fully formed.[23]

Allendes studied at UCH under Bogumil Jasinowski, José Ferrater Mora, and Marcelo Neuschlosz. Neuschlosz, in particular, gave him private lessons which soon developed into exchanges with the younger Allendes, whose knowledge of Indian philosophy greatly impressed the aging specialist in the philosophy of science. Allendes successfully completed his studies and was subsequently offered a professorship in the department. Yet reflecting on his education after more than thirty years, Allendes still regarded Ricardo Gálvez as his major influence.[24]

These four intellectuals, who would all make substantial contributions to their discipline, developed their philosophical interests outside the university and in fact did not feel entirely comfortable with the direction of philosophical studies in the 1950s. In a field that had abandoned politics as a central subject of concern, it was difficult for junior practitioners to articulate an alternative view of the discipline. They were clear, however, that criticism was lacking and that the field had been reduced to mere exposition, with limited discussion, of European philosophical currents.

LOGIC AND CRITICISM

The field of logic afforded an opportunity for philosophers to depart from and eventually criticize the type of philosophical studies available in their department. Logic had been the poor cousin in the family of Chilean philosophical concerns ever since Molina's establishment of a hierarchy of values for the subjects of philosophical concern. The neglect of logic had roots in the nineteenth-century critiques of the alleged association between logic and scholasticism, despite Andrés Bello's efforts to counter them. In the twentieth century, this neglect had a great deal to do with Molina's antipositivist orientation as well as with the resistance of academics to involve themselves with a subject that, it appeared, demanded tedious work as well as familiarity with mathematics. Only a few Chileans, most notably Juan Serapio Lois, Wilhelm Mann, Pedro León Loyola, and Marcos Flores, managed to sustain interest in the subject of logic.

This was not a problem for either foreigners, such as Gerold Stahl, who came from a philosophical tradition not hostile to logic, or for Chileans like Juan Rivano, who came from a mathematics background. The two would in time become founding members of the Chilean Association of Logic and Philosophy of Science, and introduce a variety of logical schools and authors.[25] Gerold Stahl, who was born in Germany and held a doctorate from the University of Munich, concentrated on symbolic logic and philosophy of science topics during his twenty-year tenure in Chile. Juan Rivano, while also concerned with similar topics, concentrated on dialectical logic and the British neo-Hegelian tradition inaugurated by Francis Herbert Bradley.[26]

Logic achieved an important degree of legitimacy when some well-known philosophers participated in a panel on logic, philosophy of science, and theory of knowledge at the 1956 congress. They included Willard V. O. Quine, Roderick Chisholm, Mario Bunge, Francisco Miró Quesada, and Juan García Bacca, among the visitors, and Félix Schwartzmann, Bogumil Jasinowski, Gerold Stahl, and Juan Rivano, among the Chilean representatives. In addition, as Félix Schwartzmann took the editorship of the *Revista de Filosofía* in the same year, logic and philosophy of science received an emphasis that helped balance the predominance of phenomenological and metaphysical subjects.[27]

The study of logic during the 1950s generally followed the patterns of specialized knowledge prevailing in the UCH Department of Philosophy. Scholars concentrated their attention on the introduction to logic as well as highly specialized problems in the field. But in one case, logical activity led to the use of the field as a critical instrument to assess the validity of philosophical concepts and eventually to criticize the dominant schools in the department. This was the case of Juan Rivano, whose use of logic as a critical instrument came from the neo-Hegelian authors Francis Bradley and Harold Joachim. An FFE mathematics graduate who studied under Jorge Millas, Rivano departed early from the dominant currents of philosophical activity through his work in dialectical logic and, increasingly, his critique of existentialist and phenomenological views.

The specialized vocabulary of the philosophical community in the 1950s included concepts such as "evidence," "self," and "consciousness," particularly among those who concentrated on phenomenological authors. In logic and methodology, such concepts as "identity," "difference," "analysis," "synthesis," and others also became common currency among members of the faculty. But these concepts were used as if consensus existed about their meaning. Rivano, who argued that it did not, undertook an extensive study of central philosophical concepts following the dialectical approach of the neo-Hegelians.[28]

Rivano's use of logic initially strengthened professionalism by expanding the scope and depth of philosophical studies. His work brought to the philosophical community an emphasis on methodological questions as well as a demand for accuracy in the definition of key philosophical concepts. Rivano's focus on the methods and instruments developed by the philosophical tradition for the acquisition of knowledge led him to question even the dialectical approach that he appeared to follow rather closely. This can be seen in his treatment of Bradley, whose *Appearance and Reality* he translated and annotated. In particular, Rivano criticized the British author's notion of reality, which he found abstract and detached from concrete experience. Rivano later condemned the same notion for allegedly condoning the coexistence of intolerable contradictions, particularly in the social realm, for the sake of preserving the harmony of philosophy.[29] But in the 1950s, Bradley helped him to develop a logical approach with which he criticized the philosophical practices of his own department. Rivano's interest in Bradley's ideas during this period was consistent with his growing discontent with academic thought and language. "In Bradley's philosophy," he maintained, "we find what we could find in any philosopher should they take leave from academic thought and devote themselves to thinking freely."[30] What he meant by this was that in his view Bradley had done what he believed every practitioner of the field should do: relate philosophy to human experience.

"Philosophy is not a group of disciplines which only exists in a group of treatises," he maintained, and went on to suggest that ideas were meant to enhance rather than impose upon, or live independently from, human experience.[31] He learned this lesson from his reading of Bradley, but he was not convinced that dialectics was the appropriate approach for solving all the questions related to man, knowledge, and reality. In particular, he found dialectics too abstract, and expressed dissatisfaction with the distance he perceived as existing between theoretical and moral questions in the philosophies based on dialectical assumptions. He thought that there was a great distance between the apparent harmony of dialectical systems and the facts of historical, social, and political phenomena. Harmony, he argued, was not as easily found in the reality of everyday experience, which was the area where he thought ideas should ultimately be tested. One could find a philosophy that was as coherent as Bradley's, but questions remained as to their applicability to human life.

Rivano suggested that neither the schools that he criticized nor the dialectics that he followed closely were able to provide guidance to the concrete needs of man. He retained the critical aspects of dialectics but expressed some clear discomfort with this approach and with academic philosophy generally. He made it clear that he expected philosophy to serve as a guide for human experience when he later suggested that "a philosophy that does not provide an integral orientation to our lives is worth nothing."[32] From a successful professional who had received academic recognitions such as the chairmanship of the philosophy department at the University of Concepción and the *cátedra* of logic at UCH, this was certainly a strong condemnation that needs to be explored beyond the specialized writings considered thus far.

JUAN RIVANO AND DIALECTICAL CRITICISM

In his unpublished *Un largo contrapunto* (1986), Rivano has referred explicitly to his discomfort with academic philosophy. In this autobiography he discusses the impact that the schools of existentialism and phenomenology, but particularly the latter, had on his milieu in the early 1950s. He mentions that these philosophies encouraged both a series of discussions on a so-called crisis of the West and, particularly because of the influence of Martin Heidegger, an emphasis on language, especially German and Greek, as the basis of philosophy.

In Rivano's account, the majority of philosophy students were ill-prepared to handle Greek or German, so that the result was a superficial and even frivolous application of Heidegger's views to the students' understanding of the field. Languages were not required in the philosophy curriculum, yet students were exposed early to Heideggerian and phenomenological views. The product was what Rivano depicts as an uncritical adoption of philosophical views that led scholars to distort or misuse the Spanish language in order to adjust it to German or other foreign terms.[33]

Additionally, Rivano argued, the discussions on the crisis of the West, along with those on existentialist themes such as the "being for death," and "nothingness," made sense in postwar Europe, but were out of place among the Chilean philosophy students who concentrated more on words than on context.[34] Rivano indicated that the early 1950s were the years when Chileans began to learn about the horrors of World War II. And yet the "crisis of the West" as a theme discussed by philosophy professors and students was not seen in the context of the war. It was, in Rivano's rendition of those years, an abstract problem that many of his classmates believed could be solved by researching the origins of language in a Heideggerian sense.

> In the early 1950s it was common to hear our professors talk about the crisis of the West. There were even some groups that attempted to reestablish the [historical] continuity [of the West] by returning to the origins [of language and philosophy]. But as I never heard anything about the specifics of the crisis—racial extermination, the killing of millions of human beings in gas chambers and firing squads in the very heart of Western Europe—I took that to mean that these were only words. It seems to me, then, that the matter should be put as follows: to all those responsible for our education, guidance, governance, and inspiration the events of Nazi Germany were regarded as uncontestable facts. But not uncontestable enough to challenge the presumed spiritual achievements of Western culture, let alone denounce the scandal and failure that such achievements represented when seen in the light of war. To me, there was no other choice but to conclude that such spiritual achievements, at the moment of truth, were compatible with the massive technological and industrialized extermination—later even commercialized—of millions of human beings.[35]

Rivano was no more comfortable with the department's lack of concern with national problems. In his autobiography he repeatedly indicated that there was no connection between the department's subjects of philosophical interest, even though they included man and his rights, and the conditions of poverty that prevailed in Chile. There was, he suggested, a general rejection of matters political, at least as subjects of philosophical discussion.

But no other event precipitated his critique of academic philosophy and even a change in his own philosophical posture more than the April 2, 1957, Santiago demonstrations against the economic policies of the Ibáñez administration.[36] Rivano, who was caught by accident in the whirlwind of rioting and shooting, emerged shaken but determined to seek to reconcile, or otherwise confront, philosophical endeavors and matters of national concern. Because a philosophy professor was a member of the cabinet that gave the green light to the repression that resulted in the death of several FFE students, he became convinced that the Chilean philosophical community condoned such situations while claiming to be apolitical.[37]

The University of Chile, except for the participation of students in protests against the government, remained largely isolated from the wider political situation of the country. Many of its leaders, including Rector Juan Gómez Millas, were supporters of Ibáñez del Campo and kept good relations with the government. The UCH in fact enjoyed something of a heyday during the 1950s as enrollments grew substantially[38] and the research and student aid budgets received hefty increases.[39]

Yet the situation in the larger society deteriorated at a rapid pace. Ibáñez del Campo, who had assumed the presidency in 1952 through the support of a heterodox combination of socialist and right wing groups, found himself relying heavily on the right towards the second half of his administration. Political unrest accelerated as Ibáñez upheld the Law for the Defense of Democracy and as the country faced the biggest economic slump since the Great Depression. In an attempt to control inflation, Ibáñez followed the recommendations of the U.S. Klein-Saks economic mission to curb government spending and placed ceilings on prices and salaries. These policies, which were in line with the philosophy of the International Monetary Fund, assured Ibáñez the support of the right but precipitated student and labor unrest.

Chile's economic problems were related to the failure, if not collapse, of the import-substituting industrialization policies pursued by both the popular front and radical governments that preceded Ibáñez's term in office. The Chilean population grew from 5.9 million in 1952 to 7.3 million in 1960, and massive rural-urban migration (Santiago alone grew from 1.4 to 2.1 million between 1952 and 1960) created enormous pressures for housing, employment, and political representation. Moreover, the administration itself was debilitated by the lack of organized political party support and constant cabinet changes. The invitation extended to the unpopular Klein-Saks mission pushed an already tense situation to the brink of an open social confrontation.

A bus fare increase in 1957 unleashed the worst violence Santiago had seen since the 1920s and 1930s. The government moved to secure extraordinary faculties from Congress and harshly suppressed urban unrest within days. The university, which had remained isolated from the economic problems of the larger society, found itself immersed in the violence as university students were in the forefront of the protests that raged on during the first quarter of 1957. IP students, as indicated earlier, were among the hardest hit by the repression.

University professors could, and by and large did, choose to remain detached from these events. But some, like Rivano, chose to criticize the position of their colleagues in these events and establish a link between their politics and the dominant mode of philosophical work at the university. As mentioned above, the changes in Rivano's specialized philosophical work that led to a critique of academic philosophy came from his studies of dialectical logic. But his dissatisfaction with the department and its philosophical preferences stemmed from concrete experiences in the 1950s which soon led him to abandon specialized language and to search for philosophical forms applicable to Chile. His first major work in this regard was *Entre Hegel y Marx* (1962), in which he discussed the transformation of dialectics from a critical philosophical instrument to a vehicle for social criticism and a foundation for humanism.

Rivano's *Entre Hegel y Marx* made an impact on the Chilean philosophical community both because of its treatment of Hegel and Marx on philosophical rather than political grounds, and because it contained harsh and explicit critiques of the Department of Philosophy and its major philosophical schools.[40] Such critiques were made in the context of his discussion of the philosophical transition from Hegel to Marx. Dividing the book into two major sections, "understanding and reason" and "freedom and humanism," Rivano covered Hegel's critique of understanding, his notion of reason, and the emergence of humanism as the new task of philosophy.

Hegel defined understanding as the type of thinking, prevalent in the philosophical tradition, "that can produce only limited and partial categories and proceed by their means," implying that, in his view, such an approach failed to comprehend reality.[41] While agreeing with Hegel's characterization of the notion of understanding, Rivano did not share his optimism on the supersedure of this type of thinking by his philosophy. Rivano suggested that phenomenology, positivism, empiricism, and scientism all represented thriving examples of understanding. In Chile, he maintained, philosophy students "have been domesticated by phenomenological mentors" who defended Edmund Husserl's antipsychologism and demanded that students "describe" objects in order to learn about them. "We, philosophical apprentices, did not know what to do with such 'rare' and 'irrelevant' things such as feeling and sensation."[42] Without a basis in psychology, he suggested, phenomenological description became an abstract endeavor that did not involve human participation.

Rivano extended his critique to modern logicians representing such currents as logical analysis and scientism, like Bertrand Russell and Hans Reichenbach. In his view, these authors had reduced philosophy to a theory of knowledge that described reality on the basis of mathematical concepts. Rivano charged that their views made reality schematic beyond recognition because they made possible the mere aggregation of phenomena apprehended through sense-perception.[43] In Rivano's mind, this demonstrated that the understanding defined by Hegel was still strong and that its main consequence was the lack of human concern that characterized the discipline. He traced this lack of humanism to professionalism, suggesting that the alienation of philosophers from reality was due to a professionalism that occupied them with pseudoproblems. But far more serious than the philosophers' alienation were the pedagogical implications of the professionalistic attitude prevalent in Chilean philosophy. He suggested that students, once in the department, found themselves "prisoners in a cave worse than Plato's," and went on to suggest that the "philosophy taught at our academic centers has done nothing to enhance spiritual life."[44]

Philosophy ought to be humanistic, Rivano argued, and he found support in the work of Hegel, Feuerbach, and Marx. According to Rivano, these three authors provided man with the tools for his liberation and spiritual realization by criticizing individualism, religion, and material alienation, respectively. The critique of individualism made man realize his place in the community; the critique of religion helped him question the validity of a notion of God as apart from man; and the critique of material alienation made him understand the sources and economic foundations of exploitation and spiritual alienation.

The transition from Hegel to Marx, Rivano maintained, was a transition from a speculative yet humanistic philosophical endeavor to a thoroughly humanistic view of man that heralded the advent of both reason and a new philosophy. This new philosophy, which Rivano discussed in the second part of his work, was primarily concerned with the themes of freedom, love understood in a social sense, and humanism. Here, Rivano no longer relied on the philosophers whom he used to support his arguments in the first part, and wrote in terms more distinctively his own, particularly in regard to the subject of human freedom.

Rivano examined the conception of freedom that was in his view most widely available to men: freedom as the ability to opt among alternatives. He found this conception to be based on individualism and supported by a social milieu that regarded options as the ultimate expression of freedom. Existentialism, in his view, was the philosophical expression of individualism, and as such it established a separation between man and his surroundings. The freedom that could be derived from such a philosophy was only separation and alienation from other human beings. In contrast, a notion of freedom as love put man in direct contact with other human beings and thus transcended the narrow and alienating limits of individualism.[45] It was in the experience of love that man, according to Rivano, realized his essence, reached out for other human beings, and attained freedom.

Rivano's interest in the transition from Hegel to Marx was not a Chilean peculiarity. Carlos Astrada (1894–1970) of Argentina also devoted attention to the subject in his *Marx y Hegel* (1958), although his concern about these two German thinkers was present in his 1952 work, *La revolución existencialista*. Astrada, who had studied in Germany under Martin Heidegger, Max Scheler, and Edmund Husserl, gradually moved away from phenomenology and existentialism in order to address Hegelian and Marxist ideas. To this extent, the development of Astrada's concerns paralleled Rivano's, as they evolved from the critique of phenomenology and existentialism to the examination of Hegelian and Marxist thought. Both Astrada and Rivano were professionally trained philosophers. But Rivano was a logician whose interest in the British neo-Hegelians led him to Hegel and from Hegel to Marx. Additionally, the political contexts in which they studied and worked were different. Carlos Astrada was a Peronist supporter who found himself in a precarious position after the fall of Juan Domingo Perón in 1955, and who later made a clear commitment to Marxist positions.[46] His purpose in writing about Hegel and Marx was essentially to declare the philosophy of Hegel an abstraction, to underscore the contributions of Marx to humanism, and to criticize the authors who in his view overemphasized Marx's debt to Hegel.

Rivano's view of the transition from Hegel to Marx, although not fundamentally different from Astrada's, focused more on Hegel's critique of understanding, the concept of reason, and the connection between freedom and humanism. Rivano was also more skeptical about Marx's view, taken literally by Astrada, that speculative philosophy had ended with Hegel.[47] While both authors were animated by similar concerns regarding the emergence of humanism, they went about their work in different ways. Astrada assumed a fundamental tension between Marx and Hegel, while Rivano took the work of both as important yet partial responses to the larger question of the emergence of humanism in the history of philosophy.

In Chile and abroad, critics acknowledged the importance of Rivano's book as well as its impact as a major contribution to Latin American philosophy.[48] However, most coincided in objecting to the style of the book, which they found "without any academic solemnity,"[49] "confusing" in its effort to make the book readable for a wide audience,[50] and written in "an aggressive mood that is hardly academic."[51]

These criticisms are significant because they reveal the first open clash between the emerging humanism advocated by Rivano and the academic professionalism espoused by the Chilean philosophical community. Rivano antagonized his peers by suggesting that the academic form of philosophy discouraged humanism, which he considered the most important among the discipline's aims. In his unpublished *Desde el abandono* (1963), he described the impact of academic philosophy on his thought as follows: "Long years of academic lies, dreams and irresponsible talk had crippled my capacity to look at reality directly. . . . I was trapped in a speculative labyrinth while people around me starved to death."[52] Professionalists, however, did not feel that the issue was whether philosophy should play a role outside the boundaries defined by the academic community but rather the unorthodox form of Rivano's philosophical writing.

Rivano maintained, however, a high level of specialized philosophical production, including a book on logic and essays on dialectics and the philosophy of science.[53] But increasingly he wrote for the general public, including newspaper articles in the national press.[54] Even in his specialized works, however, he provided a rationale for the closer connection he viewed as indispensible between philosophy and human reality. This approach led him to sever his ties with the dialectics of Hegel and Bradley. He did so because he felt that man's destiny rested upon finite experience rather than on the notion of absolute defended by these authors. Dialectics, as Bradley and Hegel used it, culminated in the Absolute, a process Rivano regarded as being too far removed from the concrete needs of man. He suggested that these authors' usage of dialectics, namely, the integration of opposites in an always increasing degree of universality, carried speculation "too far," meaning "going beyond the limits within which there is still a relation between speculation and life."[55]

Philosophy, he lamented, had reached levels of abstraction that were entirely alien to man's concrete reality. A conciliation between the two was needed, and he felt that dialectics could do this for as long as it remained within the confines of human existence. "Dialectics," he maintained, "is a way of living and acting intelligently; it opens the way for a true life, but *our* life."[56] Dialectics thus understood informed his subsequent writing. Criticism of academic philosophy remained an important part of his work, but he also had to respond to the questions raised by his own critique of the field. Could a humanistic philosophy, for instance, serve the human needs traditionally satisfied by religion? In his *Desde la religión al humanismo* (1965), Rivano addressed this question by first criticizing philosophy's lack of humanistic concerns and high level of abstraction. Particularly because of the abstract nature of the field, philosophy could hardly take the place of religion in man's life. Religion provided man with a sense of security, and although much emphasis was given to the centrality of God, this sense of security was the most tangible contribution of religion to human life.[57]

Religion, however, was not a complete response to man's needs. By concentrating on the affirmation of God, Rivano felt, religion was alienating because it took man's longing for fulfillment beyond his own concrete life. As he put it, "to the extent that religion is a response to man's need for security, it says important things which we must listen to seriously; but by projecting that security to heaven, religion goes from saying important things to making gratuitous assertions about man."[58]

Philosophy could and should take the place of religion, in Rivano's view, but for that it needed to take into account man's need for security. Marxism had criticized religion on material grounds, but it still lacked concern for the spiritual needs of man. Philosophy could move beyond this limited approach by giving man a sense of security through freedom understood in secular terms. Should philosophy help him realize his spiritual potential, man would achieve freedom and no longer have a need for an external God.

"Haste," "lack of university level," and "incredible frivolity," were some of the comments made about Rivano's *Desde la religión al humanismo*.[59] According to Jaime Concha, who claimed the support of Aristotle, philosophy was characterized by meditation. He found this feature missing in Rivano's work. "Everything Rivano touches," Concha suggested, "turns into futility."[60] His critique was directed against the form of Rivano's work rather than its content. No mention was made of Rivano's interpretation of humanism nor of his proposals for a meaningful philosophical endeavor in the country, but the commentary reveals the extent of the resistance to considering Rivano's work as a legitimate philosophical approach.

Rivano continued, however, to link philosophy and subjects of human concern that increasingly involved social elements. In his *El punto de vista de la miseria* (1965), Rivano rejected what he termed "theological" and "metaphysical" alienation. His view of theological alienation echoed the positivists' earlier rejection of the theological stage in the evolution of humanity and the Marxist critique of religion. But his concept of metaphysical alienation emerged as a response to decades of Chilean philosophical concern for metaphysics. At any rate, Rivano was not subscribing to any theory of evolutionary stages. Instead, he argued that the place for the realization of human needs and potentials was neither a transcendental reality nor the Absolute, but society. Only the community of man had the capacity for "reducing, eliminating or overcoming the conflictive nature of social existence."[61] Despite the conservative tendencies inherent in social institutions, the community had a "progressive" character because of its very composition: human beings.

Following Marxist ideas, to which he adhered only partially, Rivano argued that consciousness was an important instrument for the transformation of society. But consciousness could be deceived by ideologies defending the status quo. Philosophers, in particular, gave an academic justification to an unjust economic structure by directly defending or simply ignoring it. Their speculations, he charged, only perpetuated the situation of exploitation and spiritual alienation affecting society, defending the interest of a minority rather than those of the larger society.

Historically, Rivano maintained, religion and philosophy had condoned alienation and exploitation by taking speculative endeavors as their main subject of concern. Philosophy, in particular, was for him "the creature of injustice and crime,"[62] and he proceeded to examine some of the major philosophers of the century, all of them German. The purpose of his focus, he explained, was to "say something about our own philosophers and their all-inclusive and grandiose manners."[63] Through his criticism of Husserl, Heidegger, and Wittgenstein, Rivano chastised both Europeans and Chileans for their detachment from social issues.[64] He suggested that the philosophy of the European authors was not meant to resolve any of the practical needs of humanity. In addition, they lived in societies that could afford their detachment from social concerns. But in Latin America, the social, economic, and political conditions of the region made similar philosophical endeavors not only irrelevant but also dangerous. They deprived the continent, Rivano maintained, of a critical attitude that could help change the status quo.

Latin America philosophers, in Rivano's view, concerned themselves with philosophies that he found alien to the region's culture, economic needs, and history. In addition, they lacked originality and were extremely obscure in their language. These philosophers indulged in conferences, publications, and meetings that served no practical purpose to their societies and in addition served the more sinister purpose of maintaining a status quo of poverty and alienation.[65]

Despite these devastating critiques, Rivano suggested that philosophy in Latin America should not be dismissed, but rather given a humanistic orientation. He urged those interested in a meaningful philosophy in the continent to establish a continuity between "the content and doctrines of philosophy and our historical reality."[66] Such schools as existentialism and phenomenology, which he found characterized by skepticism, were products of a culture in crisis. But a continent struggling for justice, like Latin America, "cannot afford to be skeptical."[67]

Rivano's critique of Latin American and Chilean philosophy was followed by a set of recommendations, specifically addressed to students, to confront academic arguments defending the separation of social and philosophical concerns. Titled *Contra sofistas* (1966), Rivano's book on the subject consisted of the application of some basic logical principles to arguments based on overgeneralizations, false inferences, inappropriate analogies, and fallacies. He suggested that some basic distinctions, such as those between universal and particular propositions, premises and conclusions, and ideas and action, provided a helpful conceptual framework to destroy sophisms. By disarming sophistry, Rivano argued, students would be prepared to face the injustice, poverty, and abandonment prevalent in the country, and direct themselves to "a true and valuable life."[68]

Rivano suggested that "sophists" used such rhetorical devices as grandiose statements and the manipulation of emotions in order to deceive the student and protect themselves from criticism. The use of paradoxes, global perspectives, and simplifications of man's nature such as explanations based on the "death instinct," or a "will for power," were sophistic means to keep student attention away from the concrete needs of the country. Rivano called on them to demand from their professors a substantiation of their arguments and to apply logical criteria to establish their validity.

Hernán del Solar, one of the influential *El Mercurio* critics, reviewed Rivano's *Contra sofistas* on April 23, 1966. He suggested that he was accustomed to thinking of the philosopher as an "imperturbable" being having the characteristics of "severity" and "balance." Juan Rivano, however, had revealed himself as an "irate philosopher" who attacked anyone with ideas different from his own, and did so in a "strident" tone. Del Solar concluded that "the irate, passionate professor Rivano will provoke the anger of many. But some will celebrate him."[69]

Events at FFE were already showing the signs of confrontation and polarization that launched the university reform movement of 1967–1968. With his *Contra sofistas*, Rivano underscored his decision to cast his lot with students demanding participation in university affairs as well as a connection between university and society. A similar inspiration guided his *Cultura de la servidumbre*, a book based on his 1966 and 1968 lectures, which provided further arguments against the intellectual activity that he felt served to mask social conditions in the country.

Rivano's *La cultura de la servidumbre* was an explicit critique of the Chilean intellectual elite, which he accused of being frivolous and subservient to European values. In his reading of Chilean literature, intellectuals appeared as pro-European, enamored with "myths" such as individualism and history, and contemptuous of things Chilean and Latin American. But because these arguments had already been presented in many of his other writings, most important in this book was his criticism of Marxist views, which he expressed to dissociate himself from Marxist political currents gaining ground both at the university and in society generally. Rivano had visited Czechoslovakia in 1967 on the eve of the Soviet invasion of that country and subsequently denounced the invasion in Chile. His critiques against the Soviet Union and of Marxism as an ideology thus stemmed from an observer's experience. But his specific discomfort with Marxism was rooted also in this movement's philosophy of history.

Marx's major historical predictions, Rivano suggested, had all failed: the proletariat did not remain the only agent for revolutionary change, nor had the revolution spread. Capitalism, instead of dying, showed tremendous strength internationally. In addition, some of the major Marxist philosophers of history were all characterized by their contempt for Third World movements for social change, as they believed that capitalism would collapse by means of its own contradictions rather than by the liberation of poor societies. Rivano invited the dismissal of Marxist historical determinism on the grounds that "it is just another form of alienation."[70]

Rivano adhered to some Marxist views, particularly the concept of alienation, although only to develop themes of his own interest rather than to lend support to Marxism as a whole.[71] He in fact criticized the attempts by intellectuals and politicians to turn Marxism into a science or an ideology resolving all problems of history and society. But the concept of alienation, which he applied to matters of spiritual life, served him by articulating a critical view of Chilean intellectual life in general, and philosophy in particular. He used this concept to criticize all philosophies that lacked humanistic concerns and to criticize the Chilean philosophers who employed their talents to think through problems alien to the needs of the country. His department, he suggested, was "an ivory tower if seen from the outside; but the Tower of Babel if seen from the inside." In his view, neither the variety of authors taught at the department nor its professional endeavors had anything to do with, let alone had a commitment with, the social and political reality of the country. Philosophy during the period, he concluded, "was proud of its uselessness."[72]

Rivano's transition from a successful professionalist philosopher in the 1950s to a critic of his department, his colleagues, and the discipline in general during the 1960s stems from the biographical events mentioned above as well as from the internal dynamics of his philosophical work. His specialization in logic led him to probe diverse schools, particularly the dialectical logic of the neo-Hegelians. Dialectics led him first to a study of Hegel and then to Marx's interpretation of Hegel's philosophy. All along, philosophical choices were made, but dialectics remained Rivano's major subject of study. He was clearly interested in this subject because it allowed him to study both specialized philosophical problems and the social concerns which he found missing in the Chilean version of the discipline. Yet even dialectics served him only to a limited extent, as he criticized both the abstract version of Bradley and Hegel on the one hand, and its ideological usage by the Marxists on the other.

In addition, changes in Rivano's philosophical orientation mirrored the changed Latin American intellectual landscape of the 1950s and 1960s, due mainly to the spread of Marxist ideas at the time of the Cuban revolution. In Chile, the discussion of Marxism was accompanied by the growth of a leftist movement that achieved a significant presence at both national and university levels. The pressure that both the movement and the school of thought put on university intellectuals led many to resist the changes advocated by the Marxists, or, as in Rivano's case, to study the philosophical basis of Marx's views, namely, dialectics.

The presence of Marxist thought in a field that had recently achieved independence from politics marked a turning point in the recent history of philosophical professionalism in Chile. Philosophers reacted slowly to the critiques against their alleged detachment from social concerns, but react they did. They found, however, that in order to respond to criticisms they not only needed to defend their view of philosophy but also the very university model that sustained their philosophical professionalism. And at that point a university reform movement loomed large just outside their classrooms.

Chilean philosophers enjoyed a brief but significant period when they achieved both independence from politics and the ability to practice philosophy according to their perception of international standards. The field produced a complex and sophisticated program of activities during these years, yet it failed to consolidate its gains through the students. In a pattern similar to previous periods, it was the graduates of the field during the 1940s and 1950s who led the critiques against their school and who sought to change the thrust of philosophical activity.

Part of the reason for this drastic reversal resides in the desired but artificial separation between university and politics. For a short time, philosophers lived as if independent from the forces that agitated the wider society. But the events of the late 1950s combined with the critiques of one of the field's own esteemed professionals made that separation no longer tenable, or even justifiable. Still, most philosophers clung to their ideal of a separation between both philosophy and university from politics, and became further entrenched. This accentuated the growing conflict among the faculty. Ironically, in the process of avoiding the politicization of the discipline, all faculty members became politicized, not just those who sought a closer connection between philosophy and politics. In the end, most philosophers came to realize that their claim to be "above politics" was also political and that it would be just as well if they said so in the open.

V

PHILOSOPHY AND THE MOVEMENT FOR UNIVERSITY REFORM

1960–1973

Philosophers found their professionalism difficult to sustain in the face of critiques from within their own ranks and also from the renewed political activism that inaugurated the 1960s in Chile. The left had come close to winning the 1958 presidential elections, and the newly created centrist Christian Democratic Party (PDC) had gathered significant momentum since the last electoral contest. These two political groups intensified their activism as they prepared for the 1964 elections, both offering substantial, and even structural, changes in Chilean society.

As political activism reached the universities, the philosophers who had been educated under the premise that the university was the embodiment of reason, and hence above and beyond politics, reacted in a variety of complex ways. Some ignored political events and went about their business as if philosophy had nothing to do with such events. Others maintained their style of philosophical work but criticized politics, especially Marxism, along theoretical lines. Still others condemned the politicization of both university and society very explicitly, although they did so from an apparently philosophical standpoint. Their reactions were not mutually exclusive, as some, like Jorge Millas, responded in all three ways.

These philosophers, whom I call *professionalists* because of their role in the institutionalization of the highly specialized and apolitical version of the discipline in Chile in the 1950s, developed an elaborate rationale to resist the pressures for university reform that different academic and political groups were already seeking to precipitate. In addition, and in the process of reluctantly becoming involved in politics, philosophers reestablished the traditional links between philosophy and higher education in Chile, although this time to demonstrate that the apoliticism that seemed to work for the discipline could also work for the university. Philosophy once again became the vehicle for advocating views on higher education, but philosophers, particularly the professionalists, reacted strongly to the threat of a university model that, if successful, would guide philosophy rather than the other way around. They attempted to restore the place of philosophy as the guide for higher education only to discover, to their dismay, that political pressures were overwhelming enough to turn not only their faculties, but also the entire university system, into an arena where larger political forces tested their strength.

Philosophers made strenuous yet futile attempts to control the process of university reform. Either for or against it, philosophers had a sobering encounter with politics that led some to strengthen their professionalism while rejecting politics, and others to radically change their philosophical orientations. Philosophers were particularly vocal during the process of university reform because they all had firm views about the university, views which were in turn rooted in their philosophical stances. But none was fully aware of the extent to which their views, philosophical or otherwise, would be limited, or even subsumed, by a larger political process that they generally knew little about. Knowingly or unknowingly, however, they precipitated a reform movement that would have tremendous consequences not only for the discipline, but for the university and the nation.

THE PHILOSOPHICAL RESPONSE

Between the time of Juan Rivano's critiques of the discipline in the early 1960s, and 1968, when university reform at UCH began, philosophers by and large continued the trends of philosophical work that had characterized the professionalism of the previous decade. The *Revista de Filosofía*, the leading journal in the field, continued the editorial line established in the 1950s. As was the case then, phenomenology and existentialism continued to receive substantial attention, as did a variety of other metaphysical subjects. The classics, particularly Plato and Aristotle, were widely discussed. But no single author received more attention than Martin Heidegger, who was frequently translated, cited, and discussed.[1]

During the 1960s and until the journal temporarily ceased publication in 1967 due to the initiation of university reform, the *Revista de Filosofía* published several articles on Hegel, Marx, and dialectics, and others that dealt with logic and philosophy of science. The journal, however, continued to favor phenomenological subjects along with some emphasis on ethics and aesthetics. The articles made no apologies for specialization nor for their lack of reference to politics or national problems, as demanded by the work of Juan Rivano. Most philosophical production took the form of articles; the books published during the period maintained a similar tone.

For instance, Félix Schwartzmann's impressively researched *Teoría de la Expresión* (1967), neither made reference to nor reflected in any way the Chilean situation of the 1960s. The book consisted of a study of human expression as conveyed by major works of philosophy, literature, science, and art worldwide. Clearly, the subject of the book did not lend itself easily to establishing connections with the Chilean situation, but the independence of the book in this regard is itself telling. It suggests that some of the leading philosophers of the period deliberately chose to maintain philosophy as a separate, isolated sphere, and also that they preferred to use their philosophical expertise to examine problems of universal validity rather than local relevance. Schwartzmann had written on Latin American issues before from a philosophical standpoint on the eve of the era of professionalism. But in the climate of the 1960s he was, more than cautious, oblivious to the philosophical challenges that had been launched from within the philosophical community.

Humberto Giannini's *El mito de la autenticidad* (1968) was indicative of a similar attitude in that it did not reflect the problems agitating both the university and the discipline, except in the indirect way of choosing not to refer to them. Instead, it maintained ties with the professionalism developed during the previous decade, in this case by discussing a theme from Heidegger's *Being and Time*: authenticity.[2] Giannini's earlier work, *Reflexiones acerca la convivencia humana* (1965), had been written in part as a response to Rivano's *Entre Hegel y Marx*. In this volume Giannini expressed his skepticism regarding an interpretation of man that in his view ignored fundamental aspects of man's individuality.[3] Giannini's book also provided an explicit rejection of philosophies carrying political connotations because in them "the existence of man and his fellow human beings makes hardly any sense; their life and death are seen as consequences of a view perhaps more subtle than the politician's, but no less implacable."[4] This isolated reference to politics, however, was not meant to throw light on any specific Chilean situation but to underscore his view that the assertion of man's individuality took precedence over dialectical or social interpretations of his realization.

Giannini's work shared with Schwartzmann's a reference to a generic man devoid of specific regional connotations. Thus their view of philosophy, although having an application to concrete human beings, was more concerned with themes of universal validity. Furthermore, their themes of philosophical concern came from major European philosophical schools rather than from an attempt to relate the discipline to national problems.

The same can be said of such works as Francisco Soler's *Hacia Ortega* (1965) and Roberto Torretti's *Manuel Kant* (1966), which concentrated on authors dear not only to the professionalist community but to the Western philosophical tradition generally. These works represented well the type of philosophical response that made no effort to defend the field. Philosophers simply practiced it the way they best knew how.

However, other professionalists responded with a more explicit defense of a philosophical model that excluded politics. Juan de Dios Vial Larraín (b. 1924), for instance, thought it necessary to determine what philosophy and its mission were particularly at a time when phenomenology, existentialism, vitalism, and Marxism made claims on the philosophical field.[5] In his view, philosophy did not need to look outside itself to find meaning and purpose. This reaffirmed the independence achieved by the discipline since Molina's time:

> Philosophy lacks its own object because it comprehends them all: there is nothing alien to philosophical knowledge; everything falls under its domain. Philosophy is not ruled by objects nor does it in turn rule them in a Copernican way: it is in a transcendental position in respect to them. Philosophy transcends both the object of science and the object as such. It is this transcendental process in which philosophical knowledge is located that gives meaning to the name assigned to the nucleus of the discipline: metaphysics. That is, beyond physics, beyond nature and its primary substances.[6]

Vial did make an effort to relate to Chilean cultural life, but he was an exception among professionalists. In any event, his contribution in this area was an isolated one even in the context of his own work. In 1966, Vial examined the Chilean character and attempted to define it on the basis of three human types which he believed could be seen throughout Chilean history: the ideologue, the adventurer, and the soldier. Of the three, he felt that the militaristic strain provided the society and the population of Chile with its most characteristic feature. In looking at the present, he stated, while it appeared that Chile was dominated by ideologues, at the bottom one could see the militaristic Chilean character at work. For instance, he saw military "caution" and "prudence" in the Communist party vis-a-vis the Socialist. And president Eduardo Frei, in his judgment, was a Chilean General De Gaulle, a "man of authority and respect for the law, the state, and the government; that is, a military man."[7]

Vial did not spend much time documenting his claims because even in this isolated interpretation of Chilean character his main purpose was to show the primacy of spiritual life. Philosophy, of course, occupied a prominent place in expressing the spiritual basis of the culture. As he put it, "what most enduringly defines a man and a people is the action of spirituality, which expresses itself most clearly in religion, science, philosophy, and art."[8]

Philosophy, as he stated elsewhere, was a "fundamentally personal activity" whose aim was the attainment of "universal truth."[9] This communication between an individual thinker and truth across geographical and time boundaries was indeed an assumption shared by most professionalists. Such an assumption is understandable in an intellectual milieu nurtured both by philosophies that knew no borders and by a desire to have an impact beyond Chile, a desire which was often fulfilled with attendance to international congresses, occasional visiting appointments in other countries, and with the arrival in the country of distinguished practitioners of the discipline. Politics offered little more than a disruption of a style of philosophical work that allowed professionals to discuss what they believed to be the central issues of not only the field but also spiritual life and humanity. It should not come as a surprise, then, that the rejection of politics, and specifically Marxism, would be presented in conjunction with a defense of the discipline's concentration on metaphysics and spiritual issues and an affirmation of the centrality of Western cultural themes for Chilean intellectual life.

The most significant attempt in this direction comes from the work of Jorge Millas, perhaps the most widely known Chilean philosopher at the time. As mentioned earlier, Enrique Molina had recognized the talents of Millas very early on, and commented on his promise extensively in 1953. Millas had initially been trained in law, but his interests led him to philosophy. As a graduate of the University of Iowa, as a visiting professor at the Universidad de Puerto Rico and Columbia University, and as a frequent Chilean representative to inter-American congresses of philosophy, Millas had both good international contacts and a scholarly reputation that took him to the chair of the UCH Department of Philosophy, a position that he held until 1966. As one of the architects of the philosophical professionalism of the 1950s, Millas naturally came out in defense of the style and content of philosophical work almost as soon as critiques and pressures for reform appeared at FFE.

Philosophically, Millas attempted to demonstrate in his *Ensayos sobre la historia espiritual de Occidente* (1960) that what unity there was in the history of Western culture was furnished by human experience understood in a spiritual sense. He was certainly sensitive to the importance of material factors in that history, but made it clear that they were subordinated to human spirituality. "The process of human existence," he suggested, "is a process of consciousness that therefore has a spiritual profile whose elimination implies the unintelligibility of the process."[10] The achievements of Western culture from Ancient Greece through the Middle Ages demonstrated, in his view, that spirituality, as manifested by Greek rationality, Roman jurisprudence, and Christian values, was indeed the center of human existence. He concluded that human experience gave history its meaning, and that this history in turn showed a movement towards ever more complex and spiritual forms of existence. However, he found that at present spirituality had lost much ground, not the least because of materialistic doctrines clothed with a philosophical appearance. Millas regarded these materialistic doctrines as inadequate guides to the full understanding of human history.

> In effect, the entrance of materialism in the scene is due less to its philosophical value than to the progressive decadence of spiritual worldviews. Not even in its most refined form—dialectical materialism—does materialism enjoy any intellectual superiority. It is neither more objective nor more consistent; it can neither invoke the undeniable testimony of experience nor offer a richer or more elaborate interpretation of the facts. On the contrary, it starts with a larger number of assumptions and reduces the representation of human affairs to a poorer and more rigid scheme.[11]

Millas took the development of materialistic doctrines, particularly Marxism, as a challenge of mass society to spiritual life. His usage of the concept of masses comes from José Ortega y Gasset, particularly as discussed by the Spanish author in his *La rebelión de las masas* (1929). Millas made the dynamics and characteristics of the Ortegan masses extensive to society as a whole. In his *El desafío espiritual de la sociedad de masas* (1962), he developed this theme further to include Marxism, a doctrine he claimed did not provide an answer for the problems of mass society because it made class and economic systems responsible for current social ills.[12] He found this to be an imperfect answer and suggested that man should be the center of preoccupations when dealing with the problems of mass society. "In mass society," he wrote, "the spiritual condition of man has not changed fundamentally: only the surrounding concrete situation has, challenging the perennial task of the spirit. Spirituality is threatened, but the menace does not really come from without. It comes from the spirit's own impotence to carry out new tasks."[13]

Because for Millas man's spirituality remained essentially the same and only social conditions had changed to the point of threatening man's spirituality, he believed that the way to handle the challenge of mass society was for the intellect to constantly remind man about his individuality and spirituality. Intellectuals, however, needed to be alert in order not to acquire the characteristics of mass society.

Millas called on literature, art, and the university to address the spiritual needs of man so as to help him cope with the current social pressures against his individuality.

Millas was equally as concerned with maintaining the focus of philosophical inquiry on man as with rejecting Marxism. He connected these two concerns in order to underscore the threat he believed Marxism posed not only for society and its institutions, but for spiritual life itself. In the larger context of Chilean politics, Millas's views struck a receptive chord in quarters antagonistic to Marxism. Humberto Giannini, who was a professionalist and himself a critic of Marxism, objected that Millas's arguments against Marxism could be construed and were in fact read as plain anticommunist tracts by the national press.[14] Jorge Millas had been a socialist in his younger years, but during the 1940s and 1950s, perhaps as a result of his assimilation of philosophical professionalism, he had grown critical of both the doctrine and the political movement. In the 1960s, when the discipline that he had helped to become a professional endeavor stood accused for its lack of concern for the social needs of man, Millas crossed the divide between philosophy and politics to defend the field from political pressures. But his message was a distinctively political one.

The same can be said of the professionalist community as a whole. Either by ignoring politics or by explicitly rejecting politics—particularly the Marxist variety—professionalist philosophers took a stand against the mounting unrest at UCH's Faculty of Philosophy. Those who ignored politics concentrated on highly specialized problems of the field or put forth a view of man as a spiritual rather than a political being. This often entailed a partial reading of the very classics the professionalists revered, including Aristotle, who defined man as a "political animal." In the professionalist usage, man was a spiritual entity; as such, he was frequently defended as the center of philosophical concerns, and this became in fact the most characteristic theme of Chilean philosophy prior to the university reform movement of the 1967–68 period. By emphasizing man and his spiritual needs, professionalist philosophers charted a course for the field that served to balance what they believed to be a Marxist demand for the material, and therefore political, needs of the community of man. Those who explicitly rejected politics, like Jorge

Millas, gave the field its combative character, which would soon become apparent in debates on the role of the university in contemporary society.

PROFESSIONALISTS AND THE UNIVERSITY

Jorge Millas and Juan de Dios Vial Larraín were among the philosophers who reacted most strongly against the pressures for university reform. They and other authors did so out of conviction that the university, just as philosophy, should be a guide and a spiritual power within the society. The university, however, would not be able to fulfill this "mission" should it yield to partisan political pressures. These philosophers' view of the field, and their defense of its professionalistic thrust, prepared them well to defend the university from the same disrupting factors that they had encountered through their philosophical work.

Millas offered his interpretation of university reform in a speech pronounced in Panama in 1962 and published in Chile in 1963.[15] Millas suggested that prior to advocating reforms of any type, it was necessary to define the basic function of the university. He declared that function to be the "transmission of higher knowledge" in all social circumstances. Social conditions could change, but the "essence" of the university remained the same as the "community of mentors and disciples working together for the transmission of higher knowledge."[16] Since present conditions indicated that society had become a "mass society," he suggested that the mission of the university was, perhaps then more than ever before, to educate society through the dissemination of higher learning.

Millas warned that mass society threatened to transfer its own characteristics, particularly the inability to offer man a spiritual realization, to the university. The institution, according to Millas, was prepared to accept the challenges of mass society by assuming the role of an "authentic spiritual power" that would both refuse to turn the university into a mass institution, and instruct society on the correct use of social and political power.

> The university must now fulfill its task of transmitting and developing superior knowledge in the midst of a technological mass-

> society. This is what the university must accept as its destiny, and thus respond to the challenge of the new society. But there is, of course, the danger that in the process of meeting the challenge the university may itself be overwhelmed by the irresponsible powers of a society which, although representing man's greatest opportunity, is also on the way to being lost.[17]

Millas was referring specifically to the introduction of political ideologies which he deemed characteristic of mass society into the university by professors and students. He was in addition referring to "abuses of power" such as student strikes, which in his view could only upset the rational dialogue essential for the functioning of the university. Strikes, demands for *co-gobierno* (that is, for student participation in the governance of the institution), and free attendance constituted for Millas the wrong idea of reform. The university, he contended, would be of no help to mass society by becoming itself a mass institution (*universidad masificada*).

Millas's view of the university and its challenges represents a response to the expansion of university enrollments during the 1950s and 1960s. The reaction was one of alarm, as the sheer number of students, combined with politics, mirrored demographic growth and politicization in the wider society. UCH philosophers, who viewed themselves as members of an elite of knowledge, felt threatened by the pressures of a democratic society demanding increasing political participation. Philosophers at Catholic University did not share the same political and ideological pressures, nor indeed the alarm of their counterparts, who were members of a public institution heavily dependent on the state. Yet just as did the University of Chile, UC experienced tremendous physical expansion during the rectorship of Alfredo Silva Santiago, a growth that posed questions on the unity and meaning of the university in the 1960s.[18]

UC philosophers responded by fashioning a view of the university that gave central importance to philosophy and theology. In their view, it was the task of both to define the "mission" of the institution and provide coherence to the rapidly expanding university. Perhaps not surprisingly, the mission was Catholic, but a principal concern of philosophers was to use the "universal" character of the discipline to unite a university which had grown to encompass eight different campuses scattered in and around downtown Santiago in the 1960s.[19]

Despite this major concern, UC philosophy professors by and large concentrated on the specialized provinces of the field. In contrast to counterparts at UCH, however, the UC faculty ventured little, if at all, into the social secular concerns that led some UCH philosophers beyond specialization. Philosophy at UC maintained a close relationship with theology and was additionally a teaching more than a research or creative endeavor. As a result, philosophy at UC was not subject to the same social and political pressures, but some members of the faculty understood that the expansion of the institution posed significant political problems.

This was particularly the case with Juan de Dios Vial Larraín, a UC university official who was also a faculty member at both UC and UCH. He viewed the problems of the university as having been generated in part by the growth of the institution and by the pressures for the "democratization" of the university. Both made it imperative, in his view, to respond to these issues before "the competition between vested interests or political struggles destroy or distort them," and to reaffirm the university in its role in the spiritual education of man.[20] In order to do that, he maintained, the university did not need to look beyond itself to deal with current educational challenges. In fact, it needed only to make the Faculty of Philosophy the "backbone" of the institution.

According to Vial Larraín, the Faculty of Philosophy could and should provide the education society needed most, that is, the ability to practice "science" in its purest form. By "science" he meant a capacity to comprehend the principles guiding society and reality in general. With an education of this type, students could become specialists and professionals, but they first needed to learn how to value and manage knowledge. Universities could help provide, in his view, "an understanding of the profound currency of eternal truths and classical principles."[21]

Vial's idea of the science to be cultivated and promoted by the university was based on philosophy. He understood science as "wisdom" and claimed support for his view from Aristotle and Descartes. The university, he thought, could implement this notion by means of what he termed the "horizontal" and "vertical" structures of the institution. The horizontal structure was constituted by the faculties which, as he had argued before, was led or should be led by the Faculty of Philosophy, in his view the very backbone of the university.[22]

The "vertical" structure of the university was composed of faculties, schools, departments, institutes, and chairs. He assigned crucial importance to the chair (*cátedra*), and regarded it in fact as the fundamental "cell" of university life.[23] The current system of *cátedras*, or chairs held in propriety by tenured faculty members, had already been attacked by Juan Rivano, who argued that the independence of the *cátedras* and the lack of accountability on the part of the professors helped maintain the university's isolation from social problems.[24] Vial's defense of the *cátedra* system was in turn related to his overall conception of the university as an institution that would freely cultivate science in order to guide the spiritual development of man and society. The mission of the university, Vial summarized in the Ortegan vein followed by other philosophy professors concerned with university issues, was the "discovery and communication of truth."[25]

It was Félix Martínez Bonati (b. 1929), a UCH graduate and professor of literary aesthetics, who most explicitly articulated a view of the university as a guide to, yet separate from, society. In an influential essay published in 1960, Martínez Bonati expressed his discomfort with the "disorder" prevalent in Chilean society, which he understood to be the product of a lack of leadership on the part of the university.[26]

According to Martínez Bonati, education was the only solution for some of Chile's ills. Specifically, he called upon higher education to direct the orderly development of the country. This was to be achieved by teaching the future leaders of society, students, the values and the classics of the Western tradition and encouraging them to cultivate an ethical consciousness with which to guide their own lives and the destiny of their nation. The university, for him, should be "the model the nation should turn to to ask for guidance and norms of conduct."[27]

In order to fulfill its mission of guiding society, according to Martínez Bonati, the university should not become involved with other social institutions. He maintained that "an essential part of what the university owes to a corrupt society is contempt."[28] Therefore, no involvement should exist between the university and Chilean society. The only members from the outside world to be accepted into the university were the students, but only to change them and strip them of "vulgarities" brought in from the outside. The student, asserted Martínez Bonati, should not be permitted to participate in politics, because politics had no educational value, and in addition political participation hurt the student's academic performance. The university had to make sure that students received a "humanistic education, and became respectful of knowledge and the values of the spiritual tradition."[29] This was, for him, the true social mission of the university.

Philosophy, according to Martínez Bonati, was to play a special role in the relations between university and society. Philosophy was the discipline best suited to implement the spirit and the mission of the university, because philosophy was "a holistic science of that which is essential." Philosophy was the key, because the study of the classics of the discipline brought professors and students together in a "studying community which is the essence of the university."[30] Philosophical studies, in his conception, involved a knowledge of the major languages of Western culture and an acquaintance with the major works of this culture. Only in this way could the values of tradition be transmitted from the "thinking elite" to students.

The Chilean defense of the classics of philosophy, their relation to the essence of the university, and the latter's role in democratic society finds a parallel in Allan Bloom's *The Closing of the American Mind* (1987). Despite the obvious differences in the social and historical contexts of Chile and the United States, the similarities between Bloom and the Chilean professionalists of the 1960s are striking. Both were attempting to resurrect the traditional role of the discipline, at least as Plato viewed it, as the guide of society. Most importantly, both were reacting against the pressures of democratic society, which they perceived as a threat to a tradition of philosophical rationalism embodied in the university. In both cases, their reactions stemmed from university experiences that affected them equally deeply during the 1960s.[31]

Although Chilean philosophers were guided by Bloom's own concern about the discipline's loss of stature in contemporary society, they acted as if the problems of philosophy and the university were the specific result of politicization, and often Marxism. They assumed a political role, although in the name of higher aims, to reverse this situation. Their audience in Chile was not only large but powerful. For instance, present at Martínez Bonati's inaugural address at Austral University in 1965—he was rector of the institution located in the southern city of Valdivia from 1962 to 1968—were, among others, the minister of education, rectors and representatives from all other major universities in the country, the ambassadors of Great Britain and the United States, and military, religious, and civilian authorities. In his speech, Martínez Bonati reiterated his position that the mission of the university should not be determined by forces outside the institution, for the university's only commitment was to "truth."[32] The university, he insisted, had no social function other than inculcating a sense of responsibility in students through study. Any other social function belonged not to the university but to other institutions of society.

Martínez Bonati also defended the virtues of isolation, suggesting that in order to be a most effective social instrument the university should be an "ivory tower." "Seclusion," he added, "is one of the most illustrious means to establish an ample and profound contact with human reality."[33] Thus secluded, the university was in a better position to impose on society the principles of a learned existence. "The mission of the university," he maintained, "does not consist in adjusting to either the reality or the mentality of the environment. Its mission is to discipline them and whip them down to the feet of the idea of humanity."[34]

The transfer these thinkers made of their commonly shared view of philosophy to higher education resulted in a conception of the university as a power within the society and a power society should follow if it indeed wanted orderly progress and the enhancement of spiritual life in the nation. In all cases, they emphasized the need for a university "mission" informed by philosophy. They volunteered their advice because they were cognizant of philosophical views on the nature of higher education. But more than anything they were reacting to university models inspired by politics. It was impossible for them to ignore student pressures for university change taking place in their own schools, but the major reason for their stance relates to the fact that they saw their own field undermined by the increasing politicization of academic life. They feared that should the university yield to pressures for reform, there would be nothing stopping politics from encroaching upon the discipline.

THE PROCESS OF UNIVERSITY REFORM

The role of the intellectual in Latin American university reform movements has always been significant, as exemplified by the 1918 university reform process at Córdoba, perhaps the best known of all university reforms in Latin America.[35] Like their Argentine counterparts, Chilean intellectuals played a crucial role in identifying the problems of the university and in debating the institution's nature and aims. In some cases, they were active in the movement itself. But it was through other groups, both inside and outside the university, that reforms were eventually implemented during 1968–1969 in Chile. The role of philosophy and of philosophers was nonetheless of paramount importance precisely because of the preexisting conflict between professionalism and social concerns within the ranks of the philosophical community. Just as Argentine intellectuals had rebelled against positivism in the early part of the century and had attacked it by means of a university reform movement, Chilean philosophers attacked the philosophical schools that they identified with professionalism, or conversely, with politics, and in the process became involved in the larger movement for or against reform at the university.

The sequence of events leading to the university reform process at UCH was initiated in 1967, when students of the Faculty of Philosophy and Education, the largest university faculty in the country, took over their classrooms and demanded the resignation of FFE authorities.[36] They attacked the administration of the Faculty of Philosophy for its alleged inefficiency and undemocratic procedures. Professors in the Department of Philosophy were immediately polarized when the conflict exploded. Some sided with the besieged authorities and condemned what they believed to be an intolerable politicization of the university environment. Others sided with the students and supported their demands. Juan Rivano, in particular, participated actively in the reform process, becoming a representative of the professors supporting reform and eventually becoming an elected chairman of the philosophy department.

Proposals for the reform of the University of Chile had already been presented by several organized groups prior to events at FFE. University reform was on the agenda of the two center and leftist political coalitions competing for power during the first half of the 1960s, namely, the Partido Demócrata Cristiano (PDC) and the Marxist Frente de Acción Popular (FRAP) which would later in the decade become the Unidad Popular (UP). The PDC, which had won the 1964 presidential elections, proceeded to implement educational reforms to modernize and democratize the UCH. Both parties agreed on the need to make changes in an institution that began with five faculties in 1843, grew to eight faculties and twenty-six schools by 1940, and expanded into thirteen faculties and more than seventy schools by 1967, yet possessed no adequate mechanisms to represent the different interests and sectors of the institution. But the two major political groups, both with large student followings at the university, differed with respect to their views of the extent to which the institutions should be reformed. The left, particularly the Communist party, sought to transform the university into an institution actively involved in the promotion of social change,[37] while the PDC administration sought mainly to modify the university to make it more responsive to the needs of the state and more accommodating to scientific research.[38] Although the aims of university reform may have been similar, both groups remained deadlocked in constant conflict over dominance at higher political levels.

The student movement at the Faculty of Philosophy unexpectedly broke the deadlock and accelerated the process of reform. Controlled by neither of the above-mentioned groups, the students not only forced the dean to resign but also caused the collapse of the entire administrative structure of the faculty in a matter of weeks. An ad hoc committee was formed to rule the occupied premises while representative elections—until then a reformist ideal—were held within every department. The central administration of the university found this situation intolerable and threatened to demand forcible governmental intervention. Leaders of the movement at the faculty responded that they would not leave the facilities until substantial changes were made in the administrative structure of the institution.[39] This demand proved to be more than the progovernment forces were willing to accept, despite their own reformist intentions. Even the left, which naturally welcomed any disruption of the existing status quo, wavered in its support of a movement over which it seemed to have little influence. Independent of the major political parties, the movement at FFE swiftly became the controversial focus of the university reform process. Demands and rejections went back and forth between faculty and the University Council, the policy-making body of the institution composed of deans. At issue was the university's unwillingness to tolerate its own democratization.

Rector Eugenio González, a former philosophy professor and dean of FFE, found himself in a difficult predicament. Facing an unyielding University Council and an equally unyielding Faculty of Philosophy over the issue of representative elections, he resigned in May of 1968, precipitating a crisis of national proportions whose most acute phase lasted until November of 1969, when Rector Edgardo Boeninger, a Christian Democrat, was elected. During that period, the UCH saw the most intense political struggle in its history. All the major political parties of the country became involved in the conflict, easily overwhelming the more academically inspired groups that made a futile attempt to influence the process.[40] Political party leaders saw in the university reform process an opportunity to gauge the strength of the different political forces already preparing for the 1970 presidential elections. Although the PDC won this struggle, the left also made substantial gains at several university levels that heralded their upcoming victory in the presidential contest in which Salvador Allende represented the UP. Such involvement by political parties has led most scholars concerned with this issue to suggest that the university became the politicized arena where larger national issues were at stake.[41]

Profound institutional changes resulted from the movement for university reform, which was inspired by the apparent need for institutional adjustments in a changing society. The power of the tenured faculty was substantially diminished, authorities were elected by a wider university constituency, and the university became more active in public affairs. Within the Department of Philosophy, students and junior faculty gained more influence over their academic programs, which no longer depended on the sole authority of the *catedrático*.

And yet the movement for university reform, now clearly controlled by national political parties, failed to satisfy the members of the philosophy faculty who had contributed in a fundamental way by articulating the arguments for or against reform. Jorge Millas was particularly unhappy about the forces unleashed by the reform process, particularly regarding student activism. Soon after students occupied the FFE facilities, Millas wrote for *El Mercurio* that students, because of their lack of vision, experience, and sense of responsibility, were attempting to turn the university into a political instrument.[42] He thus felt it necessary to reiterate his view of the essential mission of the university: the transmission of superior knowledge. Such a mission implied that students should devote themselves to learning rather than attempting to dismantle the basis of academic authority. The university, he suggested, could and in fact was rendering a social service by cultivating and transmitting superior knowledge. Any other version of university service to society, he thought, was a mere rhetorical device to politicize the institution. At any rate, those responsible for defining the aims of the university could not be the students, but rather those academic members of the institution who were aware of the fundamental essence of higher education. "The university is already democratic," he insisted, "to the extent that it is composed of members who, either directly or indirectly connected to the interests of knowledge, teach and conduct research. Also, to the extent that it recognizes no other qualification than a moral and an intellectual capacity to belong [to the university]."[43]

Millas consistently defended his view of the university throughout the process of university reform. His critique of university politicization, however, became more pointed and specifically anti-Marxist, as he believed that the university reform movement was controlled by "Marxist and paramarxist political militants."[44] He suggested that because of this politicization the possibilities for a true reform had already been frustrated, and that the ground had been opened for a "marketplace" approach to the conduct of university affairs "where people go on hawking rather than reasoning."[45] He was referring to the creation of reform committees (*claustros reformados*) that replaced the old faculty councils for the election of representatives for each faculty. These committees, many of which were controlled by the left, elected officials with the participation of faculty, students, and staff. Millas, who viewed this situation with dismay, reported that

> the faculties of the University of Chile are amusing themselves these days by conducting education and science in semi-organic assemblies, by means of reports and ballots which will eventually give power to political groups and organized impersonality. I believe that this must be denounced as the maximum frivolity, and as a perversion of the university spirit.[46]

Millas was not alone in his unhappiness with the direction of the reform movement. He and other philosophers reacted strongly against the effects of reform on philosophy. Humberto Giannini, for instance, reacted against the reform process because he felt that it involved an attack against the hard-won achievements of his scholarly career.[47] Gastón Gómez Lasa, who was active in university affairs during the period, thought in retrospect that philosophy was pressured to respond to immediate concerns. As a result, the field became too close to ideology. As he put it, "the discipline forfeited its role of wisdom to become the shield for political platforms."[48]

The disenchantment with university reform came also from those who advocated it and even took leadership positions in the process. Juan Rivano, who had been elected chairman of the Department of Philosophy in 1968 and held the position for one and a half years, reacted against the new university statutes that emerged from the reform process, which were approved by the Congress in August 1969.[49] He pointed out that nothing had really changed at the university as far as democratization was concerned, for the statutes indicated that budget decisions and the academic structure of the institution were controlled by the University Council. In his view, this concentration of power made weaker, poorer, or politically unreliable faculties vulnerable if not indefensible with respect to financial and academic decisions made at top university levels. He summarized the situation as follows:

> What was the rationale for reform? There had been a critique and a call for changing the deficiencies [of the university]. The reformist rationale was, above all, the abolition of injustice and arbitrariness, and the creation of a new university: an ORGANIC university. . . . But the emphasis turned to "revolution," "structural change," the "committed university," "youth power," "development," and the "Chile of the future." The budget issue was brushed aside, and the [university] structure that effected the classist distribution of power remained untouched.[50]

Both Millas and Rivano, who had so little in common regarding their views on philosophy and the university, coincided in at least one respect: they were both aware that the process of university reform had come to be controlled by the dynamics of national political party struggles. It is doubtful that they would have done otherwise in regard to expressing their views about an institution for which they and other academics felt very strongly, but clearly they had no way of knowing, perhaps because of the isolation of the philosophical community to which they had become accustomed in the 1950s, that as soon as a political issue was raised at FFE, national political parties would seize the opportunity to massively intervene in university affairs. Philosophers had a sobering and disheartening encounter with politics due to the reform.

Even Catholic University faced, almost simultaneously with the University of Chile, a process of university reform that shook the very roots of the institution. Pressures for student participation and even the secularization of the university characterized a university reform process that involved both intellectuals and political parties.[51] At UC, students became politically active for reasons similar to those motivating UCH students. At issue were the role of the university in contemporary Chilean society as well as the participation of different academic groups in the selection of authorities. The reform accomplished greater freedom from the church, as archbishops no longer appointed university authorities. The first lay rector, Fernando Castillo Velasco, took office as a result of this process. As one observer has noted, however, UC became more vulnerable to the wider participation of constituents as well as more dependent upon the state.[52]

While similar to the process at UCH, university reform at UC had a different impact on philosophy. The field had been studied at the School of Education, but after the university reform philosophers achieved independence from the school and succeeded in creating their own Institute of Philosophy in 1970. Because of their greater freedom from the church, philosophers advocated a study of the field that was open to "all other disciplines as well as [attentive] to the urgent problems of our society."[53] Philosophers were substantially involved in the creation of the Institute, and in effect managed to institutionalize a highly specialized curriculum of studies. Of course, some members of the faculty objected to the trend towards a diminished emphasis on theological matters. Professor Pedro de la Noi, for instance, complained that metaphysics had been left out of the curriculum and that even Saint Thomas Aquinas received little attention in both the baccalaureate and *Licenciatura* programs.[54] Logic, linguistics, political philosophy, and history of science figured prominently in the post reform curriculum. And so did the number of lay faculty, which included several UCH graduates and professors. Contrary to the effects of reform at the University of Chile, the UC philosophy faculty found a propitious environment to implement a specialized, and significantly less Catholic, curriculum. This involved a certain degree of conflict among the faculty, but one that was mild compared to the situation at the University of Chile.

UCH philosophers, for their part, found themselves in the middle of a polarized political struggle between the leftist Unidad Popular and the Christian Democratic Party—now supported by a variety of right wing groups. From then until 1973, philosophers reacted to this situation in a variety of ways. Some, like Juan Rivano, resigned his post at the department, but stayed at FFE. Others, like Jorge Millas and Humberto Giannini, left for positions at other universities or faculties within the UCH. Still others, like Félix Martínez Bonati and Roberto Torretti, left the country altogether. A group of philosophy professors of leftist political leanings, including Jorge Palacios and Armando Cassigoli, gained ascendancy at the Department of Philosophy, an ascendancy that paralleled the growing strength of the left nationally. During the Unidad Popular years (1970–73), these philosophers would seek to adjust philosophical inquiry to the needs of a government that identified closely with Marxism, and in the process ran into conflict with a critical philosophical current that would again rise in protest against an academic policy allegedly imposed from the top.

PHILOSOPHY DURING THE UNIDAD POPULAR ADMINISTRATION

Because of the internecine struggles at UCH, Chilean philosophy during the UP years was introduced to a wider geographical area. Still, many philosophers maintained a close connection with the department at FFE, and some kept a reduced teaching schedule there. However dispersed, the philosophers who maintained a significant level of production were the same philosophers trained at UCH. Despite university reform, there was important continuity, but also a great deal of change evident in the work of Chilean philosophers.

Jorge Millas, who moved from FFE to the School of Law and then to Austral University in Valdivia during the university reform period, inaugurated the Unidad Popular years with his two-volume *Idea de la filosofía* (1970). It is clear from this book that the dust of the university reform battles had not yet settled in his philosophical work. He framed his *Idea* in the context of what he viewed as the ideological and even antirational climate of the day, although he made no explicit reference to Chile. He felt that in such a situation it was necessary to define both the essence and the object of the discipline. He found it important to do this, he explained, out of loyalty to "the rational vocation of philosophy," and out of loyalty to man, who had for centuries found realization in the discipline.[55]

Millas's definition of philosophy was closely related to the presumed rationality of man. Philosophy, in his view, "aspires to the rational integration of experience," and therefore it is "the discipline of knowledge par excellence."[56] His focus turned to philosophy per se, and to the specifics of knowledge acquisition. In discussing philosophy, he found its four major subjects to be metaphysics, logic, theory of knowledge, and axiology, which covered "the total range of problems which have always occupied philosophy, that is, being, knowledge, and value."[57] As far as knowledge was concerned, he believed it to be intimately connected with the problem of truth. He discussed in detail the connection between the two and the different doctrines of knowledge developed by the philosophical tradition. Again, the philosophical tradition he related to was mainly European, and his references to man, as well as all major philosophical themes, fall within the boundaries of that tradition.

The significance of Millas's work in the context of the university reform period and in the context of the ascendancy of the left, which he opposed, lies in the fact that it represents a return to specialization, if not a withdrawal from the political debates which had permeated his own work in the 1960s. This was by and large the philosophers' reaction to the heightening of political polarization in the country.[58] Juan Rivano himself seems to have paused to devote some attention to specialized logical themes.[59] A closer reading, however, reveals that in this period Rivano began to extend his critique of Chilean philosophical professionalism to the discipline as a whole. He criticized philosophy for failing to recognize the extent to which contemporary social and political events undermined the validity of the most fundamental logical and philosophical principles.

Rivano devoted substantial attention to this theme in his writings of the university reform period through the Unidad Popular years. In his "Tesis sobre la totalización tecnológica" (1971), Rivano took issue with what he understood to be a generalized philosophical assumption that took for granted the primacy of reason at individual human and social levels. Particularly in the case of diverse philosophies of history, and also in the case of philosophical interpretations of man, Rivano believed that unfounded assumptions were being made about the role conscious human beings had to play in the unfolding of history and their own lives. He suggested that human and social events had a dynamic of their own that did not necessarily conform to the philosophical ideal of rationality. In his view, materialistic criteria emerging from the study of contemporary events rendered criteria based on the rational bases of human history obsolete, if not useless. Even Marxism, based as it was on dialectical assumptions that viewed history as leading mankind to freedom in a classless society, made unacceptable assumptions about the nature of social change. Rivano suggested, for instance, that recent technological developments severely undermined some of the fundamental tenets of Marxism.[60]

Rivano suggested that assumptions of this nature were not confined to Marxism; they compromised the entire philosophical discipline as well. A traditional emphasis on the capacity of reason to find unity in the diversity of experience had turned into an attempt to fit reality into the categories of thought. Philosophical systems were all troubled by their tendency to generalize and establish their validity on the basis of internal coherence rather than correspondence to reality. The result was a failure to comprehend a social reality that he argued defied the coherence of philosophical systems.[61] The field had become useless to the extent that it sought to apply norms and values inspired by rationality to understand social and political reality. He thought Plato's subordination of force to reason, for instance, at best an idealistic view of politics, if not a philosophical posture susceptible to ideological manipulation. Instead, he stated, the philosopher should concentrate on human and social events even, and perhaps especially, when they did not seem to conform to the highest ideals of reason. Politics and politicians, particularly in his *Introducción al pensamiento dialéctico* (1972), emerged in Rivano's work as holding a significant clue as to how reality assumed the forms that philosophers often failed to comprehend.[62]

What philosophers, particularly Rivano and Millas, were debating was whether philosophy should maintain a professionalist focus on man, values, and the Western tradition, or whether it should concentrate on the social and political issues that agitated society in general, and Chile in particular. To be sure, philosophers like Millas devoted much attention to society, although his approach was inspired by an uncompromising defense of man's individuality and rationality as opposed to what he viewed as the alienating dynamics of politics and mass society. Other philosophers like Juan Rivano believed that fundamental philosophical assumptions on man and society were untenable, if not contradicted by politics and contemporary events. That is, Chilean philosophy had reached a point of division between those who believed that philosophy had a right and a capacity to guide society and those who believed that social events should provide the substance of philosophical thinking, even at the expense of dismissing precious philosophical principles.

The background of these conflicting views was a level of political violence that led to two takeovers of the UCH philosophy department by students who declared their opposition to the university policies of the Allende administration. This movement did not receive a great deal of press coverage, as was customary during the heights of the university reform period, possibly because the movement did not enjoy the endorsement of any major political party. The 1971 takeover, however, was registered in one philosophy student union publication which indicated that the movement was against the "bureaucrats" installed by the 1968 reform.[63] The second takeover, in 1972, seems to have been particularly violent, but was lost in the no less violent politicking surrounding the election of rector that year.[64] The Christian Democrats controlled the rectorship, but the left controlled some of the faculties, including FFE. The philosophy movement, in this context, was little more than a thorn in the side of a faculty jealously guarding its stronghold.[65]

During this period, the philosophical community stood divided, scattered, and generally unproductive except for writings—few in number but highly significant—such as those of Millas and Rivano, who emerged as the most representative authors of the professionalist and critical views that characterized Chilean philosophy. The *Revista de Filosofía* ceased publication in 1970, thus contributing to the significant drop in philosophical writing during the Unidad Popular years. Still, important transformations took place in Chilean philosophy as a result of the heavily politicized period of university reform that lasted through 1973. The professionalists became convinced that much that was wrong with the university and society was the product of the inability of both to follow the example of philosophy. After a brief but intense involvement with the very politics that they rejected, they went back to their specialized practice, although not without expressing a great deal of resentment towards the politicization that had drained so much of their energy. The critics, who extended their disenchantment with Chilean professionalism to the field as a whole, and who also rejected political affiliations and became critics of the left, were convinced that politics should not only not be ignored, but be brought to the center of philosophical attention.

Politics drove a wedge between philosophers who now had little in common beyond a dissatisfaction with the turn of events after the reforms of 1968–69. The abyss between the two major currents was political, philosophical, and apparently insurmountable, as each group felt entirely alienated. Philosophers remained divided much as did the rest of Chilean society until a bloody military coup put an end to political confrontations, at least temporarily. As in the wider society, these conflicts did not disappear after the coup: they only acquired a more sinister character that forced philosophers to face their darkest hour.

VI

CHILEAN PHILOSOPHY UNDER MILITARY RULE

The military junta headed by General Augusto Pinochet intended to do away with the country's organized political activity, including that at the universities, after the coup of 1973.[1] Still, it had to contend with the legacy of a highly active and articulate university constituency.[2] The philosophical community, in particular, had a recent history of participation in university affairs. Partly because of this history, but generally because of its interest in keeping tight control over the university, the new government placed special emphasis on maintaining the country's philosophers at arm's length. The military predicted, perhaps accurately, that the discipline's potential for social criticism could provide a source of dissent within the university. Consequently, the military authorities took a series of measures to ensure that members of the philosophical community would not become vocal critics of military rule nor of military intervention in higher education institutions.

However uninformed about the complexities of Chilean philosophical history, the military understood clearly that there was a difference between professionalists and critics, particularly with regard to their political attitudes. Military authorities thought it best initially to bank on the antagonism between the two groups in order to isolate the critics and then turn against the professionalists themselves in favor of a group of academics loyal to the government that was willing to implement the regime's university policies. I call these academics *officialists,* and describe in this chapter how the military reliance on this group alienated the traditionally apolitical professionalists, who were not viewed as trustworthy by the regime. Because of these developments, the Chilean philosophical landscape seems to have changed fundamentally within a few years of military rule. Critics had been persecuted, professionalists alienated, and a new officialist current established. Yet the central purpose of depoliticizing the discipline, as well as university life in general, remained an open question at best.

CHILEAN PHILOSOPHY AFTER 1973

As seen in the previous chapter, the disputes concerning the objectives of philosophy and those of the academic disciplines in general became highly antagonistic during the university reform period. But the full extent of such disputes became dramatically clear with military intervention in the universities in 1973. Inevitably, the violent character of this intervention, particularly at the Faculty of Philosophy and Education, known still as the Instituto Pedagógico, posed the question about which conception of philosophy would coexist with military rule.

For those who viewed philosophy as a professional and academic exercise, the military intervention represented a much-wanted restoration of the peace broken during the 1960s and early 1970s at the universities. It also meant the possibility of cultivating a conception of philosophy free from the social and critical demands that characterized the discipline during the premilitary coup period. This view of philosophy was by definition exempt from any need to question the legitimacy of the military intervention and from expressing opinions that could be construed as political.

For those who viewed philosophy as a critical instrument responsive to national problems, the situation under military rule became not only precarious but openly dangerous. In the aftermath of the intervention, professors and students who maintained this view of philosophy were either forced to resign their teaching positions or expelled. Some were imprisoned, exiled, or both imprisoned and exiled.

The hostility of the military to the Department of Philosophy and to the professors and students who shared a critical philosophical approach might be explained by the role they played in the university reform process and by the fear that they could form a locus of opposition against military intervention. There are, however, other factors that explain this antagonism. Firstly, the military sought to dismantle the participatory university model that emerged from the reform period. Many of those who had been part of it and who remained at the Department of Philosophy were looked upon with suspicion, if not hostility. Secondly, the existing tension between professionalist and critical philosophers on political grounds justified, at least initially, the military support for the former and the persecution of the latter.[3]

While the military made few explicit references to the role of philosophical activity in public discourse before 1977, it made it abundantly clear from the outset that politics would no longer be accepted at the universities. The principal instrument of military university policy became the *Rectores delegados,* or university rectors directly appointed by the government, usually officers in active service. The primary objective of military intervention was political demobilization, an aim that was pursued by means of sharp reversals in the participation of students and academics in the governance of the universities. The left was naturally made a target of repression, but members of the Christian Democratic Party (PDC) and even independents and conservatives were soon targeted as well.[4] The repression of nonleftist academics, particularly PDC members, was the result of a larger conflict between the party, which had supported the 1973 coup, and the military. Christian Democrats, including former president Eduardo Frei, became vocal critics of military rule when it became clear that the promised restoration of democracy was not in sight. Pinochet's government retaliated by attacking the party and harassing its leaders.[5]

By the mid-1970s, even sectors of the right had become alienated from the military, in part because of the severity of the regime's neoliberal economic policies. Widespread disenchantment with the overall economic program would not become a major issue of right wing discontent until the recession of 1981.[6] But unhappiness about the impact on specific areas such as higher education set in early. Drastic budget cuts to the universities as well as plans to charge tuition antagonized the middle class and provided a focal point for discontent. As a result, a broader, and perhaps more threatening, political opposition against military rule developed after 1975, with tangible consequences for both national politics and the universities. Military distrust of politicians, even previously sympathetic ones, translated into heavy reliance on their own military personnel and zealous civilian followers.[7]

The impact of these national developments was quickly felt in the philosophical community. Professionalist philosophers the caliber of Jorge Millas and Humberto Giannini were not asked by the military to take key administrative positions at the department or at the Faculty of Philosophy. Instead, the military appointed professors who were marginal to or altogether unknown in the Chilean philosophical community. Although they did not have the international or even national reputation of the professionalists, these new professors shared with the professionalists the view that the discipline was fundamentally academic and apolitical. Perhaps more important, these professors supported the military fully and were willing to work in administrative positions under military supervision.

In turn, the military gave full institutional support to these officialists and their philosophical preferences. At the same time, it alienated those who, because of their philosophical professionalism and prestige, had expected to become the dominant figures of Chilean philosophy. The intervention in the universities made it clear to them that the military's aim was not philosophical professionalism but a model of philosophical activity compatible with the political objectives of the regime. The new official philosophy was expected to excise social and critical elements from its activity. The military found many academics willing to do just that, but only after alienating the leading professionalist philosophers and eliminating the critical ones.

A group of increasingly disenchanted philosophers, some of whom had already been removed form the University of Chile, were interviewed by the opposition magazine *Hoy* in May 1978. These included Jorge Millas, Gastón Gómez Lasa, Humberto Giannini, Edison Otero, and the priest and Catholic University philosophy professor Arturo Gaete. They were asked to speak about the role of philosophy in society, the nature of Chilean philosophy, and the relationship between philosophy and ideology. The philosophers avoided any reference to the current situation under military rule, but an expression of discontent emerged from their responses. They underscored the importance of philosophy for society, particularly when it helped to establish human commonalities above and beyond ideological differences. They also drew a sharp distinction between ideology and philosophy by criticizing the political usages of the former. Philosophy, as they presented it, was a dialogue whose only condition was a free and spontaneous disposition on the part of those willing to engage in it.[8]

However oblique, the philosophers' responses underlined what they thought was missing in their society. They expressed a view of philosophy as dialogue, but they did so in order to imply that this definition did not apply in Chile. They suggested that the discipline had lost its place in society and that it was also threatened by ideology. Philosophers were disgruntled but did not, or could not within the confines of the *Hoy* interview, come around to explicitly relating their discontent to military rule. Even their consensus on the importance of dialogue was overshadowed by disagreements on whether philosophy in Chile could be distinct from philosophy in other areas. Professionalists like Millas, for instance, reaffirmed their long-held positions on the universal character of both philosophy and human nature. The *Hoy* interview revealed a state of shock, confusion, and lack of common purpose on the part of nonofficialist philosophers. Their agreement on dialogue, however, was significant in that it represented an attempt by this group of philosophers, particularly the professionalists, to focus on the more social aspects of the discipline. Equally significant was the attention devoted to their thoughts by an opposition magazine of wide national circulation.

By 1978, the leading figures of Chilean philosophy were either out of the country or increasingly at odds with the regime. The entire field had been subject to dramatic changes. Surely, the old tension between a professionalist and a critical view of philosophy persisted. However, the changes in the field after 1973 became so substantial that one must test the strength of the distinction between professionalists and critics in light of the following developments: First, while critiques against professionalism took place within academic circles during the pre-1973 period, opponents of military rule and official philosophy since that time were physically removed from the universities. Second, philosophical production outside the universities grew, despite the scarcity of channels for the publication of philosophy-related essays.[9] Finally, as mentioned above, a significant rapprochement emerged between professionalist and critical philosophers outside the universities. Faced with the challenges of military rule, the two main currents of Chilean philosophy, along with the new officialist current, developed their own distinct responses to the new social and political situation in the country.

THE OFFICIAL PHILOSOPHERS

The emergence of an officialist philosophical current represents the most important change occurring in the field of Chilean philosophy after 1973. The military encouraged its creation and provided it with an agenda. General Agustín Toro Dávila, rector of the University of Chile, outlined the military government's expectations for the work of Chilean philosophers in 1977. Philosophy, he assured his audience at the Second National Congress of Philosophy, had an important role to play in the new society. Chile had just emerged from a period of "profound confusion." Fortunately, he stated, the country had been "saved from falling into a system that would have invaded consciousness and destroyed the spiritual values that lend meaning and dignity to human existence."[10]

Toro Dávila did not identify them by name, but he was referring to both Marxism and the Salvador Allende administration. He explained that having saved the country from the threat of Marxism, the current government was engaged in a task of institutional reform that required the participation of intellectuals. The task of academics in general, and philosophers in particular, was to educate the young in accordance with the government's goal of "civic and moral reconstruction of the community." He called on philosophers to promote among the young a "critical mind" and "authenticity."

> A critical mind so that they will not be seduced by foreign ideologies or false prophets. Authenticity to make them appreciate our own cultural values, and to guide their search for those ways of changing society that are appropriate to our idiosyncrasy and our level of development . . . The purpose, in general, is to find in our tradition and history—as well as in the major postulates of the Christian Western civilization—the inspiration and guidance needed to create a sense of national unity. The aim is to build a society that is more just, more Christian, and which provides for an adequate balance between human rights and duties.[11]

Official philosophers read accurately from Toro's statements that the foreign ideologies to be rejected were Marxist. They received from the military government the signal that they could work on any other philosophical school. That is, this latitude was allowed as long as philosophers kept in mind that the discipline should emphasize spiritual values and promote the reconstruction of society through adherence to the general principles of the military government.

An important aspect of the activity of the officialists became the attempt to reinterpret Chilean philosophical history along apolitical, and particularly anti-Marxist lines. The first major effort in this direction was by Roberto Escobar (b. 1926) in his *La filosofía en Chile,* published in 1976.[12] The effort was hardly new or original. Enrique Molina had produced his account of Chilean philosophy in the 1950s in order to advance a professionalistic view of the field. In the climate of the 1970s, Escobar wrote his version in order to advance a similar aim, but most significantly to either remove from the roster those philosophers who had identified themselves with Marxist positions in the past or to dismiss their work as ideological. Even some of the professionalists, such as Marco Antonio Allendes and Gastón Gómez Lasa, received scant attention or were simply not included despite their caliber and contributions. In Escobar's depiction, philosophy had deteriorated badly from 1971 to 1973 due to the general influence of "Soviet communism" on society but had begun a dramatic recovery in 1974. No mention was made of the military coup nor its impact on the philosophical community.

A similar omission was made in two other officialist versions of Chilean philosophical developments by Santiago Vidal Muñoz (b. 1918), and Joaquín Barceló Larraín (b. 1927).[13] Vidal's involvement with Chilean philosophy had been mainly through the SCF. After the military coup, he assumed professorships in the faculties of Philosophy and Education, and Human Sciences at UCH. In 1977, he advanced a view of Chilean philosophy that did not depart significantly from his earlier (1956) work on the subject and that attempted to emphasize the continuities of Chilean philosophical work since the 1930s. In his account, no breaks of any sort had occurred in Chilean philosophy, not even in 1973. Barceló had been an unproductive scholar whose published work was limited to articles, translations, and book reviews at a time when the field turned out the largest and most important production in its history. In the period 1974–1975, however, he was appointed professor and dean of the Faculty of Philosophy and Education and emerged as one of the leading voices of the group of officialists. In his short rendition of Chilean philosophical developments, Barceló pointed out that the most significant feature of Chilean philosophical activity was the institutionalization of the field in the country's universities. The "professionalization" of the field, the creation of the Sociedad Chilaen de Filosofía, the publication of philosophical journals, and the celebration of congresses were all important products of this process of institutionalization. He expressed some concern over an economic model that placed little importance on the field but made no connection between economics and the military regime.[14]

Barceló's rendition of recent Chilean philosophical history was accurate in some respects, but significantly omitted 1973 and the consequences of military rule for both the university and the field. Barceló's purpose in this rendition was to reaffirm, if not return to, the rationale developed during the 1950s which separated the field from politics and defined the discipline's proper areas of endeavor. As for his view of the teaching of philosophy, Barceló also echoed the calls of the 1950s: to return to the classics of Western philosophy, to work directly with the sources produced by the great philosophers.[15] In the context of the evolution of Chilean philosophical history, this view had precedents. But in the context of military rule, the reduction of the field to textual analysis underscored the importance attached by officialists to the extrication of philosophy from politics.

Depriving philosophy of political content did not mean the termination of political concerns on the part of philosophy students at the Instituto Pedagógico. After a wave of repression in the early period of military rule, students staged protests against the presence of security forces on the campus beginning in 1978. IP students received the support of students from other campuses, thus in effect producing the first indications of a generalized student movement. As these protests led to arrests and repression involving allegations of torture, unrest built to a climactic point in 1980, when students confronted Dean Barceló with demands for the termination of repressive activities.[16] After mutual accusations of unwillingness to listen, negotiations broke down, and the reorganization of the Faculty of Philosophy was declared the same year. Graduate philosophy studies were moved to the La Reina campus, in the outskirts of Santiago, while the old IP became an Academia Superior de Ciencias Pedagógicas offering only professional degrees. Student unrest provided the government motivation for not only the dissolution of the Faculty of Philosophy but also for the revamping of higher education in early 1981.[17]

The field of philosophy, it appeared, could not be entirely safe from political involvements. The officialists established themselves in the quieter surroundings of La Reina, where the philosophy program concentrated on the study of the classics as recommended by Barceló, who became dean of the new faculty.[18] However, unrest on the part of students as well as the larger society prompted interest in political problems even among the officialists. At La Reina, a master's degree in moral and political philosophy was established in 1982, with courses and seminars taught by professors with solid anti-Marxist credentials, including Mario Ciudad and Barceló himself. The approach of the officialists to the discussion of political matters was pointedly antipolitical and anti-Marxist. In an essay discussing "Alienation and Politics," for instance, philosophy professor Fernando Valenzuela (b. 1928), a lawyer by training, made the argument that alienation had nothing to do with political systems or class interests. Utilizing the language and concepts of Heidegger, he argued instead that alienation was intrinsic to human existence.[19] This line of thinking was not new, but it helped the officialists to address political issues at a time when politics could no longer be ignored.

Still, despite the more propitious environment as well as the officialists' own concern for political issues, even the La Reina campus was shaken by student unrest in 1985 and 1986. Fernando Valenzuela, now dean of the Faculty of Philosophy, Humanities and Education, inaugurated the 1986 academic year with a speech that condemned the unrest experienced by the faculty in recent years. He advised his listeners, and especially students, to be more understanding of the national situation and not to use disruptive tactics. After all, he argued, the rationale for student protest was not valid: the system of *Rectores delegados,* for instance, was perfectly appropriate for the circumstances. Additionally, the use of police on the campus was justified on the grounds that force should be used to prevent "greater evils."[20]

Despite their efforts and despite government support that allowed them to change their location as needed to avoid politicization, the officialists found themselves besieged by political unrest by the mid-1980s. The same politicization that they had condemned in previous regimes was now evident at their very campus. It became clear that even under the watchful eyes of the military, the apolitical university model was unworkable. Yet the officialists remained in control.

Just as their ideal university model faltered, official philosophers failed to establish enduring philosophical schools or institutions. They resorted to the philosophical schools of the past and used the same publication channels established by their predecessors. While it is true that official philosophers attempted to join the mainstream of Chilean philosophical production by going back to the professionalistic model of the 1950s, in some cases resurrecting the very schools and thinkers studied in that era, this attempt can be described as regressive. The model of the 1950s had even been abandoned by the very professionals who introduced it to philosophical studies. The derivative approach of the officialists became apparent not only in the emphasis on such schools as phenomenology and authors such as Martin Heidegger, but in the overall effort to link national philosophical production with foreign philosophical models.

An examination of the work of officialists shows a dramatic drop in philosophical production after 1973. Books became few and far between, and even articles in the *Revista de Filosofía* filled only one yearly issue as opposed to the quarterly format of the 1950s and 1960s.[21] Philosophy graduates also became few and, most significant, their theses concentrated on the great Western philosophers and rarely, if at all, on philosophical problems or issues involving various thinkers or a tradition of scholarship. Heidegger and Ortega y Gasset received the greatest amount of attention by officialist faculty and their students.[22]

Directly related to the lack of both productivity and philosophical innovation on the part of officialists is the dependence of this current upon the institutional bases established by the military principally at the University of Chile. Having no major connection with the development of the discipline in Chile, this current of philosophical activity has not developed a life of its own and depends on the continued support of the regime to maintain its academic presence and its present level of activity.

The significance of the official philosophers rests not on philosophical grounds, as their production is derivative and not fundamentally different from that of the 1950s. Rather, it rests on their ability to implement a model of philosophical teaching that is consistent with the government's view of philosophy and higher education. Moreover, this current remains significant because its followers occupy most major academic positions in at least one of the leading universities. But however dominant this current may be at UCH, its dominance is based on the political conditions created by military rule and might thus disappear when such conditions change. At any rate, UCH is no longer in the forefront of philosophical production, as many professionalists and critics reestablished their work either outside of academe or in other universities in the country. Official philosophy may nevertheless outlive its present importance at the university, for it has already had fifteen years to educate students along the lines required by the regime.

THE PROFESSIONALIST PHILOSOPHERS

Military intervention in the universities forced the established professionalist philosophers to stand perhaps the most difficult trial of their careers. Although generally opposed to the views of the critical philosophers as well as to the philosophers' involvement in politics, many professionalist philosophers reacted in one way or another to military rule in general and to the intervention of the universities in particular. The spectrum of these reactions is wide, ranging from support of, to opposition to, military rule. In all cases, however, professionalist reactions were slow to develop. This delay may have been due to their uncertainty about how long the military intervention at the universities would last as well as to their hope of having the military sanction their own philosophical approach.[23]

Some professionalists reacted favorably to military rule, like Juan de Dios Vial Larraín, until recently the dean of the Faculty of Philosophy at the Catholic University and formerly a professor at UCH and Austral University. A law graduate of the Catholic University who developed his philosophical interests at UCH but maintained ties with UC throughout his career, Vial entered the Ministry of Foreign Relations as an aide to minister Hernán Cubillos in 1979.[24] He also represented the government at various meetings of the Organization of American States (OAS) and the United Nations Educational, Scientific and Cultural Organization (UNESCO). However close to the military regime politically, Vial can still be considered a professionalist by virtue of his long-standing membership in the Chilean philosophical community. Since 1950, Vial had sustained a philosophical production that earned him a reputation in the field of metaphysics.[25] As did other professionalists, he opposed the alleged politicization of both the university and the field in the 1960s. Unlike other professionalists, however, his rejection of the changes in his field and university led him to embrace the larger aims of the military and accept various government appointments.

In addition to conducting his work on metaphysics, Vial retained an active interest in the university as a concept and as an institution after 1973. As was the case with other professionalist philosophers, Vial's view of the university placed the institution in a central position of guidance to the larger society. Professionalists during the 1960s and 1970s defended this view of the university against social pressures for reform. After 1973, some professionalists viewed military control over the institution as yet another, and perhaps more dangerous, form of pressure. Vial, however, maintained the traditional view and even underscored the university's exclusive character as a repository of universal knowledge. In Vial's view, the mission of the university and its central position in society was not affected by the advent of military rule. On the contrary, this mission became even more important in the current situation. Vial expanded on these themes when addressing a group of university students in 1980, reminding them that Marxism had been responsible for the social and political deterioration of the early 1970s. "There was no coup d'etat nor seizure of power here, but rather the assumption of authority where authority had been forsaken."[26] The university now had the opportunity to contribute to the reconstruction of society. Students, in particular, were given the chance to find new forms of representation and pluralism under military rule. In a tribute to the military, Vial closed his remarks by stating that "one of the most important lessons I ever received on the mission and responsibility of the University of Chile came from a General of the Republic who now carries high government responsibilities."[27]

Vial expressed his support for the government on various other occasions, but his political opinions were separate from his philosophical work.[28] His views on higher education, however, combined his political and philosophical positions. This had been true of other philosophers, who found in the university a link to the larger society. But Vial was an exception in that he perceived no incompatibility between his field, his concept of higher education, and military rule. In October 1987, during the most critical phase in the relations between university and government since 1973, Vial was appointed rector of the University of Chile by the military government. Vial assumed the position with the conviction that philosophy would inform his actions as university rector because, after all, the university was "eminently a philosophical institution."[29]

The appointment of a philosopher to one of the most important public positions in the nation was certainly not a new event in Chile. The philosopher's own desire to influence society via education was far from a novelty. But Vial was unusual in that no professionalist was as willing to associate himself so closely with the military government. By and large, professionalist philosophers avoided identifying themselves with the regime. But they avoided criticizing it as well. Félix Schwartzmann, for instance, who only recently accepted a position under the rectorship of Vial Larraín, maintained a distance with respect to the military regime and the official academic circles. In his work both before and after 1973, Schwartzmann maintained a line of thought whose basis he established in his acclaimed *El sentimiento de lo humano en América,* which owes little or nothing to the themes and the schools of thought promoted by the officialists.

After 1973 Schwartzmann's work continued to refer to contemporary issues, but in a universal fashion that makes it difficult to gauge the extent to which his thought has been affected by the period of military rule. An examination of his writings reveals an interest in the application of philosophy to the understanding of contemporary social problems such as the forms of human interaction, the role of the state, and the effects of rapid technological change.[30] Often the problems he addresses derive from current sociological literature in Europe and the United States. In particular, these include such issues as scientific advances and their impact on society, the problems of pollution, and the relationship between science and philosophy. In Schwartzmann's work, philosophy emerges as a discipline that dwells on contemporary social issues. However, his assertions are either so general or so oriented towards the problems of technologically more advanced societies that connections between his philosophy and specific national problems are elusive.

Even when in 1982 he discussed national identity and character, Schwartzmann only vaguely referred to the situation of Chile under military rule. National culture, in his view, was at a disadvantage in a society that favored habits of consumption. This view, which could be construed as a veiled critique of the military's neoliberal economic model, made no specific reference to Chile under military rule.[31]

Schwartzmann's lack of specificity did not escape the attention of the press, particularly at a time when other philosophers had made explicit references to military rule. In an interview published by *El Mercurio* in 1983, the writer Enrique Lafourcade asked Schwartzmann why Chilean philosophers "say nothing" to either "dissent or applaud" the actions of the military regime. Schwartzmann's laconic answer was: "I have never been silent." Schwartzmann had indeed never been silent, as Lafourcade implied, but under military rule he managed to devise a language that allowed him to refer in an oblique manner to current events while still remaining solidly within the boundaries of the discipline. As Schwartzmann put it in his response to Lafourcade, "To speak of Einstein's philosophy means more for democracy than to talk about non-performing loans."[32]

This type of indirect reference to the conditions of the country under military rule can also be found in Gastón Gómez Lasa, who was removed from his post at the University of Chile after the coup and took a position in ancient philosophy at the Austral University in Valdivia. Like Schwartzmann, Gómez Lasa today enjoys a considerable professional reputation thanks to his work on, and direct translation of, Plato. Unlike Schwartzmann, the impact of Chilean events after 1973 strongly affected the contents of Gómez Lasa's philosophical work. This can be seen in two different ways. First, through research on Plato's dialogues Gómez Lasa has sought to contribute from the field of philosophy to the politically relevant question of dialogue being discussed in other areas of national life. He has concentrated on the study of the Platonic dialogue for most of his academic life, thus reflecting an interest in the subject that went beyond the political moment. Still, the relevance and the implications of such study have not escaped him nor the attention of the wider public. The organized opposition to military rule, in particular, has made dialogue with the government one of its leading demands since 1978.[33]

Second, Gómez Lasa's choice of texts revealed a view of philosophy which not only paid attention to the political aspects of the philosophical tradition, but gave them the stature of central themes within that tradition. After 1973 Gómez Lasa translated and published Plato's *Seventh Letter* and *Socrates' Apology,* works that focus on the dilemmas facing the philosopher before authoritarian rule.[34] Gómez Lasa's concern with this issue became more explicit in the book *Platón: Primera Agonía,* where he discussed the *Gorgias,* one of Plato's most profound reflections on the limits of philosophy in relation to political power. ''The cardinal question of power,'' explained Gómez Lasa, ''is not just another theme within the dialogical process; nor simply a question to be discussed in essentialistic terms; nor a problem of definitions. As the *Gorgias* presents it, the question of power is a *factum* which provides the very basis for adopting a definitive decision regarding human life. Power not only lays out man's fate, but it also determines his human condition even beyond his life on earth.''[35]

Gómez Lasa's focus on power and the legitimacy he gave it as a genuine subject of philosophical concern represents an attempt by Chilean professionalists to use the philosophical tradition to understand the contemporary social and political situation of the country. However, Gómez Lasa has referred to this situation only indirectly. Similarly, his public comments on Chilean philosophy before 1980 were few and only to remember his colleagues during the period when he was chairman of the UCH Department of Philosophy, between 1962 and 1965. Since that was the period when academic philosophy was being questioned, Gómez Lasa's reference to the past reveals a view of philosophy that runs contrary to that of the official philosophers. Specific references to Chilean philosophy, however, are missing, and Gómez Lasa himself acknowledged in a 1983 interview that his ''silence of years might very well be a considerable mistake.''[36]

Despite his admittedly reserved attitude with respect to military rule, Gómez Lasa has made his unhappiness about it clear, particularly in the 1980s. In various interviews, Gómez Lasa has made references to the situation of philosophy and higher education that suggested discontent with military control over the universities. His discontent, however, was not confined to military rule; it included the treatment accorded to the university by other political systems as well. That is, he viewed the deterioration of university life in the context of social upheaval in the last few decades. The reform period, for instance, pushed the field of philosophy dangerously close to ideology.[37] This exposure to external social pressures, including the pressures of the military, made the university suffer. In this sense, Gómez Lasa's rejection of military rule is part of a tradition of professionalistic discontent with the impact of politics and society on higher education.

Gómez Lasa's philosophical work since 1973, on balance, has been strongly affected by military rule. This is apparent in his use of Greek philosophy to address the predicament of the discipline before authoritarian power. But references to the current situation in Chile are lacking. In contrast, other professionalist philosophers have made specific references to the problems of the country, the university, and philosophy, but without substantially altering the contents or the themes of their philosophical activity. Such is the case of Marco Antonio Allendes, a professor of philosophy at the University of Concepción. His philosophical production after 1973 did not change in any fundamental way. Allendes, who concentrated his attention on aesthetics and Eastern philosophy, departed little from his central concerns. For instance, one of his important writings after the coup included an essay on the unity of art and science.[38] This is an interesting theme from the point of view of specialized philosophy, but one that has little to do with the specific situation of Chilean philosophy.

Still, Allendes is among those professionalist philosophers who went beyond the limits of the academic discipline to address the concrete problems of the university. In September of 1979, for instance, Allendes publicly expressed his discontent with the expulsion of professors from the university, referring specifically to his colleague Humberto Otárola. He regarded Otárola's firing as unjustifiable and repudiated military decrees for the governance of the university.[39] Subsequently, Allendes labelled the military intervention at the universities "irrational" and called for the return of the institution to civilians on the grounds that the appointment of *Rectores delegados* was damaging to Chile's international image. He further added that both the man of the cap and gown and the man of the sword had respectable yet not interchangeable professions. On account of the misplaced expertise of military men at the universities, Allendes concluded that the experience of military intervention was "deplorable."[40] His increasingly outspoken criticism eventually led to his removal from the university in 1986.

Similarly, Humberto Giannini, another professionalist philosopher with a well-established reputation in philosophy, went beyond the limits of academic philosophy to address some of the abnormalities he perceived as resulting from military intervention. On several occasions Giannini manifested his disagreement with the authoritarian handling of student conflicts at the universities.[41] He also expressed his preference for a democratic government and became an active member of the Chilean Commission for Human Rights. In 1985 he produced his most explicit criticism of the situation of philosophy under military rule. His opinions on the subject were made in the context of published statements by Juan Rivano. In an interview with Rogelio Rodríguez, a former student of Rivano and a critic himself, Rivano underscored the tenuous position of the professionalists, who in his view were hard-pressed to reconcile their interest in such perennial subjects of philosophy as freedom and human dignity with the daily realities of repression.[42] Giannini agreed with Rivano that Chilean philosophy had by and large remained silent, but that there was not much that could have been done. "The great majority," responded Giannini, "of Chilean philosophy professors and thinkers would have wanted to say something, but the situation at the university was such that they had to make the choice [of remaining silent]."[43]

Giannini was not entirely happy with the situation of Chilean philosophy, and referred specifically to the officialist current. Not only were the officialists in agreement with the military government but they also justified its actions. "They are not, however, professional philosophers in my view."[44] According to Giannini, Chileans were accustomed to looking upon the university as the center of intellectual activity, but the situation had now changed. Professional philosophical activity was to be found outside the universities and in other countries where Chilean philosophers resided. As for himself, Giannini retained his university positions at both UC and UCH but developed connections with other institutions, such as the Academia de Humanismo Crisitiano. He also edited the journal *Teoría,* which later became *Escritos de Teoría,* where he provided a forum for various nonofficial philosophers. But insofar as his own philosophical work was concerned, Giannini remained attached to a traditional and professionalist philosophical orientation. Even though he wrote on such themes as nationalism and ideology, more representative of his work in philosophy is his *Tiempo y espacio en Aristóteles y Kant* (1982), which deals with the most traditional aspects of the discipline.[45]

Giannini's latest work confirms this professionalist orientation. His *La ''reflexión'' cotidiana* (1987) is a reflection of long-standing philosophical concerns. It is also an attempt to bring professionalism closer to human life and daily realities. In this book, Giannini seeks to define a common ground for human experience on the basis of spacial and temporal coordinates. He thus discusses man's daily affairs at home, at work, and at the public square as well as his perceptions of time. Giannini's aim with this approach is to establish the basis for a human communication that is grounded on shared experiences. Philosophy emerges from this work as a discipline that is outwardly oriented and seeks to contribute to the elucidation of significant aspects of human life. In this respect, the links of Giannini's latest book with his previous works are stronger than the links with the current political situation. Despite Giannini's references to the latter situation outside the field, the contents of his philosophical work have not, overall, been affected by military rule.[46]

Unlike Giannini, Jorge Millas's philosophical work was most profoundly affected by military intervention. Among the professionalists, it was Jorge Millas who assumed an outspoken critical position. However, the differences between Jorge Millas and the critical philosophers are still quite substantial, particularly during the pre-1973 period and during the first years of military rule. In 1974, for instance, in a prologue to William Thayer's *Empresa y universidad,* Millas described the last ten years at the university as years of disorder. Prior to this, Millas had actively resisted the attempts to reform both the discipline and the university from his position as chairman of the Department of Philosophy in the 1960s. For him the advent of military rule represented in many ways a new beginning for the universities. As he stated in the aftermath of the military coup, ''once again we ask ourselves about the identity of the university, and about the forms of interaction and efficiency that it requires to be saved.''[47] These cautious words of hope, however, turned into bitter disappointment by 1976. At that time, Millas not only changed the orientation of his philosophical work but he also became one of the most outspoken critics of military intervention at the universities.[48]

In his philosophical work, Millas expressed his concern for the situation of contemporary Chile in his writings on violence.[49] Violence, he explained, is not only a legitimate theme of philosophical inquiry but one of particular relevance in Chile, where ignoring it ''might accentuate the dangerous manicheanism and pharisaism of the moment.''[50] Even more significant was his willingness to gauge the value of the different philosophical schools according to their capacity to account for the concrete problems of society. This demand was repeatedly made by the critical philosophers during the 1960s, when phenomenology and existentialism, in particular, were viewed as orientations that ignored such problems. Phenomenology, popular among the official philosophers in the midseventies, came under the attack of Millas, who had himself been instrumental in introducing it in professional circles.

The reason for Millas's change of orientation lies in the nature of his focus, for the problems of violence, in his view, could not be treated in phenomenological terms. A phenomenological study of violence, according to Millas, was merely analytical and led to ''talking about worlds that are not in this world.''[51] With phenomenology in mind, Millas proceeded to attack those philosophical schools, Marxism included, which he viewed as compatible with violence. Without openly acknowledging it, Millas belatedly agreed with the foremost critical demand of the 1960s: to judge the value of a given philosophical school not so much for its internal coherence as for its capacity to address the problems of society.

Expelled from Austral University for expressing opinions contrary to the interests of the military regime in the city of Concepción in 1980, Millas returned to his teaching position only after a flurry of protests from academics around the country threatened the precious peace sought by the military at the universities. Still, he was stripped of his administrative responsibilities. These events led him to devote the last two years of his life to the critique of military rule and its implications for the universities. Although an opponent of political involvements for several decades, Jorge Millas became a political figure once again after he resigned from Austral University in 1981 to meet his own demand for "authenticity."[52]

The same man who had denounced the heavily politicized university of the reform period as well as the "committed university" of the Salvador Allende administration now attacked the "university under surveillance" and the "barracks university" of the Pinochet regime.[53] In Millas's view, all of these models of the university violated the essentials of a genuine university life. But the current situation of the universities seemed to him to be a reflection of an even graver problem, for he considered the university problem to be "one of the most serious in the grave spiritual prostration of the country."[54] His reasons for resigning were that given the "autocratic" powers of the rectors appointed by the military government and the massive expulsion of academics, "one's presence approves of this situation."[55] His resignation, he explained, had become a matter of moral and intellectual integrity.

Millas's concern for Chile's universities reflected the philosopher's traditional interest in the concept of higher education as well as his own views, developed over the decades, on the university. In 1981, he published *Idea y defensa de la universidad,* a compilation of his major articles on the subject over a period of two decades.[56] There is remarkable continuity in Millas's thinking in this regard, for he remained uncompromising in his position that no one other than the university itself should define the fundamental mission of the institution, let alone interfere with its pursuit of truth. Millas's criticism of the military was primarily a critique against the government's handling of higher education. He did develop a more comprehensive basis for criticizing military rule, but the transition from cautious approval to outspoken criticism was precipitated by university affairs. As follower of a philosophical tradition that had been nourished by both the concept and the institution of the university, Millas felt the impact of military rule as a direct blow against a lifetime of philosophical work.

After his resignation from Austral University, Millas became founder and president of the Academia Andrés Bello, an association of academics and intellectuals that took a critical stand with respect to the military regime. Millas also taught private seminars and often expressed his critiques of the government through the opposition media. Unlike the work of Allendes and Giannini among the professionalists, Millas's philosophical work could no longer be separated from his political opinions. For instance, by 1982 Millas was finishing a book on Friederich Von Hayek, an author whose economic neoliberalism was being promoted by official circles. But apparently the coming together of philosophy and politics in Millas was not enough to sustain him. He had always managed to have his opinions heard, but increasingly, as in Concepción in 1980, Millas found it difficult even to find a room in which to address the public. When the University of Concepción denied him use of the facilities, he was forced to find a room in a city parish and lecture in quarters surrounded by police.[57] Moreover, his resignation from the university and, in the words of Humberto Giannini, the "systematic and devastating war" waged against him because of his critiques of the military government, apparently caused him great sorrow.[58] He died at the age of sixty-five in November of 1982.

With Millas's death the future of professionalist philosophy is presently unclear, due to the general tendency of this group to abstain from actions and opinions that might be interpreted as political. Additionally, their long isolation has taken its toll. For fifteen years, most professionalists have worked in universities other than UCH, often in the provinces. But even when working in Santiago, like Humberto Giannini, they find themselves in an isolated and disadvantaged position. "It's a very precarious situation," Giannini said in an interview. "I have found meaningful philosophical friendships only outside the university."[59] Their written work, as a result, has been the product of long-standing concerns rather than the outcome of an intellectual climate created by peers. Moreover, several professionalists have recently retired or are rapidly approaching retirement age. They thus find their labor of decades to be unfinished, their institutions changed or destroyed, and their chances of regaining control over the discipline to be few indeed.

THE CRITICAL PHILOSOPHERS

Under military rule, professionalists like Millas became critics, and hence significant overlap exists between these two groups during the period. However, the most important distinguishing factor between the two remains the resistance of professionalists to allowing changes in their philosophical orientation due to social and political events. Critics had waged a long battle to incorporate social and political concerns into the field and sustained this attitude, although not without exceptions, during the years of military government. Unlike the professionalists, the critical philosophers did not expect a restoration of professional philosophical activity from the military government. The very nature of their writings reveals their awareness of the implications of military rule for national and university life.

However significant, the critical current was never very strong in university circles; with military rule, it was nearly wiped out. The most important example is that of Juan Rivano, who had been a critic of the "committed" philosophy propounded by leftist academics at the UCH Faculty of Philosophy. He had also taken part in a university-based opposition movement against the authorities of that faculty, then headed by a historian and Communist party leader, the late Hernán Ramírez Necochea. Supported by such professionalist philosophers as Gastón Gómez Lasa and Cástor Narvarte and basing their arguments on the principles of the 1968 university reform, which included the academic autonomy of the departments, Rivano and others resisted repeated attempts to introduce a Marxist-inspired curriculum without departmental consensus.

Such opposition against the university policy of the Unidad Popular government did not make critics any more acceptable to the military. The new authorities concentrated instead on the critical activities of these philosophers and the potential they represented for similar opposition against military intervention at the universities. Both Rivano and Edison Otero (b. 1945), a junior philosophy professor, were interrogated by military personnel and expelled in 1974 amidst the silence, if not hostility, of the professionalists. The sense of collegiality that had existed among professionalists and critics as members of the philosophical community, however precarious it might have been prior to 1973, suffered a serious breakdown under military rule. Despite the lack of support from members of the profession, the absence of charges against Rivano and Otero helped them to return to their teaching posts, although they were removed again in 1975. In that year, Edison Otero was expelled from the university and Juan Rivano was expelled and imprisoned, in both cases without charges.

A significant current of Chilean philosophical thought was thus purged from the university and forced to exist beyond the academic world. This current, however, maintained a remarkable level of productivity, given the serious obstacles presented by the lack of academic resources and, in the case of Rivano, by exile. Because of the nonacademic situation of this group, such intellectuals as Juan Rivano and Edison Otero sought alternative means of expression, which led them in turn to establish connections with social science fields and organizations.

The creation, consolidation, and growth of several private, nonprofit research institutions has been one of the most significant developments for intellectual life in Chile under military rule. These organizations sheltered many academics after the coup and moved in to fill the vacuum left by the harassment and in some cases elimination of university-based social science research. The Catholic church provided significant support to these organizations, as did the Konrad Adenauer Foundation, the Ford Foundation, and others. These centers and institutions include the Corporación de Promoción Universitaria (CPU), the Academia de Humanismo Cristiano (AHC), the Instituto Chileno de Estudios Humanísticos (ICHEH), and the Facultad Latinoamericana de Ciencias Sociales (FLACSO).[60] They have all given an important impulse to the study of the social sciences removed by the military from the universities. Research in philosophy, however, has not been a priority in these institutions, partly because of the discipline's isolation in the past, which prevented it from establishing lasting ties with the social sciences. Military rule changed this relationship significantly, if unintentionally.

Through CPU and its publications *Documentos de Trabajo* and *Estudios Sociales,* Edison Otero began, in 1976, to develop the basis for closer links between philosophy and the social and natural sciences. In his writings, Otero also offered both a critique of the obstacles that in his view had kept the disciplines separated and an attack against academic and professionalist practices in general. "These days," Otero stated in 1978, "official academic philosophy neglects the development of connections [with other sciences] and instead affects an air of self-sufficiency by cultivating the scholastic study of its own past."[61] Further evidence of Otero's interest in themes that are the province of other social sciences can be found in his concern with the subject of violence. He coauthored with Jorge Millas the book *La violencia y sus máscaras,* in which the problem of violence was accorded the character of a genuine subject of philosophical inquiry. Unlike Millas, however, he used the results of the social and natural sciences to present his views on this phenomenon. The same approach became apparent in Otero's subsequent book on the theme of violence, *Los signos de la violencia* (1979), in which he argued in favor of interdisciplinary research and advanced a view of intellectual activity which, he submitted, could counter the effects of violence.[62] Reflection, in his view, provided an effective instrument against the violence unleashed in the name of ideological and political convictions.

However successful Otero was in presenting his views through private research groups, the absence of a university affiliation limited the circulation of his work. In 1979 he created and edited the journal *Carnets,* which was closed down by the military regime after publication of the first issue. After his expulsion from the University of Chile, Otero found himself joining the ranks of university professors who taught in secondary schools to make a living. Eventually, as an outgrowth of his interest in communications media, he found employment in an advertising agency. He remained active in private research groups such a CPU and ICHEH, but the weight of years of separation from the university as well as constant limitations on his endeavors took their toll. Otero began to increasingly move away from a critical perspective. His latest book, a collection of citations from various intellectuals titled *Los derechos de la inteligencia* (1985), shared the traditional professionalist position that "intelligence" can play a fundamental social role provided that intelligence itself defines the nature of the link with society. Professionalists called it "spiritual life," and Otero's concept is similar in that a distance is created in both cases between the activities of the mind, which pressumably has its own dynamics and rights, and the interests of society.[63] An even sharper reversal from a critical position came with Otero's contribution to a government publication designed to promote, worldwide, the cultural activities of the regime.[64] Like the work of the professionalists, who may not necessarily support the military government and who go about their work as if independent from politics, Otero's latest work found accommodation with, if not the approval of, the administration.

The military government, however, has been largely intolerant of critical activities and has struck out against intellectuals who have assumed a critical position. This was the case of Renato Cristi (b. 1941), a University of Toronto Ph.D. who returned to Chile to teach philosophy at the University of Chile. Prior to his return, Cristi voiced criticisms against the political views of Jaime Guzmán, one of the chief ideologues of the military government.[65] Once in the country, Cristi made public his advocacy of democracy and, like Jorge Millas, took issue with Friederich Von Hayek's neoliberalism. In his opinion and that of his coauthor Carlos Ruiz, Hayek's ideas were being promoted by official circles because they coincided with the economic policies of the military government. Furthermore, they believed, such ideas were being used to justify "the overwhelming prevalence of the free-market economy," ideas which they questioned on moral and ethical grounds.[66] In 1981, Renato Cristi was expelled from his teaching position. Before leaving the country to accept a visiting professorship in Canada, he declared that "only the philosophy which [the military] believes serves to legitimize the present is guaranteed peace."[67]

The strongest military retaliation against the critics involved Juan Rivano, who has lived in exile since 1976. Unlike Otero and Cristi, Rivano can neither return to Chile nor regularly publish there. He was abducted by the secret police in 1975 and was moved to some of the most notorious prison camps set up by the military after the coup. Despite international pressure for his release, the military retained him without charges for a year. Upon his release, Rivano moved to Israel and finally to Sweden, where he was granted asylum. Once in a position to resume his work, Rivano continued the line of thinking that characterized his production during the early 1970s; that is, an effort to reconcile philosophical concepts with contemporary social, political, cultural and economic developments or else reject those concepts.

Rivano's production after 1973 falls under three major categories: logic and epistemology; social and political philosophy; and literature. The theme uniting these writings concerns Rivano's conviction that the complexity of human and social experience can be apprehended logically. All along, he has argued that logical categories can be devised so that such complexity can be handled and understood rather than simplified or obliterated, as he claims happens with formal, mathematical, and even dialectical logic. This has led him to explore a variety of examples, mainly from the contemporary social and political world, which in his view illustrate how traditional philosophy and logic fail to provide an intelligent apprehension of reality. Although he uses a number of findings from the natural and social sciences, it is clear that his major sources come from the field of logic. Even his literature is more often than not a vehicle for the expression of his logical concerns. Logic has continued to serve him to address disciplinary and extradisciplinary subjects.

A prolific writer, Rivano has met heavy censorship, as exemplified by the military authorities' threat to confiscate an issue of *Estudios Sociales* which included an article by him in 1982.[68] The *Revista de Filosofía,* which he had edited in the past, now refused to publish his work. It has been mainly through the activities of former students like Rogelio Rodríguez that Rivano's work has circulated in Chile after the coup. Also, partly because no other scholar of his stature and training has emerged in the field of logic under military rule, his work again began to be published in Chile in the 1980s. A second edition of his *Lógica elemental* appeared in 1985 and his *Perspectivas sobre la metáfora* in 1986.[69] In the first book, Rivano paid homage to Pedro León Loyola and Marcos Flores, his mentors in the field, in an attempt to underline the continuity of logical studies in the country. Logic, indeed, has been one of the casualties of the discipline, since officialists lack the interest or the training to maintain even a minimal level of activity in this area.

Rivano's work on political philosophy has found more obstacles to publication, but several of his articles have appeared in the CPU journal *Estudios Sociales.*[70] One major interview appeared in *Pluma y Pincel,* where Rivano issued his critique of Chilean philosophy under military rule, particularly its professionalist strain. But the bulk of his production in exile remains unpublished, including a massive work titled *Un largo contrapunto* (1986), in which Rivano recounts much of his intellectual development as well as Chilean cultural history since the 1930s. The work consists of a personal account of the education, culture, and politics of the nation beginning with his primary education in the provinces, his work in philosophy in Santiago, and his critiques of the literary and philosophical production of Chile. Félix Schwartzmann had earlier produced a comprehensive and scholarly analysis of Chilean cultural history from a philosophical standpoint. But Rivano's *Contrapunto* is written in an autobiographical form which emphasizes the clashes between contending cultural and political forces in the nation. In this work he argues that the culture of Chile as promoted by the educational system and presented in a large body of literature and philosophy is derivative at best, and is oblivious to the overwhelming imbalance between higher aims and material conditions. As he had sketched in his earlier *Cultura de la servidumbre* in the 1960s, Chilean culture reemerged in his *Contrapunto* as a culture divided, a culture in which contradictory tendencies uneasily coexist and often bring their differences to the political arena.

Rivano's case shows that despite imprisonment, censorship, and the hostility of the military government, the critical current has maintained a significant level of production and presence in the country. This current, however, is threatened by the prolonged separation from the university. Without access to students and channels for publishing important parts of their work, critics face a difficult future. Yet unlike the officialists, who require the political and financial support of the government to maintain a minimum level of philosophical activity, critics sustain theirs with little if any support. Critics as well as professionalists, in this sense, have been able to remain central currents of Chilean philosophy despite fifteen years of military rule.

The military manifested its hostility against the critics early for reasons having to do with the regime's fear of opposition activities at the university. The attitude towards the professionalists was more ambivalent, evolving from support to neglect, and ultimately to harassment and repression in those instances where the professionalists moved to critical positions. To the military, only the officialists proved to be reliable, as the regime's interest in the discipline and the university required the unqualified support of members of the university community. The military thus undermined the institutional basis that had supported the development of philosophical studies in Chile. Yet however draconian this university policy may have been, it did not lead to the total destruction of the community of philosophers, who found alternative means of expression as well as more hospitable institutions. Chile, in this sense, has been more fortunate than Argentina, where repressive military policies between 1976 and 1983 took a heavier toll on university life and intellectual work. Both countries shared a similarly repressive military experience, but university constituencies in Chile and Argentina have fared very differently. As Tulio Halperín-Donghi has shown, this is due to the different processes of institutionalization of culture in both nations.[71] Chilean universities remained remarkably stable for most of their history. This allowed Chileans to continue to work in university settings and even to reconstitute working groups outside the university to an extent that Argentina could not even approach. Chilean philosophy may provide a case in point to the extent that by and large it continues to function in an institutional context. However scattered or isolated, the major philosophical figures of the pre-1973 period continue to be prominent in the field and have made efforts to salvage some of the philosophical centers and publication channels.

Some qualifications are in order, however, as the Chilean philosophical community has been fundamentally disrupted in important ways. Professionalists and critics both lost control over the discipline at UCH to the officialists. The military also struck a major blow against UCH by means of successive purges and budget cuts. In addition, the interests of the officialists went beyond the universities to better respond to the needs of the military. The fragmentation of the Faculty of Philosophy and its separation from the old Instituto Pedagógico provides one example of institutional collapse due to military rule and the willingness of officialists to go along with it.

Chile still differs from Argentina in that some level of continuity has been maintained. The professionals of the past continue to recognize their peers and continue to use the standards that allowed them to function as a coherent group during the 1950s and 1960s. They remain productive, they pointedly distance themselves from the officialists, and they continue to set the pace for Chilean philosophical activity. They may no longer work at their traditional university, but their influence over the field is still unequaled by any other group. More important, the long period of military rule has brought closer together the professionalist and critical views of the discipline, which seemed to be so thoroughly incompatible during the 1960s. Both views and their followers have borne the brunt of government censorship and repression. Although they remain totally separate in philosophical outlook, professionalists and critics maintain ties and connections which have in effect kept professional philosophy alive, thus providing a measure of continuity with respect to the historical development of the discipline.

Beyond the creation of an officialist current, military rule has unintentionally introduced other important changes in Chilean philosophy. Military rule has prompted many, including the professionalist philosophers, to pay increasing attention to such themes as violence and power. These concerns have in turn made philosophers more responsive to the findings and work of other social scientists as well as more responsive to the notion that their professional calling includes pronouncements on the situation of the country and its higher education institutions. What all of this means and where it will lead is not apparent under the present conditions of military rule. What is obvious, however, is that a significant part, if not the greater part, of Chilean philosophical activity takes place outside official philosophical circles. The main conflict, then, is no longer between professionalist and critical philosophy, but between official philosophy, supported by military rule, and a largely nonacademic yet free critical and professional view of the discipline.

Conclusion

When Plato concluded that the best king was a philosopher-king, he set out to establish the ideal republic with the help of his disciple Dion. The endeavor was to be made easier by Dion's influence over Dionysius, ruler of Syracuse, and the latter's favorable disposition towards philosophy. Instead, Plato's involvement in politics nearly cost him his life. Embittered, he returned to Athens to create the Academy and to devote the rest of his life to philosophy. Philosophers and kings, just as philosophy and politics, have led an uneasy coexistence ever since.

Plato's experience with the king and politics has haunted Chilean philosophers since Independence. Few have been willing to be as close to politics as Plato once was, let alone allow politics to dictate the nature of their philosophical concerns. But Chilean philosophers resemble Plato in that they have devoted an important part of their thinking to politics in order to attempt to guide society according to philosophical principles. When confronted with the specifics of political maneuvering and ideology, however, they have reacted with exasperation and withdrawal.

And yet Chilean philosophers have had few problems with politics as long as it was kept separate from their philosophical activity. As seen throughout the book, many of the most important philosophers of the nation have held high-level political positions. Their rejection of politics, then, relates more to what they believe should be the object of philosophy than to a total rejection of political involvement. In fact, they have not shunned political commitments during those times when they believed that their views on the discipline and the university were threatened. They may not have been the best or the most effective politicians, but they have certainly been among the most vocal defenders of their interests.

Why then their effort to keep philosophy separate from politics? Philosophers have been interested in this separation for different reasons. One is the understandable fear of being at odds with the policies of changing governments of different ideological persuasions. During the nineteenth century, the religious issue was delicate enough to make philosophers cautious about their religious opinions. But as soon as they perceived that the secular state had the upper hand in the conflict, they were merciless in their critiques of Catholicism. During the twentieth century, philosophers attacked Marxism because, in fact, most administrations during the period were suspicious of, if not antagonistic to, Marxist politics. Under military rule, philosophers thought it best not to behave politically under a government suspicious of politics altogether. Philosophers have all along been perceptive readers of the political changes that can affect their interests.

Another reason for this separation is the limited claim politics has on a field that boasts a long tradition of concerns on issues that transcend politics, such as metaphysics. Philosophers, at least Chilean philosophers, have traditionally been more at home discussing the intricacies of metaphysics than the grey and often intractable areas of politics. They revolted against positivism for its rejection of metaphysics and insisted that philosophy had nothing to do with either practical or political endeavors. Philosophy, they have emphasized, requires a special calling closer to meditation than to the action associated with practical politics. Philosophical careers, in addition, are not built on the basis of political expertise but rather on knowledge of specialized, if not esoteric, philosophical subjects. During the twentieth century, philosophers have found support for this view in some of the most distinguished practitioners of the field internationally.

But perhaps the most important reason for the separation of philosophy from politics concerns the degree of mobility that it has allowed Chilean philosophers. Because of this separation, philosophers have been able to devote their full energies to both endeavors simultaneously or find refuge in one sphere at times of turmoil in the other. Clearly, they have preferred to work in their specialized practice, but they have also made certain that the door to—although not from—politics was left wide open. Be it in the form of political appointments or in the form of access to political channels for the defense of their philosophy or university interests, philosophers have crossed the boundaries between philosophy and politics frequently and eagerly. Not a few of the philosophers have occupied the highly politicized office of rector of the university, as well as important cabinet positions in different governments. Still, philosophical professionalism has attracted them more than any other concern, even to the point of their becoming political to defend it. Not only have they felt part of the distinguished community of thinkers who form the Western intellectual tradition, but they have also enjoyed the prominence that their specialization has allowed them in the form of publications, congresses, and a great deal of national attention.

One of the most significant effects of military rule has been the undermining of this separation. All philosophers except the officialists have reached the point where they find that they can no longer maintain their specialized concerns. Their professionalism was founded on the basis of a dynamic interaction with a university model that favored specialization and allowed philosophers a great deal of control over their academic programs and activities. Under military rule they have lost control over the university, and even those philosophers with the most impeccable anti-Marxist credentials, like Jorge Millas, have suffered persecution. Their mobility has been restricted, forcing them to think politically about the ways to recover control, at least over the discipline. Their task is not an easy one, however, and they must calculate well whether to join other political forces, taking into consideration the lessons of the university reform period, or remain fragmented, powerless, and unable to do much of the specialized philosophical work that took them so long to establish.

Chilean philosophical activity has traditionally been related to such central national problems as the relationship between religious and secular thinking during the nineteenth century and between intellectual activity and politics during the twentieth. However, philosophers have found their inspiration to approach these problems in the field itself, and usually in European authors whom they have read selectively. During the brief period in which they did not feel the pressures of politics, they became accustomed to treating the major philosophical themes of the Western tradition as if they were their own and were applicable to Chile. The massive political changes that have restricted their philosophical activity since the university reform period have not convinced them that their philosophical focus should be changed. A few have become motivated to understand politics and the national situation better. But most continue to think of philosophy as beyond national circumstances. The irony of their effort is that the dialogue that they wish to maintain with the Western tradition has been more of a monologue on their part. Their work is only rarely translated and is practically unknown beyond Chile. In addition, Chilean philosophers find it increasingly difficult to carry on a type of philosophical work that has little impact, if any, on an international constituency that maintains only a limited interest in their efforts.

Still, philosophers have articulated subtle developments in the educational, cultural, and political history of their country. Whether at the university, in the national press, or in politics, they have addressed much that is important to know about a nation's effort to define its intellectual tradition, its major problems, and the meaning of its changing political landscape. It remains to be seen, however, whether the philosophical tradition established by Chilean philosophers will survive the ravages of the military period and, if so, what lessons they will learn from it, particularly with regard to social and political issues. But they are likely to volunteer their opinions and involvement in the still uncertain future of their nation.

Notes

Introduction

1. The bibliography on this subject is very extensive. Some of the most important works include: Francisco Romero, *Filosofía de ayer y de hoy* (Buenos Aires, 1947); Frondizi, "¿Hay una filosofía Iberoamericana?" José Ferrater Mora, "El problema de la filosofía americana," *Filosofía y Letras* 18 (1950): 379–383; Rivano, *El punto de vista;* Augusto Salazar Bondy, *¿Existe una filosofía de nuestra América?* (Mexico City, 1968); Leopoldo Zea, *La filosofía Americana como filosofía sin más* (Mexico City, 1969); Francisco Miró Quesada, *El problema de la filosofía latinoamericana* (Mexico City, 1976); and "Posibilidad y límites de una filosofía latinoamericana," *Revista Interamericana de Bibliografía* 27 (October–December 1977): 353–363. Jorge J. E. Gracia and I have summarized the debates and the major approaches to Latin American philosophy in "The Problem of Philosophical Identity," and in our *Filosofía e identidad cultural en América Latina.* (Caracas, 1988).

Chapter I. Philosophy, the Secularization of Thought, and Higher Education

1. Allen Woll, *A Functional Past.* A concise, yet particularly valuable study that focuses on the period under study is Collier, "Evolución política, institucional, social y cultural de Chile." See also his "Chile from Independence to the War." The bibliography for the period is extensive, but its major sources have been collected and commented on by Collier in "The Historiography of the 'Portalian' Period."

2. Donoso, *Las ideas políticas en Chile,* 186.

3. Ibid., 216–217, and Krebs, "El pensamiento de la iglesia frente a la laicización del estado en Chile, 1875–1885," in *Catolicismo y Laicismo*, edited by Krebs, 29.

4. The best studies of the Instituto Nacional are by Domingo Amunátegui Solar. See his *Los primeros años; El Instituto Nacional*, and *Recuerdos del Instituto Nacional*. Further information about IN can be found in Labarca, *Historia;* Campos Harriet, *Desarrollo educacional;* Jobet, *Doctrina y praxis;* and Margaret Campbell, "Education in Chile: 1810–1842."

5. Amunátegui Solar, *Los primeros años*, 156–157.

6. A detailed study of scholasticism in Latin America is O. Carlos Stoetzer, *The Scholastic Roots of the Spanish American Revolution* (New York, 1979). The most important study of Chilean colonial philosophy is Walter Hanisch Espíndola, S. J., *En torno a la filosofía en Chile*.

7. Mario Góngora, "Origin and Philosophy of the Spanish American University," in *The Latin American University*, ed. Maier and Weatherhead, 17–64; Medina, *Historia de la Real Universidad*.

8. Jobet, *Doctrina y praxis* 144–45.

9. Amunátegui Solar, *Los primeros años*, 162.

10. Quoted in Amunátegui Solar, *Los primeros años*, 231. This and all other translations in the book, unless otherwise indicated, are mine.

11. For a discussion of Egaña's educational and political views, see Julio César Jobet, *Doctrina y praxis*, 131–135; Collier, *Ideas and Politics*, 260–286; and Raúl Silva Castro, "Ideario Americanista de don Juan Egaña," *Revista de Historia de las Ideas* 2 (October 1960): 31–53.

12. Collier, *Ideas and Politics*, 274–275.

13. For a discussion of Lozier's role at IN, see Amunátegui Solar, *Los primeros años*, 291–359.

14. Ibid., 265.

15. Ibid., 691.

16. Egaña, *Tractatus*. This textbook was primarily on logic, and covered neither metaphysics nor ethics, as suggested by the title.

17. Amunátegui Solar, *Los primeros años*, 378.

18. Juan Egaña demonstrated his proximity to this school by suggesting that "*analysis est optima methodus inveniendi veritatem; et ex compara-*

tione idearum simplicium per intimas, et succesivas consequentias proceditur ad examinandas causas rerum, convenientiasque idearum,'' in the *Tractatus,* p. 28.

19. The Idéologues were followers of Condillac who concentrated on the analysis of ideas, which they believed to be derived from sensations. The movement, which included such figures as Cabanis and Destutt de Tracy, was popular in France between the last years of the eighteenth century and the first two decades of the nineteenth. See Boas, *French Philosophies.*

20. Amunátegui, *Don José Joaquín de Mora,* 108.

21. Hanisch, *Rousseau,* 94 and 106.

22. Meneses' rectorship of IN has been discussed by Amunátegui Solar in *Los primeros años,* 361–425. Meneses (1785–1860) supported the Spanish monarchy during the War of Independence; he returned to Chile to become a priest in 1822. Figueroa, *Diccionario,* 5: 255–256.

23. Every important Liceo in Santiago taught philosophy by 1830. The Instituto Nacional had sixty-eight philosophy students by 1830; the Liceo de Chile, twenty-seven; the Colegio de Santiago, seventeen; the Colegio Juan Antonio Portés, ten; the Convento San Francisco, thirty-two; and the Recoleta Domínica, three. That is 157 students out of a total of 772 students in the Santiago secondary schools. See Francisco Solano Pérez, ''Estado general de las escuelas de primeras letras y de su enseñanza en el distrito de Santiago en el mes de Diciembre de 1830,'' *El Araucano* no. 18, January 15, 1831, and Campos Harriet, *Desarrollo educacional,* 76. At the Instituto, attendance in the philosophy class was second only to attendance in the law class.

24. The *Ideología* consisted of four parts: history of philosophy, ideology, general grammar, and logic, in addition to separate comments by Varas and Marín. An appendix featured the program and examinations for the philosophy course. The first and third sections were written by José Miguel Varas, the second and fourth by Ventura Marín.

25. Juan Carlos Torchia Estrada indicates that Manuel Belgrano and Bernardino Rivadavia had close ties with the Ideology school and recommended their teaching in Argentina. Rivadavia, in particular, was a correspondent of Destutt de Tracy. See Torchia's *La filosofía en la Argentina.*

26. For an examination of Laromiguière's position in nineteenth-century French philosophy, see Boas, *French Philosophies,* 35. One of Laromiguière's students, Juan Antonio Portés, joined Mora's Liceo de Chile

in 1829. At the inauguration of the philosophy class he summarized the main tenets and accomplishments of the Idéologues and culminated his presentation with praise to the "inmortales lecciones" of Laromiguière. His speech is included in Stuardo Ortiz, "El Liceo de Chile." For a comment on Portés and his role in Chilean philosophy, see Hanisch, *Rousseau,* 143–145.

27. Varas and Marín, *Ideología,* 80.

28. Marín, *Filosofía* (1834), 1: i–ii.

29. Varas and Marín, *Ideología,* 119.

30. Francisco Encina has covered the period extensively in his *Portales,* 2 vols. (Santiago, 1934).

31. The events leading to the creation of the Liceo de Chile and the subsequent deportation of Mora have been described in detail by Miguel Luis Amunátegui's *Mora.* Stuardo Ortiz's "El Liceo de Chile" covers the same events in vols. 115: 162–217, and 116: 50–91, of the *Revista Chilena de Historia y Geografía.* See also Margaret Campbell, "Education in Chile."

32. No one has been more adamant in this regard than José Victorino Lastarria. See his *Recuerdos literarios,* 125–126. See also Amunátegui Solar, *El progreso,* 43–44.

33. Indeed, the course that would normally be called philosophy was called Ideology at Mora's Liceo. The main authors studied included Condillac and Destutt de Tracy. Mora himself taught the course to students in their fifth year. See Stuardo, "El Liceo de Chile," 64.

34. Monguió, *Mora y el Perú,* 4.

35. Ibid., 145.

36. Mora, *Cursos,* v. The pages of Mora's introduction to the first edition of the book are unnumbered. Following the practice of Luis Monguió, I will give Roman numerals to these pages.

37. See Boas, *French Philosophies,* particularly chapters 4 and 5. On Cousin and Eclecticism, see Alan B. Spitzer, "Victor Cousin and the French Generation of 1820," in *From Paranassus: Essays in Honor of Jacques Barzun,* ed. Dora B. Weiner and William Keylor (New York, 1976), 177–194, and W. M. Simon, "The 'Two Cultures' in Nineteenth-Century France: Victor Cousin and Auguste Comte," *Journal of the History of Ideas* 26, no. 1 (January–March 1965): 45–58.

38. Mora, *Cursos,* vii.

39. Monguió, *Mora y el Peru,* 139.

40. Quoted in Hanisch, *Rousseau,* 137–138.

41. Labarca, *Historia,* 96.

42. Amunátegui Solar, *Los primeros años,* 476–478.

43. Marín, *Filosofía,* 1: iv–v.

44. Ibid., 1: 258–260. According to Guillermo Feliú Cruz, this fear had some basis up to Ramón Briseño's time. He explains that "the very few minds that attempted to emancipate themselves from that [scholastic and theological] intellectual tutelage in order to teach philosophy according to other schools were, if not persecuted, at least isolated and silenced by the clergy," in Ramón Briseño, 65.

45. Bello's review was published in *El Araucano* no. 222, December 12, 1834, and no. 266, October 9, 1835. It has also been included in his *Obras,* 3: 580–582. Although there was a Chilean edition of Bello's complete works in 1881, I will use the more widely available Caracas edition for the purposes of citation.

46. Bello, *Obras,* 3: 582.

47. Amunátegui Solar, *El Instituto Nacional,* 43.

48. Ibid., 95–96.

49. Marín, *Filosofía,* 1: xiii.

50. Mental breakdowns seem to have been a common occurrence among intellectuals in the nineteenth century. One may venture to say that the demands made of these intellectuals, as their multiple activities in politics and education suggest, took a heavy toll on these men. Amunátegui Solar presents a more challenging interpretation when he suggests that such breakdowns were the product of "the intellectual and religious crisis endured by many of the most cultivated minds of the century." In the specific case of Ventura Marín, he suggests that "there was a struggle between two opposite tendencies, that of the saint fathers [of the church] and that of the eighteenth century philosophers. . . . Marín's intelligence succumbed in the fight." See Amunátegui Solar, *Los primeros años,* 530–531. Even the serene Ramón Briseño was forced to partial retirement due to a "congestión cerebral," as he put it, in 1871.

51. Briseño's *Curso de Filosofía moderna* was published in two volumes under the pseudonym N.O.R.E.A. and had four parts: psychology, logic, ethics, and philosophy of law. Briseño reedited the *Curso* in 1854 and reduced it to one volume. The philosophy of law section included in the second volume of the first edition was reedited in 1866 and published with a section on the history of philosophy translated from a book by Géruzez, who was partial to Scottish philosophy and its French interpreters. There was yet another edition of Briseño's philosophy of law in 1870.

52. The creation of the University of Chile did not entail the elimination of IN, which still housed higher education teaching. The university, however, was now in charge of supervising not only the Instituto but also all schools at all other levels of education, in accordance with article 154, chapter XI, of the 1833 Constitution. The university was also charged with the promotion of research on science and the humanities. See "Ley Orgánica de la Universidad de Chile," *Anales de la Universidad de Chile* (henceforth *AUCH*) 1 (1843–1844): 3. In essence, UCH was originally an academic and supervisory body whose teaching component was not inaugurated until a decade later. On the creation of the UCH, see Barros Arana, *Un decenio;* Pacheco Gómez, *La Universidad de Chile;* Feliú Cruz, *La Universidad de Chile;* and the works already cited by Amunátegui Solar (*El Instituto Nacional*), Labarca, Góngora, and Campos Harriet. For the study of FFH, there is a very useful compilation of the *Actas* of 1843–1862, edited by Ana Guirao Massif. See also her introductory work, *Historia.* The best source for the study of the UCH continues to be the *Anales de la Universidad de Chile,* published annually since 1843.

53. Amunátegui Solar, *El Instituto Nacional,* 113–115.

54. This view has roots in Diego Barros Arana, justly recognized as an authority on the period, who suggested that the UCH took "las corporaciones de esa clase en Francia" as its model. See his *Decenio,* 1: 323. Most scholars concerned with the subject have since referred to the French background of the UCH. See, for instance, Labarca, *Historia,* 108–110; Feliú Cruz, *La Universidad,* 73; Guirao, *Historia,* 5, and Góngora, "Origin," 57–58. For the purposes of comparison, see Joseph N. Moody, *French Education Since Napoleon* (Syracuse, 1978).

55. Juan David García Bacca, "Introducción general a las obras filosóficas de Andrés Bello," in Bello, *Obras Completas,* 3: xviii. Important biographies of Bello are by Amunátegui, *Vida de Bello,* and by Rafael Caldera, *Andrés Bello* (Caracas, 1935). Important studies of the multiple aspects of Bello's thought and career are by Feliú Cruz, ed., *Estudios;* Lynch, ed., *Andrés Bello;* and the volumes published by the Fundación La

Casa de Bello, *Bello y Caracas* (Caracas, 1979); *Bello y Londres,* 2 vols. (Caracas, 1981); *Bello y Chile,* 2 vols. (Caracas, 1981); and *Bello y la América Latina (Caracas, 1982).*

56. Quoted by Fernández Larraín, *Cartas a Bello,* 76–77.

57. Richard B. Sher, *Church and University in the Scottish Enlightenment: The Moderate Literati of Edinburgh* (Princeton, 1985).

58. The *Filosofía del entendimiento* was part of the first volume of the Chilean edition of Bello's *Obras Completas,* published in 1881. Walter Hanisch indicates that the philosophical pieces published by Bello in *El Crepúsculo* in 1843 and 1844 correspond roughly to the first 137 pages of the Chilean edition. See Hanisch's "Andrés Bello," in *Bello y Chile* 1: 264.

59. Particularly, his review of Ventura Marín cited in note 45, and his critique of the 1832 reform at IN authored by Montt, Marín, and Godoy. Bello criticized the program in an article published in *El Araucano* on January 21, 1832, in which he voiced his concern about the timing of logical and philosophical studies.

60. Bello, *Filosofía del entendimiento,* 5.

61. An interesting account of Bello's association with the *Edinburgh Review* while in London is J. R. Dinwiddy, "Liberal and Benthamite Circles in London, 1810–1829," in *Andrés Bello,* ed. Lynch, 119–136. Julio César Jobet has suggested in his *Doctrina y praxis,* 159–160, that Bello's educational ideas can be traced to his tenure in England.

62. Sher, *Church and University,* 212. Another useful comment on the connection between philosophical and educational ideas in the clerically based Scottish Enlightenment is Davie, *The Democratic Intellect.* See also Eric Ashby's *Technology and the Academics: An Essay on Universities and the Scientific Revolution* (London, 1966).

63. Stewart R. Sutherland, "Andrés Bello: The Influence of Scottish Philosophy," in *Andrés Bello,* ed. Lynch, 100.

64. Bello, "Discurso," 139–152. For an analysis of Bello's educational ideas, based primarily on the inaugural speech, see Kilgore, "Notes," 555–560.

65. Bello, "Discurso," 142; Sher, *Church and University,* 151–152.

66. Bello, "Discurso," 140–141.

67. This accomplishment is all the more remarkable when one considers that the UCH emerged virtually unscathed from the civil wars of 1851

and 1859. Surely, the strong backing of the government helped, though critics like Barros Arana suggested that this connection made UCH quite vulnerable to governmental control, particularly in the area of firing academic personnel. See his *Decenio,* 1: 326. Vicente Pérez Rosales also criticized the university as nothing more than an appendage of the state in his *Recuerdos.* Still, as was the case for most of the nineteenth century, university and government enjoyed a prolonged honeymoon that was closely related to the successes of UCH in several areas of interest to the government, particularly the supervision of education, the pursuit of scientific research, and the recruitment of political leaders. Cooperation rather than conflict characterized the relations between university and government, particularly during the period of establishment and consolidation of UCH.

68. Articles 1 and 3, "Ley Orgánica," *AUCH,* 3–4. Compare these responsibilities of the University of Chile to those outlined by Joseph Moody for the French, *French Education,* 12.

69. Briseño, *Curso,* 2: 118. His religiously motivated philosophical thought is made even more explicit in his "Consideraciones."

70. Briseño, *Curso,* 2: 216.

71. Cifuentes, *Memorias,* 1: 28.

72. Feliú Cruz, *Ramón Briseño,* 68.

73. Session of April 23, 1845, in *Memorias de los egresados,* 120. See also Guirao's comment in her *Historia,* 40–42.

74. Bello's review was published in numbers 757, 759, and 760 of February 21, March 7, and March 14, 1845, respectively. It is also included in his *Obras Completas,* 3: 593–613.

75. Ibid., 595–596.

76. Bello, *Filosofía del entendimiento,* 529.

77. In addition to his personal religious convictions, Briseño was politically aligned with the *pelucones* who split from the Montt-Varista ruling coalition in the 1850s on religious grounds. This added an element of militancy to his already high proclerical inclinations. See Feliú Cruz, *Ramón Briseño,* 46–48.

78. Andrés Bello, "Memoria leida por el Rector de la Universidad de Chile en el aniversario solemne del 29 de Octubre de 1848," *AUCH* 5 (1848): 179.

79. Juan Bello, *AUCH* 10 (1853): 399–408.

80. Sessions of January 11 and 18, 1848, in *Memorias de los egresados,* 140–141. After the debates, Bello reviewed the textbook extensively and made it clear that in his view Rattier's physiological section needed substantial revision. In addition, he pointed out that several areas of ethics needed expansion. Still, he regarded the book as "one of the best for teaching elementary philosophy in our country." See Bello's "Filosofía, Curso completo, de Mr. Rattier," published originally in the *Revista de Santiago* in 1848–1849, and included in his *Obras Completas,* 3: 657–691.

81. "Acuerdos de las Facultades," *AUCH* 5 (1848): 67–68.

82. Session of August 22, 1848, in *Memorias de los egresados,* 152.

83. Feliú Cruz, *Ramón Briseño,* 67.

84. Bello's philosophical publications during the 1840s and 1850s are contained in volume 3 of his *Obras Completas.* They are mainly reviews of significant philosophical works or textbooks considered for school adoption. His quinquennial reports of 1848, 1853, and 1859 also contain comments, if not directives, on philosophical developments. See volumes 5, 10, and 16, respectively, of *AUCH.* Bello's students were no less influential, although many of them cultivated other fields or were his antagonists in philosophy. However, Salvador Sanfuentes and Aníbal Pinto, both involved in the examination of philosophy textbooks, were close to Bello's philosophical approach. Aníbal Pinto, in particular, who later became president of Chile, wrote a highly professional piece titled "Consideraciones sobre el método filosófico," in *AUCH,* which can only be compared to some of Bello's own pages on the subject in his *Filosofía del entendimiento.*

85. Two older, but still useful, biographies of Lastarria and Bilbao are Fuenzalida Grandón, *Lastarria y su tiempo* and Donoso, *Bilbao y su tiempo.* See also Oyarzún, *El pensamiento de Lastarria,* and Lipp, *Three Chilean Thinkers.*

86. Lastarria, "Investigaciones sobre la influencia social de la conquista y del sistema colonial de los españoles en Chile," 199–271.

87. Andrés Bello published his response in *El Araucano* in 1844. It has been included in the Chilean edition of his *Obras Completas,* 7: 71–88. The statutes Bello referred to is article 28 of the organic law, *AUCH* 1 (1843–1844): 9. The historiographical implications of the Lastarria-Bello controversy have been discussed by Allen Woll in his *A Functional Past.*

88. Bilbao was never very explicit about his own, much less the university's, view of philosophy, although he used the term sparingly. During his trial in 1844, when he stood accused of blasphemy, he in turn accused his prosecutors in the name of "philosophy." See the "Defensa del artículo 'Sociabilidad chilena,' " in *Obras Completas,* ed. Bilbao, 1: 50. However, the closest he came to defining philosophy was as a concept radically opposed to Catholicism. See his "La América en peligro," in *Obras Completas,* 2: 201.

89. Alberdi, "Ideas," in *Escritos póstumos,* 15: 607. A good examination of Alberdi's philosophical views vis-a-vis Bello's is by Ardao, "Bello y la filosofía latinoamericana," in *Bello,* 179–191.

90. All members of the faculty were asked to pledge "to obey the Constitution of the Republic and to fulfill the obligations imposed by my membership to the University of Chile, according to its statutes, and especially, to promote the religious and moral instruction of the people," *AUCH* 1 (1843–1844): 98. The promotion of religious and moral instruction was in fact one of the criteria for judging philosophy textbooks. The commission composed of Salvador Sanfuentes and Antonio García Reyes charged with the examination of Briseño's *Curso,* for instance, recommended approval because "it found nothing in the whole book that could offend the morality or the religious conscience of our society," *AUCH* 16 (1859): 253.

91. Session of December 6, 1860, in *Memorias de los egresados,* 214.

92. Session of September 26, 1860, Ibid., 210.

Chapter II. The Era of Positivism

1. The different aspects of the confrontation between church and state at the time of positivist influence have been discussed by Ricardo Krebs, editor and contributor to *Catolicismo y laicismo.* See also Ricardo Donoso, *Las ideas políticas.*

2. Lastarria, *Recuerdos literarios,* 270. For a discussion of Lastarria's encounter with positivism, see Woll, *A Functional Past,* 175–180; and Bader, "Early Positivistic Thought," 376–393. On Latin American positivism, see Zea, *Dos etapas,* and *Pensamiento positivista.* See also Ralph Lee Woodward, ed., *Positivism in Latin America,* and Kilgore, "Positivism," 23–42.

3. Lastarria, *Recuerdos,* 461–62 and 492–99.

4. Bader, "Early Positivistic Thought," 381.

5. Lastarria, *Recuerdos,* 419.

6. Ibid., 489–91.

7. Cifuentes, *Memorias,* 2: 53–66.

8. Galdames, *Historia,* 456–57; Cifuentes, *Memorias;* Alfredo Riquelme Segovia, "Abdón Cifuentes frente a la laicización de la sociedad. Las bases ideológicas," in *Catolicismo y Laicismo,* ed. Krebs, 119–151.

9. Cárter, "El liberalismo," 87–141.

10. Larraín Gandarillas, "Examen," 740.

11. For discussions on Catholic and positivist perspectives on education, see Ricardo Krebs, "El pensamiento," and María Eugenia Pinto Passi, "El positivismo chileno y la laicización de la sociedad, 1874–1884," both in *Catolicismo y laicismo,* ed. Krebs, 7–74 and 211–255, respectively.

12. Campos Harriet, *Desarrollo educacional,* 80–84.

13. Fogg, "Positivism in Chile," particularly chapter 6, titled "Positivism in Santiago from the late 1870's through 1891," 167–220.

14. Juan Enrique Lagarrigue, "Necesidad," 388.

15. Ibid., 392.

16. Labarca, *Historia,* 163 and 168.

17. Pontificia Universidad Católica, *Presencia de la filosofía,* 47–48.

18. Levy, *Higher Education,* 80–81.

19. Ibid., 81.

20. Jorge Lagarrigue, "La filosofía positiva," 638.

21. Jorge Lagarrigue, "Una conversión," 228–246.

22. Ibid., 236.

23. Ibid., 237–238.

24. Ibid., 231.

25. Ibid., 244.

26. Jorge Lagarrigue, "Trozos del diario íntimo," in Zea, *Pensamiento positivista,* 159.

27. Allen Woll, *A Functional Past,* 182; Zea, *Dos etapas,* 210–215. For a summary of the Balmaceda administration see Blakemore, "Chile," *The Cambridge History,* 5: 499–551.

28. Sehlinger, "Cien años," 78; and Lipp, *Three Chilean Thinkers,* 88–89.

29. The most important biography of Valentín Letelier is Galdames, *Valentín Letelier y su obra.* Other important sources on Letelier are Sehlinger, "Thought and Influence," Jobet, *Doctrina y praxis,* 283–347, and his *Letelier y sus continuadores.* Also, Lipp, *Three Chilean Thinkers,* 53–100, and Sehlinger, "Cien años," 72–85.

30. Campos Harriet, *Desarrollo educacional,* 83.

31. Jorge Lagarrigue, "Trozos," 160.

32. William Walter Sywak has extensively studied the German educational features that Chileans, and particularly Letelier, introduced in Chile. See his "Values."

33. Letelier described the foundation of the Instituto Pedagógico in detail in his *La lucha por la cultura,* 355–419.

34. Ibid., 398.

35. Ibid., 397–98.

36. Ibid., 393.

37. Ibid., 389.

38. The strongest critique against German influences in education in general, and the German professors in particular, is by Eduardo de la Barra, who was himself a positivist and a proponent of secular public education. See his *El embrujamiento alemán.* See also Carl Solberg, *Immigration and Nationalism,* 75–80. On the reaction of the Faculty of Philosophy and Humanities to IP, see Guirao, *Historia,* 84.

39. Feliú Cruz, "El Instituto Pedagógico," 11–43.

40. Letelier was imprisoned as a result of his opposition while in Congress to the government of José Manuel Balmaceda. The last edition of the *Filosofía de la educación* was published in Buenos Aires in 1927. For an analysis of this book in the context of Latin American educational thought, see my "The Influence of Positivism," in *Latin American Education,* ed. Nystrom 58–72.

41. Letelier, *Filosofía,* 141.

42. Ibid., 123.

43. Ibid., 276–78 and 286.

44. The political and ideological influence of positivism in various Latin American countries has been discussed in Davis, *Latin American Thought,* 97–134; Jorrín and Martz, *Political Thought and Ideology,* 121–153; and Hale, "Political and Social Ideas," *The Cambridge History,* ed. Bethell, 4: 367–643.

45. Letelier, *Filosofía,* 345.

46. Sehlinger, "Educational Thought," 158–59; Campos, *Desarrollo educacional,* 84, and Guirao, *Historia,* 36.

47. Letelier, *Filosofía,* 295–97.

48. Universidad de Chile, *AUCH* 14 (1857): 81–82.

49. Briseño, *Curso.* Tomo segundo.

50. Jourdain, *Nociones de filosofía,* 2d rev. ed., 8. This philosophy text was used in the provinces as well. Enrique Molina, who was a secondary school student in La Serena in the 1880s, complained that the text did not even fulfill the purpose of clarifying such issues as the immortality of the soul and the existence of God. See Molina, *Lo que ha sido el vivir,* 36.

51. Ibid., 242–43.

52. Universidad de Chile, "Plan de estudios y programas para la enseñanza secundaria clásica en los liceos y colegios de Francia," *AUCH* 61 (1882): 249–326.

53. Universidad de Chile, "Programa para el estudio y los exámenes de Filosofía, según el texto de Mr. Jourdain traducido en Chile," *AUCH* 66 (1884): 86–98.

54. Marín, *Elementos de la filosofía* (1872), 5.

55. Ibid., 10.

56. Larraín Gandarillas, "Examen," 852.

57. Ibid., 740.

58. Universidad de Chile, "Decretos y otras piezas sobre instrucción pública, *AUCH* 68 (1885): 782.

59. Pontificia Universidad Católica, *Presencia de la filosofía,* 21.

60. Francisco Ginebra, S. J., *Elementos de filosofía,* 6th ed., 2 vols. (Barcelona, 1915), 1: 5–6. Historian Luis Galdames used Ginebra's textbook for his philosophy course while a secondary school student in the 1890s. Indicating that Ginebra's book was of no use because of its esoteric nature, he could not understand how it could "still be used to torture the brains of the young" at the time of writing in 1912. He used this example to advocate reforms in the teaching of philosophy. See his *Educacion económica,* 164–165

61. Fernández Concha, *Filosofía.* This book was re-edited in 1888 and 1966. In 1900, Fernández Concha authored a comprehensive interpretation of man in response to positivist and rationalist currents titled *Del hombre en el orden sicológico, en el religioso y en el social.*

62. Lagarrigue, "Necesidad," 387.

63. Universidad de Chile, *AUCH* 70 (1886): 297.

64. Letelier, *Filosofía,* 294.

65. Ibid., 410.

66. Ibid., 413.

67. Jobet, *Doctrina y praxis,* 296–99.

68. Letelier, *Filosofía,* 384.

69. Ibid.

70. Universidad de Chile, "Boletín de Instrucción Pública," *AUCH* 86 (1893): 145–46.

71. Bello, *Filosofía del entendimiento* in *Obras completas,* 3: 512–521.

72. Lois, *Elementos.*

73. Figueroa, *Diccionario,* 4: 86–89.

74. Lois, *Elementos,* 1: 5–56.

75. Figueroa, *Diccionario,* 4: 88.

76. On Schneider's career, see Letelier, *La lucha por la cultura,* 405–408; Montebruno, "Don Jorge Enrique Schneider," 175–207; and Mann, "Jorge Enrique Schneider," 1–17.

77. Universidad de Chile, "Memoria del decano de la Facultad de Filosofía," *AUCH* 86 (1893): 363.

78. Consejo de Instrucción Pública, *Programas de instrucción secundaria* (Santiago, 1893), 187–196.

79. Montebruno, "Don Jorge Enrique Schneider," 197–98.

80. De la Barra, *El embrujamiento,* 46.

81. Figueroa, *Diccionario,* 2: 124–126.

82. De la Barra, *El embrujamiento,* 148.

83. Mann's view of philosophy, particularly in regard to secondary school teaching, was an encompassing one that provided a synthesis of the knowledge acquired by students in other fields. The pillars of philosophy for him, however, were psychology and logic. He believed that other subfields, including metaphysics, could be subsumed under these two subjects of study. He presented his views on philosophy in his "El espíritu general," 643–707, and specifically on psychology and logic in his "La enseñanza," 939–977. On Wilhelm Mann's career in Chile, Sommerville, et al., "Una fase importante," 206–237.

Chapter III. The Founders of Chilean Philosophy

1. Gracia, ed., *Latin American Philosophy,* 13–18; Francisco Romero, *Sobre la filosofía en América* (Buenos Aires, 1952), 63.

2. Gracia, *Latin American Philosophy,* 18.

3. The most representative thinker of the antipositivist reaction in Chile is Enrique Molina, discussed below. He addressed the links between philosophy and higher education in his *Discursos universitarios.*

4. On Enrique Molina's career, see Lipp, *Three Chilean Thinkers;* Armando Bazán, *Vida y obra del maestro Enrique Molina* (Santiago, 1954); Miguel Da Costa Leiva, "El pensamiento filosófico de Enrique Molina," (Ph.D. diss., Universidad Complutense de Madrid, 1978); and "El pensamiento de Enrique Molina Garmendia," in *Bio-Bibliografía,* ed. Astorquiza, 95–112. The journal *Atenea: Revista Trimestral de Ciencias, Letras y Artes* published a special issue (No. 376) in 1957 devoted to Molina's thought and career. Miguel Da Costa Leiva has compiled 14 volumes of Molina's correspondence as well as 17 volumes of his unpublished works. Together they constitute one of the most important sources for the study of Molina's thought. An autobiography by Enrique Molina titled *Lo que ha sido el vivir* (1949) was scheduled to appear in print in 1974 but

remains unpublished to this date due to the censorship of the military-designated authorities of the University of Concepción. The Molina family has generously provided me with access to this source as well as permission to cite it in this book.

5. Donoso, "El Instituto Pedagógico," 9. On Molina's role at the Liceo de Talca, see also Arturo Torres Rioseco, "Don Enrique Molina, Rector del Liceo de Talca," *Atenea: Revista Trimestral de Ciencias, Letras y Artes* 128, no. 376 (1957): 221–226.

6. On Molina's educational ideas, see Jobet, *Doctrina y praxis*, 387–397.

7. Enrique Molina, *Filosofía americana: Ensayos* (Paris, 1914), 273.

8. Gracia, *Latin American Philosophy*, 33.

9. Molina, *Filosofía americana*, 17.

10. Molina, *La filosofía en Chile*, 16.

11. Molina's essay was first published by *AUCH* in 1910. It became part of his *Filosofía americana*, 167–216.

12. Molina, *La filosofía en Chile*, 18; *Lo que ha sido el vivir*, 108–109.

13. These lectures were published in *AUCH* vols. 138 and 139 and later included in a book titled *Dos filósofos contemporáneos: Guyau-Bergson*.

14. Molina, *Dos filósofos contemporáneos*, 362.

15. Ibid., 368.

16. Ibid., 372.

17. Molina, *De lo espiritual, 64*.

18. Molina elaborated on his views on Marxism in *La revolución rusa y la dictadura bolchevista* (Santiago, 1934).

19. Molina, *De lo espiritual*, 210–213.

20. Molina, *Confesión filosófica*. The book was based on Molina's speech when he became academic member of the Faculty of Philosophy and Education at UCH in 1941. José Ferrater Mora commented on Molina's speech in *Atenea: Revista Trimestral de Ciencias, Letras y Artes* 67, no. 199 (January 1942): 87–90.

21. Molina, *Confesión filosófica*, 49.

22. Ibid., 63.

23. Ibid., 62.

24. Ibid., 89.

25. Ibid., 156–57.

26. On Finlayson's career and thought, see Manuel Atria, ''El pensamiento metafísico de Clarence Finlayson,'' *Mapocho* 23 (1970): 71–82; Roberto Escobar, ''Clarence Finlayson: el filósofo que regresó del silencio,'' *Inter-American Review of Bibliography* 20, no. 4 (1970): 459–463; Agustín Martínez, ''Clarence Finlayson (1913–1954),'' *Finis Terrae* 1, no. 3 (1954): 53–56; and the prologue by Tomás MacHale to Finlayson, *Antología,* 9–19.

27. Finlayson, ''Expresión de la cultura americana,'' in *Antología,* 36.

28. Finlayson, ''Mensaje a los fenomenólogos llamados católicos,'' in *Antología,* 176.

29. Frondizi and Gracia, eds., *El hombre y los valores,* 42–43.

30. Gracia, *Latin American Philosophy,* 27.

31. Finlayson, ''Consideraciones sobre los tiempos actuales,'' in *Antología,* 226.

32. Ibid., 223.

33. Finlayson, *Hombre, Mundo y Dios,* 53.

34. Ibid., 174.

35. Millas, *Individualidad,* 120.

36. Ibid., 127.

37. Molina, *La filosofía en Chile,* 93.

38. Millas, *Individualidad,* 170.

39. Ibid., 213.

40. Ibid., 214–15.

41. Ibid., 224.

42. Millas, ''Carta a José Ortega y Gasset,'' *Atenea: Revista Trimestral de Ciencias, Letras y Artes* 38, no. 147 (September 1937): 571.

43. Millas, *Individualidad,* 223–24.

44. Drake, ''Chile, 1932–1958,'' (University of California, San Diego, typescript), 33–34 and 41, forthcoming in *The Cambridge History.* See also his *Socialism and Populism.*

45. Ibid., 55.

46. Loveman, *Chile,* 268–70; Drake, "Chile, 1932–1958," 8–9 and 49.

47. Drake, "Chile," in *Spanish Civil War,* ed. Falcoff and Pike, 254–56.

48. Loveman, *Chile,* 285–92; Drake, "Chile, 1932–1958," 50–53. See also Claude G. Bowers, *Chile Through Embassy Windows.*

49. "Recuerdo del paso por Chile del filósofo José Ortega y Gasset," *Occidente* 301 (May–June 1983): 32–38.

50. Molina, *Discursos universitarios,* 33. Some of his ideas on higher education were presented earlier in his *De California a Harvard,* particularly the notion that universities should offer a haven for spiritual growth and values, pp. 253–260, and the support for the strengthening of faculties in matters of educational policy, p. 140.

51. Molina, *Confesión filosófica,* 72.

52. Molina, *La revolución rusa,* 50.

53. Ibid., 171.

54. Molina, *La filosofía en Chile,* 52–53; *Lo que ha sido el vivir,* 186–187.

55. Molina, "En el Ministerio de Educación Pública," *Atenea: Revista Trimestral de Ciencias, Letras y Artes* 128, no. 376 (1957): 28; *Lo que ha sido el vivir,* 218.

56. Molina, *Lo que ha sido el vivir,* 219. In order to leave no doubt about his convictions in this regard, Molina repeated these points on national radio. See his "Discurso de Enrique Molina Garmendia como Ministro de Educación, en cadena nacional de emisoras," in *La obra inédita,* vol. 3. Early in 1948, Carlos Vicuña Fuentes, Santiago Aguirre, and Santiago Labarca of the National Committee of Solidarity and Defense of Public Liberties addressed a letter to Molina asking him not to be a part of the persecution against Communist teachers. Molina responded on January 29, 1948 that Communist teachers were not exactly idealistic saviors of humanity but advocates of a Soviet regime that had no regard for public liberties. See the *Epistolario,* Vols. XI and XIII. On March 18, 1948, Molina signed a directive to public education officials requiring that all teaching personnel be notified of the incompatibility between teaching and communist activities, and that failures to comply be reported to the Ministry of Education. See the appendix "Circular a los directores generales de educación pública" in *Lo que ha sido el vivir,* 285–286.

57. Finlayson, "Consideraciones," in *Antología,* 236.

58. Millas, *Individualidad,* 30.

59. Ibid., 202.

60. Ibid., 148.

61. Frei, *La política y el espíritu,* introduction by Gabriela Mistral, 83–84.

62. Ibid., 55.

63. Frondizi and Gracia, *El hombre y los valores,* 20. See also my "El pensamiento de Eduardo Frei Montalva," *Estudios sociales* 32, no. 2 (1982): 123–28.

64. Frei, *La política y el espíritu,* 184.

65. Campos Harriet, *Desarrollo educacional,* 197–201; Labarca, *Historia,* 350–355.

66. Sommerville, et al., "Una fase importante," 232.

67. Wilhelm Mann, "El espíritu general," 648.

68. Ibid., 653.

69. Ibid., 691.

70. Ibid., 668. He elaborated further on his views on the importance of logic and psychology for philosophy teaching in his "La enseñanza," 939–977.

71. Ibid., 682–83.

72. Ibid., 688.

73. Ibid., 690.

74. Ibid., 701.

75. Loyola, *Hechos e ideas,* 19–21.

76. Ibid., 30.

77. José Echeverría, *La enseñanza de la filosofía,* 67; and Campos Harriet, *Desarrollo educacional,* 178–182.

78. Campos Harriet, *Desarrollo educacional,* 177.

79. Munizaga, *Filosofía de la educación secundaria,* 12–14.

80. Loyola, *Lógica formal.*

81. Ibid., 25.

82. Ibid., 6.

83. Loyola, *Hechos e ideas,* 59.

84. Ibid., 82.

85. Ibid., 40–41.

86. Ibid., 25–26.

87. Ibid., 41.

88. Ibid., 33–34.

89. Ibid., 47.

90. Loyola addressed key problems in the philosophy of science in his *Una oposición fundamental.*

91. Roberto Munizaga summarized the influence of Loyola on generations of students in his "Discurso de Recepción," which is included in Loyola's *Una oposición fundamental,* 17–31.

92. Oyarzún, *Temas,* 161.

93. Pontificia Universidad Católica, *Presencia de la filosofía,* 75–105.

94. Ibid., 79.

95. José Echeverría, *La enseñanza de la filosofía,* and Jorge Gracia, "Panorama general de la filosofía latinoamericana actual," in Círculo de amigos del Instituto Goethe, *La filosofía hoy en Alemania y América Latina* (Córdoba, 1983), 142–195.

96. Frondizi, "Philosophy," *Handbook of Latin American Studies,* no. 10 (1944), 390.

97. José Luis Abellán, *Filosofía española,* 22.

98. José Ferrater Mora published several books during his stay in Chile. These include the second edition of his *Diccionario de filosofía* (Mexico City, 1944); *Unamuno: bosquejo de una filosofía* (Buenos Aires, 1944); *La ironía, la muerte y la admiración* (Santiago, 1946), and *El sentido de la muerte* (Buenos Aires, 1947). Ferrater departed for the United States in 1949.

99. Gastón Gómez Lasa, interview with author, Santiago, Chile, July 1985.

Chapter IV. The Institutionalization and Critique of Philosophical Professionalism

1. Enrique Molina, *La filosofía en Chile,* 135–140; Vidal, "Apuntes," 58.

2. "Estatuto orgánico," *RF* 1 (August 1949): 98–101.

3. Santiago Vidal Muñoz, "La Sociedad Chilena de Filosofía," *RF* 1 (August 1949): 95–97.

4. The article was by Oyarzún, "Lastarria," 27–56; more representative articles during Ciudad's tenure are Mario Ciudad, "La filosofía como hecho filosófico," *RF* 2 (April–June 1952): 27–43; Alberto Wagner de Reyna, "La palabra como analogía," *RF* 3 (October 1955): 15–24; and Karla Cordua, "La existencia como fuente de la verdad," *RF* 3 (July 1956): 62–76.

5. Vidal, "Apuntes," 53–54.

6. José Echeverría, letter to author, October 15, 1987.

7. Juan Rivano, letter to author, August 19, 1987.

8. See *Atenea: Revista Trimestral de Ciencias, Letras y Artes* 128, no. 376 (1957).

9. "El Departamento de Filosofía de la Universidad de Chile: Cátedras actuales," *RF* 3 (July 1956): 101–103.

10. "Estatuto da Sociedade Interamericana de Filosofia," in Congresso Internacional de Filosofia, *Anais,* 3 vols. (São Paulo, 1956).

11. Some of Jorge Millas's publications prior to 1956 include *Idea de la individualidad; Goethe y el espíritu de Fausto* (Rio Piedras, Puerto Rico, 1948); "El problema del método en la investigación filosófica," *RF* 1 (August 1949): 9–25; "Para una teoría de nuestro tiempo," *RF* 2 (April–June 1952): 65–80; "Sobre la visión historicista de la historia de la filosofía," *RF* 3 (October 1955): 2–14; and "Kierkegaard o el vértigo prefilosófico," *RF* 3 (July–December 1956): 3–18.

12. "Primer congreso de la Sociedad Interamericana de Filosofía," *RF* 3 (July 1956): 105.

13. "El Congreso Interamericano de Filosofía," *RF* 3 (December 1956): 118–124.

14. Levy, *Higher Education,* 79–80.

15. Pontificia Universidad Católica, *Presencia de la filosofía,* 116–118.

16. Ibid., 129. In addition to the major philosophical centers at UCH and UC, the Department of Philosophy of the University of Concepción, founded in 1958, advanced the institutionalization of professional philosophical studies in Chile. Like its counterparts in Santiago, the philosophy department at Concepción featured a sophisticated program that included regular philosophy courses for University of Concepción students as well as extension courses for the general public. Most philosophy faculty in Concepción were UCH faculty or UCH graduates. They included Marco Antonio Allendes, Luis Oyarzún, Juan Rivano, and Roberto Torretti. Jorge Millas, Félix Schwartzmann and Juan de Dios Vial Larraín taught in Concepción as visiting faculty. The annual reports of the University of Concepción provide useful summaries of philosophy-related activities. See Universidad de Concepción. *Memoria presentada por el Directorio de la Universidad de Concepción,* years 1958–1962.

17. Some of Schwartzmann's publications include "Sistemas cerrados y leyes de la naturaleza," *RF* 3 (December 1956): 28–40; "Significado de las relaciones entre naturaleza e historia para el conocimiento histórico," *RF* 4 (December 1957): 28–37; and "Sentido de la expresión en el arte budista," *RF* 5 (May 1958): 3–14, among others during this period. For a discussion of his work see Margarita Schultz and Jorge Estrella, *La antropología de Félix Schwartzmann* (Santiago, 1978). See also Sarti, *Panorama,* 599–600, and Vidal, "Apuntes," 50–53.

18. A distant exception is Jorge de la Cuadra, who, although trained in law, developed an interest in philosophy that led to his writing and publication of *La filosofía de la realidad.* This work used many philosophical references and attempted to provide an interpretation of contemporary Western civilization. He believed that however sophisticated modern life may have become, it had essentially failed to enhance human happiness. The work is most significant in that it represents an attempt to identify the central issues of the time, in this case material versus spiritual progress, and use philosophy to point out the shortcomings of modern life. In his book, De la Cuadra also introduced some concepts of Indian philosophy, which his nephew Marco Antonio Allendes de la Cuadra would discuss

more systematically in the 1950s and 1960s. For a comment on De la Cuadra's *Filosofía* see Molina, *La filosofía en Chile,* 114–130.

19. Fuenzalida, "Reception of 'Scientific Sociology,' " 95–112.

20. Gastón Gómez Lasa, interview with author, Santiago, Chile, August 1985. See also my "La vocación filosófica."

21. Humberto Giannini, interview with author, Santiago, Chile, August 14, 1985.

22. Rivano, *Un largo contrapunto,* 254–255.

23. Marco Antonio Allendes graduated in 1953 with a thesis on *La experiencia mística.* He later published the "Relación entre religión y filosofía en el pensamiento hindú," in *AUCH,* 131–152.

24. Marco Antonio Allendes, interview with author, Concepción, Chile, March 7, 1987.

25. The Association was founded in 1956, shortly after the Inter-American Congress of Philosophy. It later became the Chilean Society of Logic, Methodology, and Philosophy of Science. See *RF* 3 (December 1956): 125, and "Tres años de la Soc. de Lógica, Metodología y Filosofía de las Ciencias," in *Boletín de la Universidad de Chile* 39 (June 1963): 52.

26. For a brief discussion of Chilean logic, particularly symbolic logic, see Jorge J. E. Gracia, Eduardo Rabossi, Enrique Villanueva, and Marcelo Dascal, eds., *Philosophical Analysis in Latin America* (Dordrecht, Boston, Lancaster, 1984), 365–369, and Gracia, "Philosophical Analysis in Latin America," *History of Philosophy Quarterly,* 111–122.

27. Schwartzmann initiated his editorship of *RF* in 1956. He included in the December issue Gerold Stahl's "La suficiencia de la lógica bivalente para la física de los cuantos" his own "Sistema cerrado y leyes de la naturaleza," and Juan Rivano's "Análisis crítico de algunas concepciones de la conciencia y el yo." This issue also included several reviews on logic and philosophy of science topics.

28. The early works of Juan Rivano included "Análisis crítico de algunas concepciones de la conciencia y el yo," *RF* 3 (December 1956): 41–53; "Sobre el principio de identidad," *RF* 4 (April 1957): 34–48; "Sentencia, juicio y proposición," *RF* 5 (May 1958): 15–30; "Ciencia, realidad y verdad," *RF* 5 (December 1958): 43–58; "Sobre la naturaleza general del método científico," *RF* 6 (July 1959): 43–77; and "El principio de la evidencia apodíctica en la filosofía de E. Husserl," *RF* 6 (December 1959): 45–57. Towards the end of the 1950s and into the early 1960s, Ri-

vano increasingly focused on Francis Bradley's work. At a seminar on this author in 1959, Rivano announced that "philosophical criticism is the subject of this seminar. I believe that Bradley is perhaps the best mentor in this respect. No one that I can think of has concerned himself so carefully with the techniques of critical thinking," in his unpublished "Curso monográfico sobre el tema 'Appearance' según el texto de Bradley, *Appearance and Reality,*" (Santiago, 1959, typescript). Rivano went on to translate Bradley's work and added an extensive study of Bradley's philosophy. See his "Sobre la filosofía de Bradley," in *Apariencia y Realidad* by Francis H. Bradley, 2 vols. (Santiago, 1961), xiii–lxxi. See also his "Motivaciones para la filosofía de Bradley," *AUCH* 119 (1961): 7–14. For a full discussion of Juan Rivano's work during this period, see Iván Jaksić, "The Philosophy of Juan Rivano."

29. Rivano, *Filosofía en dilemas,* 3, 7.

30. Rivano, "Sobre la filosofía de Bradley," xiv.

31. Rivano, "Experiencia del error y doctrina del conocimiento," *RF* 8 (June 1960): 93–136.

32. Rivano, *Desde el abandono.* (unpublished).

33. Rivano, *Un largo contrapunto,* 186–189.

34. Ibid., 77–78.

35. Ibid., 192.

36. The political and economic background of the 1957 protests has been discussed by Paul W. Drake in his forthcoming "Chile, 1932–1958," in *The Cambridge History,* and by Brian Loveman, *Chile,* 294–295. The political and educational background for the protests has been discussed by Frank Bonilla and Myron Glazer, *Student Politics in Chile,* 139–203.

37. Rivano, *Un largo contrapunto,* 233–234, 253–254, 258, 263–264.

38. Figures provided by Fernando Campos Harriet indicate that enrollment at UCH grew from 10,928 in 1950 to 13,919 in 1956. See his *Desarrollo educacional,* 204.

39. Between 1953 and 1958, the student aid budget increased from 1 million to 36 million pesos. The research budget was funded, beginning in 1956, with 0.5% of fiscal revenues from customs duties and export taxes. See Corporación de Promoción Universitaria, *Juan Gómez Millas: Estudios y consideraciones sobre universidad y cultura* (Santiago, 1986), 193–194.

40. Juan Rivano had discussed Hegel earlier in his "La filosofía hegeliana de la historia," *RF* 8 (November 1961): 57–84, but in his *Entre Hegel y Marx,* Rivano discussed Marx extensively for the first time.

41. G. W. F. Hegel, *The Science of Logic,* trans. William Wallace (London, 1962), 58.

42. Rivano, *Entre Hegel y Marx,* 27.

43. Ibid., 46.

44. Ibid., 54.

45. Ibid., 137.

46. Frondizi and Gracia, *El hombre y los valores,* 153. See also Hugo E. Biagini, "Pensamiento e ideologías en la Argentina (1950–1959)," *Ideas en Ciencias Sociales* 6 (1987): 39–54.

47. Rivano, *Entre Hegel y Marx,* 71.

48. Marco Antonio Allendes, "Comentario crítico a *Entre Hegel y Marx,* de Juan Rivano," *RF* 10 (January 1963): 125–133; Humberto Giannini, "Reflexiones en torno a una obra de Juan Rivano," *RF* 10 (January 1963): 135–143; Fernando Uriarte, review of *Entre Hegel y Marx* by Juan Rivano, *Mapocho* 2 (February 1963): 256–257; Angel García Martín, "Juan Rivano: *Entre Hegel y Marx,*" *Documentación Crítica Iberoamericana* 5 (October–December 1965): 667–671.

49. Uriarte, 258.

50. García Martín, 668.

51. Allendes, "Comentario," 126.

52. Rivano, *Desde el abandono,* 39–40.

53. Rivano, *Curso de lógica antigua y moderna* (Santiago, 1964); "Dialéctica y situación absoluta," *Mapocho* 3 (March 1963): 110–124; "Sobre la clasificación de las ciencias," *Atenea: Revista Trimestral de Ciencias, Letras y Artes* 158 (January–March 1965): 23–68.

54. During the mid-1960s, Rivano wrote nearly fifty newspaper articles covering a variety of topics of national interest, mainly for the editorial page of *Las Noticias de Ultima Hora.* For a complete listing of these articles, see Jaksić, "The Philosophy of Juan Rivano," 254–256.

55. Rivano, "Dialéctica y situación absoluta," 114.

56. Ibid., 123.

57. In addition to his *Desde la religión al humanismo,* he also discussed this issue in "Religión y seguridad," *Mapocho* 8 (February 1965): 165–173.

58. Rivano, *Desde la religión al humanismo,* 36.

59. Jaime Concha, review of *Desde la religión al humanismo* by Juan Rivano, *Atenea: Revista Trimestral de Ciencias, Letras y Artes* 163 (April–June 1965): 257–258.

60. Ibid., 260.

61. Rivano, *El punto,* 23.

62. Ibid., 68.

63. Ibid., 69.

64. Ibid., 73.

65. Ibid., 111. Rivano devoted chapters 6, "Los teóricos de América," and 8, "Jornadas metafísicas en Tucumán," to discussing the works and themes of a variety of Latin American philosophers.

66. Ibid., 145.

67. Ibid., 148.

68. Rivano, *Contra sofistas,* 10.

69. Hernán del Solar, review of *Contra sofistas* by Juan Rivano, *El Mercurio,* April 23, 1966.

70. Rivano, *Cultura de la servidumbre,* 161.

71. Rivano, *Enajenación: Una clave para comprender el marxismo* (Santiago, 1969), 2d ed., 1971.

72. Juan Rivano, letter to author, May 29, 1979.

Chapter V. Philosophy and the Movement for University Reform

1. The following translations of Heidegger's work appeared in the *Revista de Filosofía* (RF) during this period: "La pregunta por la técnica," trans. Francisco Soler, no. 1 (1958): 55–79; "Poéticamente habita el hombre," trans. Ruth Fisher de Walker, no. 1–2 (1960): 77–79; "El habla," trans. Francisco Soler, no. 2–3 (1961): 127–140; "Aletheia," trans. Fran-

cisco Soler, no. 1–2 (1962): 89–108; ''Identidad y diferencia,'' trans. Oscar Mertz, no. 1 (1966): 81–93; ''La constitución onto-teo-lógica de la metafísica,'' trans. Luis Hernández, no. 1 (1966): 95–113; and ''Hegel y los griegos,'' trans. Ian Mesa, no. 1 (1966): 115–130. Among the articles critical of Heidegger's philosophy appearing in *RF* are Jorge Eduardo Rivera, ''La critica de Zubiri a Heidegger,'' no. 1–2 (1964): 41–66, and Juan Rivano, ''Gunter Grass y Martín Heidegger,'' no. 1 (1969): 75–88. This latter issue of *RF* included excerpts from speeches by Martin Heidegger while a member of the German National Socialist party during 1933–1934. In a philosophical community that revered the work of the German philosopher, the publication of these fragments represented a sharp, if not unwelcomed, reversal of the consistently laudatory approach to the study of the German thinker. Recently, Chilean scholar Victor Farías has published *Heidegger et Le Nazisme* (Paris, 1987), a book that discusses the German philosopher's connections with National Socialism. Although Farías, who was trained in Germany in the 1960s, may have been familiar with Chilean critiques of Heidegger, his work does not stem from the Chilean philosophical production of that decade. The critique of Heidegger in Chile at that time was both a critique of the German thinker, and a critique of a large segment of the Chilean philosophical community that made no attempt to relate Heidegger's political and philosophical views. The critique of Heidegger, therefore, was part and parcel of a critique against the professionalist custom of separating political from philosophical issues.

2. Giannini, *El mito de la autenticidad,* 11.

3. Giannini, *Convivencia humana,* 12, and ''Reflexiones en torno a una obra de Juan Rivano,'' *RF* 10 (January 1963): 135–143.

4. Giannini, *Convivencia humana,* 10.

5. Vial Larraín, ''Consistencia metafísica,'' 47.

6. Ibid., 53.

7. Vial Larraín, ''Militares, aventureros, ideólogos,'' in *El carácter chileno,* ed. Godoy Urzúa (Santiago, 1976), 489.

8. Ibid., 490.

9. Vial Larraín, ''Acerca de la filosofía,'' 91.

10. Jorge Millas, *Ensayos,* 23.

11. Ibid., 13.

12. Millas, *El desafío espiritual.* There is an English translation of this book by Millas, *The Intellectual and Moral Challenge of Society,* trans. David J. Parent (Ann Arbor, Mich., 1977).

13. Ibid., 49–50.

14. Humberto Giannini, "Comentarios Críticos: *El desafío espiritual de la sociedad de masas,*" *RF* 10 (July 1963): 121–123.

15. Millas, "Discurso," 249–261.

16. Ibid., 253.

17. Ibid., 257.

18. Pontificia Universidad Católica, *Presencia de la filosofía,* 109.

19. Ibid., 111–114.

20. Vial Larraín, "Universidad y educación," 43–59.

21. Ibid., 59.

22. Vial Larraín, "Idea de la universidad," in *La universidad,* 12.

23. Ibid., 11.

24. Rivano, *El punto,* 166.

25. Vial Larraín, "Idea de la universidad," 8. He and other philosophers made constant references to José Ortega y Gasset's essay "Misión de la universidad," first published in Spain in 1930. Chileans borrowed from Ortega the idea that the primary function of the university, which he described as "the intellect of society," was the formation of professionals with a strong cultural background. According to Ortega, every discipline, either scientific or humanistic, should provide students not only with the means to become efficient professionals but also with a larger understanding of their culture. Ortega was mainly reacting against what he thought to be an excessive emphasis on scientific research at the contemporary university, and he outlined ways of turning science into a useful activity within the institution. But Chilean intellectuals took from his ideas what best suited their own purposes. They particularly responded to the suggestion that the university should become one of the spiritual powers in society. To this idea they added their own conviction that philosophers should lead society from within a university free of disturbing external factors.

26. Martínez Bonati, "La misión humanística," 114–137.

27. Ibid., 117.

28. Ibid., 122.

29. Ibid., 128.

30. Ibid., 132, 136.

31. Allan Bloom, *The Closing of the American Mind: How Higher Education Has Failed Democracy and Impoverished the Souls of Today's Students* (New York, 1987).

32. Martínez Bonati, *La situación universitaria,* 27.

33. Ibid., 43.

34. Martínez Bonati, "La misión humanística," 137.

35. Walter, "The Intellectual Background," 233–253. See also John P. Harrison, "The Role of the Intellectual in Fomenting Change: The University," in *Explosive Forces in Latin America,* ed. John J. TePaske and Sydney Mettleton Fisher (Columbus, Ohio, 1964). University reform did not begin with the Córdoba movement. See Mark J. Van Aken, "University Reform Before Córdoba," *Hispanic American Historical Review* 51 (1971): 447–462. Most literature on university reform movements has concentrated on student politics. See, for instance, Glaucio Ary Dillon Soares, "Intellectual Identity and Political Ideology among University Students," in *Elites in Latin America,* ed. Lipset and Solari, 431–453; Kalman H. Silvert, "The University Student," in *Government and Politics in Latin America,* ed. Peter G. Snow (New York, 1967), 367–385; Robert E. Scott, "Student Political Activism in Latin America," in *Students in Revolt,* ed. Seymour M. Lipset and Philip G. Altbach (Boston, 1969), 403–431; Dani B. Thomas and Richard B. Craig, "Student Dissent in Latin America: Toward a Comparative Analysis," *Latin American Research Review* 13 (1979): 71–96; and Levy, "Student Politics," 353–376. Sources covering a wider range of higher education issues in the region include Harold Benjamin, *Higher Education in the American Republics* (New York, 1965); Dooner and Lavados, eds., *La universidad latinoamericana;* Maier and Weatherhead, eds., *The Latin American University;* and Levy, *Higher Education.*

36. These events, like all others related to the Chilean university reform movement, were widely covered by the national press. *AUCH* compiled most of these articles in addition to documents and pamphlets related to the reform in No. 146 (April–June 1968), and No. 147 (July–September 1968). Interpretive sources on the university reform movement of 1968 include: Huneeus Madge, *La reforma;* Fagen, *Chilean Universities;* Salcedo, *La Universidad de Chile;* Michaels, "Chilean Politics," in *Universities and the New International Order,* ed. Spitzberg, 4: 14–40; Manuel Antonio Gar-

retón, "Universidad y política," 83–109; Flisfisch, "Elementos," and Jaksić, "Philosophy and University Reform," 57–86.

37. Ramírez Necochea, *El partido comunista.* An important source on the National Technical University (UTE), written by a prominent Communist party leader is Enrique Kirberg, *Los nuevos profesionales.*

38. Fagen, *Chilean Universities,* 11–15.

39. These events took place between September and October of 1967. On September 9, 1967, the newspaper *Las Noticias de Ultima Hora* reported that "Estudiantes de Alemán, Física y Filosofía se tomaron locales." A month later, Hernán Ramírez Necochea replaced FFE Dean Julio Heise on an interim basis. See *AUCH* 146 (April–June 1968): 33–44.

40. The most significant of such groups was ADIEX (Asociación de Docentes, Investigadores y Agregados de Docencia de la Universidad de Chile), founded in May 1968 and headed by Fernando Vargas Figueroa. The group, which came to be known as the "Varguistas," collapsed in June 1969 as a result of pressures from within and without to follow the policies of the major parties in conflict. See Huneeus, *La reforma,* 223–228 and 326–27.

41. This point is largely accurate, but one is left with an obscure idea of the initial motivations for reform as well as the key role played by FFE. Scholars emphasize economic factors among the motivations for reform, particularly Bonilla and Glazer, *Student Politics in Chile,* 310; and Michaels, "Chilean Politics," 15, but they agree with Huneeus, Garretón, Flisfisch, and Kirberg in viewing the events of 1968 as an expression of a larger political struggle between the major political parties of the country.

42. Millas's article appeared in *El Mercurio* on October 3 and 4, 1967. This and other articles by Millas on the university have been included in a volume titled *Idea de la universidad* (Santiago, 1981), 40–41. I will use this latter reference for the purposes of citation.

43. Millas, *Idea de la universidad,* 50.

44. Ibid., 56.

45. Ibid., 68.

46. Ibid., 76.

47. Giannini, interview with author, Santiago, Chile, August 14, 1985.

48. Gastón Gómez Lasa, "Nuevo reto a la filosofía," *Ercilla,* January 9, 1985.

49. Rivano, "El anteproyecto," 23–31. This issue of *RF* (No. 1, 1969), known as the "revista negra," was devoted to the process of university reform. It presents a critical view of the direction of the movement and its also outlines the philosophical views of the faculty who initially advocated reform.

50. Ibid., 24.

51. Brunner and Flisfisch, *Los intelectuales.* See also Manuel Antonio Garretón, "Universidad y política" for a discussion on university reform at Catholic University.

52. Levy, *Higher Education,* 89–90.

53. Pontificia Universidad Católica, *Presencia de la filosofía,* 145.

54. Ibid., 148.

55. Millas, *Idea de la filosofía,* 1: 13.

56. Ibid., 50.

57. Ibid., 108.

58. There were few philosophical works published during this period, but the specialized approach prevailed. This is the time when Juan de Dios Vial Larraín wrote his *Metafísica cartesiana* and compiled the *Meditaciones metafísicas de René Descartes* (Santiago, 1973). Gastón Gómez Lasa wrote a series of studies on Plato during this period, including *Del Protágoras al Gorgias,* Escritos Breves, No. 7 (Santiago, 1972); *Buscando la inmortalidad del alma. Comentario sobre el Fedón,* Escritos Breves, No. 11 (Santiago, 1972), and *Sobre el Parménides: Las aporías en torno a las ideas,* Escritos Breves, No. 14 (Santiago, 1972). Other works include Humberto Giannini, *Vida inauténtica y curiosidad,* Escritos Breves, No. 3 (Santiago, 1971), and Gerold Stahl, *Elementos de metamatemáticas.*

59. Rivano, *Lógica elemental; Introducción al pensamiento dialéctico* (Santiago, 1972). The second edition of his *Curso de lógica antigua y moderna* appeared in 1972.

60. Rivano, "Tesis sobre la totalización tecnológica," in *En el límite,* ed. Centro de Alumnos de Filosofía, Universidad de Chile (Santiago, 1971), 57–58.

61. Rivano, *Filosofía en dilemas,* 3–10.

62. Rivano, *Introducción al pensamiento dialéctico,* 84–91. In an interview with the author in August 1980, Rivano contested that politics

could be understood on the basis of philosophical principles and emphasized that the politician whom he had been taught to despise during his formative years understood social reality better than philosophers. See Jakšić, ''The Philosophy of Juan Rivano,'' 241–244.

63. Centro de Alumnos de Filosofía de la Universidad de Chile, ''Al Margen,'' in *En el límite,* 103.

64. Ricardo López, interview with author, Santiago, August 1985. Professor López was a member of the philosophy student government in 1972.

65. The political polarization affecting the university has been amply described by Danilo Salcedo, Carlos Huneeus, and Manuel Antonio Garretón. The politics of the Unidad Popular period have been covered by Loveman, *Chile,* 333–348; Sigmund, *The Overthrow of Allende;* Garretón and Moulian, *La Unidad Popular;* and Nathaniel Davis, *The Last Two Years;* among many others. Paul W. Drake has compiled a useful bibliography of works in English on the period and beyond. See his ''El impacto académico,'' 56–78.

Chapter VI. Chilean Philosophy under Military Rule

1. For discussions on Chile under military rule, including opposition activities, see Alan Angell, ''Chile After Five Years of Military Rule,'' *Current History* (February 1979): 58–61; Arturo Valenzuela, ''Eight Years of Military Rule in Chile,'' *Current History* (February 1982): 64–68; Hojman, ed., *Chile after 1973;* Valenzuela and Valenzuela, ed., *Military Rule in Chile;* particularly chapters five and six by Manuel Antonio Garretón and the Valenzuelas respectively; Pamela Constable and Arturo Valenzuela, ''Is Chile Next?,'' *Foreign Affairs,* no. 63 (Summer 1986): 58–75; Loveman, ''Military Dictatorship,'' 1–38; and Garretón, ''The Political Evolution,'' in *Transitions from Authoritarian Rule,* ed. O'Donnell, Schmitter, and Whitehead, 95–122.

2. The actions of the military government at the universities have been discussed in a special report prepared by Michael Fleet for the Task Force on Human Rights and Academic Freedom of the Latin American Studies Association (LASA). The results were published in the *LASA Newsletter* 8, no. 2 (June 1977): 23–38, under the title ''Academic Freedom and University Autonomy in Chile.'' Professor Fleet noted that the major aim of the military government was to ''depoliticize'' higher education in the

country in order to put the system in line with the regime's political priorities. The unfortunate record of means used to achieve this aim is examined in the report, which is of particular relevance for the study of higher education under authoritarian regimes. Other important sources for the study of Chilean universities under military rule are: Levy, "Chilean Universities," 95–128; Garretón, "Universidad y política," 83–109; Brunner and Flisfisch, *Los intelectuales;* and Brunner, *Informe;* Correa, Sierra, and Subercaseaux, *Los generales del régimen,* particularly the chapter on the universities; and Programa Interdisciplinario de Investigaciones en Educación (PIIE), *Las transformaciones educacionales.*

3. The manner in which the purges were conducted university-wide has been described by Michael Fleet in his report to LASA. He found that military prosecutors (*Fiscales*) conducted hearings on the basis of which dismissals or suspensions of academic personnel were decided. Fleet indicates that the prosecutors acted on the basis of often anonymous denunciations which in some cases "were made by undercover informants, and in others by academics fueled as much by jealousy and professional ambition as by ideological fervor." (p. 26) Although the Faculty of Philosophy and Education at the University of Chile was among the hardest hit by purges in the aftermath of the coup, numbers reported by *Mensaje* (Chile) suggest that the higher education system as a whole stood a substantial politically inspired reduction of its personnel during the first few months of military intervention: 30 to 35 percent of the academics, 10 to 15 percent of the staff, and 15 to 18 percent of the students. That is, approximately 18,000 people. Jaime Ruiz-Tagle, "Universidades: De las purgas a la privatización," *Mensaje,* no. 287 (March–April 1980): 92.

4. Levy, "Chilean Universities," 107.

5. Loveman, "Military Dictatorship," 16–17.

6. Ibid., 18–19.

7. Levy, "Chilean Universities," 107.

8. The interview was conducted by the senior staff of *Hoy,* including Emilio Filippi, Abraham Santibáñez, and Guillermo Blanco. See "Exploradores de la verdad," *Hoy,* May 10–16, 1978, 34–36.

9. Various independent journals such as *Pluma y Pincel, Estudios Sociales,* and *Estudios Públicos* were publishing philosophy essays in the 1980s. This situation changed dramatically with the declaration of a renewed state of siege in November, 1984, when various journals were shut down. In addition to articles, philosophers have had their interviews pub-

lished in news magazines such as *Hoy, Ercilla, Huelén* and newspapers such as *El Mercurio* and *El Sur* (Concepción).

10. Agustín Toro Dávila, "Discurso de inauguración del II Congreso Nacional de Filosofía," *135 aniversario de la Universidad de Chile* (Santiago, 1977), 26.

11. Ibid., 27–28.

12. Escobar, *La filosofía en Chile*. This book was commissioned by the Organization of American States (OAS) in 1972, but as the author indicates, it was revised, expanded, and updated in 1975.

13. Santiago Vidal Muñoz, "La Filosofía en Chile," 19–44. Joaquín Barceló Larraín, "La actividad filosófica en Chile en la segunda mitad del siglo XX," in *Bio-bibliografía de la filosofía en Chile desde el siglo XVI hasta 1980,* ed. Fernando Astorquiza (Santiago, 1980), 109–112.

14. Ibid., 112.

15. Barceló, "Observaciones acerca de la enseñanza de la filosofía en la educación superior," in *La filosofía en América,* ed. Ernesto Mayz Vallenilla, 2 vols. (Caracas, 1979), 1: 53–54.

16. Odette Magnet, "El festival de la una," *Hoy,* November 26–December 2, 1980, 21–23.

17. The statutes of the new system of higher education in Chile, including that of the Academia Superior de Ciencias Pedagógicas, are in Secretaría General del Consejo de Rectores Universidades Chilenas, *Nueva Legislación Universitaria Chilena* (Santiago, 1981). For an analysis of the new legislation, see Levy, "Chilean Universities," and Brunner, *Informe,* 55–64. As both these authors show, the motivation for the changes in higher education was also economic.

18. Barceló, "Los programas de postgrado de la Facultad de Filosofía, Humanidades y Educación de la Universidad de Chile," *Revista Chilena de Humanidades* 2 (1982): 11–18. See also the UCH master's program brochure "Programa de Magistratura en Filosofía," Departamento de Filosofía, Facultad de Filosofía, Humanidades y Educación, 1982.

19. Fernando Valenzuela Erazo, "Alienación y Política," *RF* 25–26 (November 1985): 57–68.

20. Valenzuela, "Discurso de inauguración del año académico 1986," *Revista Chilena de Humanidades* 8 (1986): 11–19.

21. The *Revista de Filosofía,* which appeared regularly for more than twenty years, dropped to a trickle during the 1970s, to reemerge in an annual format in the 1980s. Prominent among the professors who publish regularly in the *RF,* but also in such other journals as the *Revista Chilena de Humanidades* and *Occidente* are Jorge Acevedo, Joaquín Barceló, Héctor Carvallo, Mario Ciudad, Jorge Estrella, and Ramón Menanteau. For a full bibliography of these authors, see Astorquiza, ed., *Bio-bibliografía* (1980) and the sequel *Bio-bibliografía de la filosofía en Chile desde 1980 hasta 1984* (Santiago, 1985).

22. Both the *Revista Chilena de Humanidades* and the volumes edited by Fernando Astorquiza include listings of philosophy theses. Heidegger and Ortega y Gasset figure prominently in the UCH theses. At the Universidad Austral, largely because of the influence of Gastón Gómez Lasa, a large number of graduates concentrate on ancient philosophy. The Catholic University in Santiago graduates fewer philosophy students than UCH, but the subjects of study are varied. Theses include works on Saint Thomas Aquinas and other Catholic thinkers like Jacques Maritain, but they also include works on Karl Popper, Edmund Husserl, Albert Camus, and Enrique Molina. Officialists are not as strong in such major philosophy centers as those at UC, the University of Concepción, and the Universidad Austral in Valdivia. Many professionalists who were removed from UCH or who found the university inhospitable moved to these institutions, especially Jorge Millas and Gastón Gómez Lasa. The Universidad Austral philosophy program has contributed numerous books on ancient philosophy, aesthetics, and philosophy of science. In addition to Gómez Lasa's books, examples include Juan Omar Cofré's *Becker: Estética y metafísica románticas* (Valdivia, 1979); Miguel Espinoza, *Análisis de la imaginación* (Valdivia, 1981); and Manuel Atria, *Tres ensayos de filosofía de la ciencia* (Valdivia, 1981). The Institute of Philosophy in Concepción, headed by Miguel Da Costa Leiva, publishes the journal *Cuadernos de Filosofía* and has an active program of conferences. The Institute of Philosophy at UC, which offers a master's degree, has a core faculty with a long established tenure at UC. They include Osvaldo Lira, Arturo Gaete, and Pedro de la Noi. Other active UC faculty (some of whom hold graduate degrees from abroad) include Oscar Velázques, Raúl Velozo, and Pablo Oyarzún.

23. When professionalists reacted against military rule, their opposition was part and parcel of a more generalized opposition against the regime beginning in 1976. At that time, the middle class that had initially supported the coup began to gradually move towards the opposition. The professionalist philosophers, however, were not merely voicing middle class discontent. Inherent in their view of philosophical professionalism was a

conception of the university that fully supported their activities: a university devoted to the cultivation of pure knowledge, the free pursuit of truth, and the creation of values for the rest of society. As the military introduced other objectives, mainly a desire to keep the university under control, professionalist philosophers found it impossible to function professionally. It was then that they proceeded to react.

24. *Hoy,* June 20–26, 1979, 4.

25. In addition to the works cited in the previous chapter, Vial published *La filosofía de Aristóteles como teología del acto* (Santiago, 1980) and *Una ciencia del ser.*

26. Vial, "El designio histórico," 42.

27. Ibid., 44.

28. See the interviews titled, "La Constitución no es ningún texto sagrado," *Hoy,* August 24–30, 1983, 52–53; and "Buscar dividendos políticos es hacerle el juego a los criminales," *Hoy,* April 15–21, 1985, 9.

29. Juan de Dios Vial Larraín, interview with author. Santiago, Chile, July 28, 1988. On Vial's appointment, see Blanca Arthur, "El rector para la paz," *El Mercurio,* November 1, 1987; P. O'Shea, "De Federici a Vial," *¿Qué Pasa?,* November 5–11, 1987, 6–8.

30. See, for instance, Félix Schwartzmann's "La función social del estado en el último cuarto del siglo XX," Separata de *Escritos de Teoría,* 1979, 24 pp.; "Cultura nacional," 113–120; "Subdesarrollo, ciencia y anticiencia," *Trilogía* 4, no. 7 (December 1984): 7–12; and "Utopía, fin de mundo y tercer mundo," *Estudios Sociales* 45, no. 3 (1985): 83–102.

31. Schwartzmann, "Carácter nacional," 27–34.

32. Schwartzmann's comments about "non-performing loans" (*carteras vencidas*) refer to the considerable debt amassed by Chile's private sector, a debt that many view as the product of the regime's economic policies. See his interview with Enrique Lafourcade in *El Mercurio,* February 20, 1983. Another interview with Félix Schwartzmann was conducted by Rogelio Rodríguez, *Bravo,* no. 64 (July 1982): 4–6.

33. This became apparent in the aftermath of the first serious breakdown of military unity in mid-1978 which led to the resignation of general Gustavo Leigh, one of the original members of the junta that toppled Salvador Allende in 1973. The publicity surrounding the crisis provided a precedent for an increasingly vocal opposition against the regime. The weekly *Hoy,* in particular, joined *Mensaje* in voicing criticism against the govern-

ment. Dialogue, or lack thereof, was often mentioned as the major problem facing government and opposition.

34. The *Seventh Letter* was published in the first and only issue of *Carnets: Revista de Reflexión e Ideas* 1 (August 1979): 28–46; the *Apología de Sócrates* was published in 1979. Even though Gastón Gómez Lasa is a long-standing member of the Chilean philosophical community, his visibility increased only during the period of military rule. Prior to 1973, his activity concentrated more on teaching than on writing.

35. Gómez Lasa, *Platón: Primera Agonía* (Valdivia, 1979), 166. Other books by Gómez Lasa include *Platón: El periplo dialógico* (1978), *Aporías dialógicas* (1978), *La institución del diálogo filosófico* (1980), *El expediente de Sócrates* (1980) and the edition of Plato's *Gorgias* (1982), and *La república* (1983). During an interview with Gómez Lasa in March 1987, he mentioned to the author the preparation of an autobiographical essay titled *El periplo de la metafísica.*

36. *Ercilla,* February 16, 1983, 21–24.

37. *Ercilla,* January 9, 1985, 22–25.

38. Allendes, "La imaginación creadora," 37–44.

39. *Hoy,* September 12–18, 1979, 69.

40. *El Sur,* (Concepción) July 8, 1983.

41. "Mediación en Campus Macul," *Hoy,* December 3–9, 1980, 15.

42. Rogelio Rodríguez, "Un filósofo en el exilio," *Pluma y Pincel,* no. 10 (October 1983): 32–36.

43. Rogelio Rodríguez, "Un filósofo que no calla," *Pluma y Pincel,* no. 16 (July 1985): 12–14.

44. Ibid., 13.

45. Some of Humberto Giannini's recent writings include *Desde las palabras* (Santiago, 1981); "El nacionalismo como texto," *RF* 19, no. 1 (December 1980): 37–45; "La Sociedad de Dios," *Escritos de Teoría* 5 (October 1982): 55–69; "Hacia una arqueología de la experiencia," *RF* 23–24 (1984): 41–57; "Acerca de la dignidad del hombre," *Anuario de Filosofía Jurídica y Social* 2 (1984): 77–87; and "Esquema de una teoría del acto," *RF* 27–28 (November 1986): 7–14.

46. Giannini, *La "reflexión" cotidiana.*

47. Jorge Millas, prologue to William Thayer A., *Empresa y universidad* (Santiago, 1974), 12.

48. Jorge Millas attracted immediate national attention when he published a strong critique of military intervention at the universities. See his "Imperativo de confianza en la universidad chilena," *El Mercurio,* January 3, 1976.

49. Millas, "Las máscaras filosóficas de la violencia," in Millas and Otero, *La violencia y sus máscaras.*

50. Ibid., 10.

51. Ibid., 20.

52. *Hoy,* June 17–23, 1981, 15.

53. *Hoy,* November 17–23, 1982, 15.

54. *Hoy,* July 8–14, 1981, 73.

55. *Hoy,* November 17–23, 1982, 15.

56. Millas, *Idea y defensa.* I have reviewed this book for *Estudios Sociales* 39, no. 1 (1984): 140–143, and have also discussed it in my "The Politics of Higher Education in Latin America," *Latin American Research Review* 20, no. 1 (1985): 209–221.

57. Marco Antonio Allendes, interview with author, Concepción, Chile, March 6, 1987.

58. Giannini, "Jorge Millas, o del difícil ejercicio del pensar," *Hoy,* November 17–23, 1982, 14.

59. Humberto Giannini, interview with author, Santiago, Chile, August 14, 1987.

60. For a listing of private research organizations in Chile, see María Teresa Lladser, *Centros privados de investigación en ciencias sociales* (Santiago, 1986). For an analysis of social science research in Chile, see Manuel Antonio Garretón, *Las ciencias sociales en Chile* (Santiago, 1982) and Corporación de Promoción Universitaria, *Las ciencias sociales en Chile, 1983: Análisis de siete disciplinas* (Santiago, 1983).

61. Edison Otero, "Vigencia y crisis," 120.

62. Otero, *Los signos de la violencia.* A similar approach is followed in his subsequent book titled *Televisión y violencia* (Santiago, 1984), written in collaboration with Ricardo López, his associate in this and other writings. Although in this work Otero concentrates on media and its social

consequences, his primary focus continues to be violence. As in other books, here he argues that the causes of violence are to be found in a web of social, political, and ideological factors. Other writings by Otero include "El pensador en la caverna," *Estudios Sociales* 31, no. 1 (1982): 79–108; "Reivindicación de la filosofía," *Estudios Sociales* 48, no. 2 (1986): 195–200; and "Los filósofos y el poder: Un anecdotario," *Estudios Sociales* 50, no. 4 (1986): 47–56. On the subject of violence, see also Cástor Narvarte, *Nihilismo y violencia* (Santiago, 1982).

63. Otero, *Los derechos de la inteligencia* (Santiago, 1985).

64. Otero, "Televisión," in Ministerio de Relaciones Exteriores, Dirección de Asuntos Culturales e Información Exterior, *Chile cultural* (Santiago, n.d.), 47–52.

65. *Hoy,* November 28–December 4, 1979, 75.

66. Renato Cristi and Carlos Ruiz, "¿Hacia una moral de mercado?" *Mensaje* 30, no. 299 (June 1981): 244.

67. *Hoy,* September 23–29, 1981, 17.

68. Patricio Dooner, interview with author, Santiago, Chile, August 1985. Dooner is the editor of *Estudios Sociales.*

69. Rivano, *Lógica elemental; Perspectivas sobre la metáfora* (Santiago, 1986); and "Globalización y estrategias lógicas," *Cuadernos Americanos* (Mexico) 265, no. 2 (March–April 1986); 72–85. Unpublished writings on logic include "Escuela de Copenhagen: Implicación y totalidad," (Lund, 1981); "Peter Zinkernagel y el fracaso de la filosofía," (Lund, 1982); "Lógica práctica y lógica teórica: Esbozo sobre las ideas de Stephen Toulmin," (Lund, 1984); "Polanyi: Doctrina del conocimiento tácito," (Lund, 1985); and "Repetición, reflexión y ambiguedad," (Lund, 1987).

70. Rivano, "Cliché y sociedad moderna," *Estudios Sociales* 41, no. 3 (1984): 129–173; "Remnant y falacia de personalización," *Estudios Sociales* 45, no. 3 (1985): 103–155; "Thomas S. Szazs: Psiquiatría e inquisición," *Estudios Sociales* 47, no. 1 (1986): 171–196; "Goudsblom: Nihilismo auténtico y nihilismo al alcance de todos," *Estudios Sociales* 51, no. 1 (1987): 77–104; and "Karl Popper: Sociedad abierta," *Estudios Sociales* 53, no. 3 (1987): 135–183. See also his *Mitos: Su función social y cultural* (Santiago, 1987).

71. Tulio Halperín Donghi, "Estilos nacionales." See also Gregorio Weinberg, "Aspectos del vaciamiento de la universidad argentina durante los recientes regímenes militares," *Cuadernos Americanos* (Nueva Epoca) 6, no. 6 (November–December 1987): 204–215.

Bibliography

The following bibliography is divided in two major sections: a bibliography of philosophical sources, and a bibliography of secondary sources. The first bibliography lists only those philosophical sources that are directly relevant to the subject of this book. It is not a comprehensive list of philosophical writings by the authors discussed in the book. Where appropriate, additional writings by philosophers have been cited in the notes. The bibliography of secondary sources includes mainly printed materials on the political, educational, and intellectual history of Chile and Latin America. Many of the sources cited in these two sections and the notes, plus additional important information on the history of Chilean philosophy has been obtained from the following repositories and individuals:

Libraries and Archives

Archivo Nacional de Chile

Biblioteca Central de la Universidad de Chile, Sala Domingo Edwards Matte

Biblioteca Central Luis David Cruz Ocampo, Universidad de Concepción, Sala Universitaria

Biblioteca Central "Profesor Eugenio Pereira Salas," Facultad de Filosofía, Humanidades y Educación, Universidad de Chile

Biblioteca de la Fundación La Casa de Bello, Caracas, Venezuela

Biblioteca del Centro Bellarmino

Biblioteca del Congreso Nacional

Biblioteca Museo Pedagógico, Dirección de Bibliotecas, Archivos y Museos, Ministerio de Educación

Biblioteca Nacional de Chile

Seminario Pontificio Mayor, Arquediócesis de Santiago, Arzobispado de Santiago

Chilean Newspapers and Periodicals

Alternativas (title changed to *Opciones* in 1984)

Anales de la Universidad de Chile

Anuario de Filosofía Jurídica y Social

El Araucano

Atenea: Revista Trimestral de Ciencias, Letras y Artes (title changed to *Atenea: Revista de Ciencia, Arte y Literatura* in 1970)

Boletín de la Universidad de Chile

Cuadernos de Filosofía (Concepción)

Ercilla

Estudios Públicos

Estudios Sociales

Finis Terrae

Historia

Hoy

Huelén

Mapocho

El Mercurio

Las Noticias de Ultima Hora

Occidente

Pluma y Pincel

¿Qué Pasa?

Realidad

Revista Chilena

Revista Chilena de Historia y Geografía

Revista de Educación

Revista de Filosofía

Revista de Santiago

El Siglo

El Sur (Concepción)

Teoría (title changed to *Escritos de Teoría* in 1976)

Trilogía

Interviews

In addition to formal interviews, I have benefited from my correspondence with most of the following philosophers between 1979 and 1988:

Allendes, Marco Antonio

Echeverría, José

Giannini, Humberto

Gómez Lasa, Gastón

Otero, Edison

Rivano, Juan

Schwartzmann, Félix

Vial Larraín, Juan de Dios

Philosophical Sources

Alberdi, Juan Bautista. "Ideas para presidir la confección del curso de filosofía contemporánea." Vol. 15 of *Escritos póstumos de Juan Bautista Alberdi*. Buenos Aires: Imprenta Juan Bautista Alberdi, 1900.

Allendes, Marco Antonio. "La imaginación creadora en la ciencia y el arte." *Atenea: Revista de Ciencia, Arte y Literatura* 442 (1980): 37–44.

———. "Relación entre religión y filosofía en el pensamiento hindú." *Anales de la Universidad de Chile* 135 (1965): 131–152.

Bello, Andrés. *Filosofía del entendimiento y otros escritos filosóficos.* Vol. 3 of *Obras completas.* Caracas: Ediciones del Ministerio de Educación, 1951.

______. "Discurso pronunciado por el Sr. Rector de la Universidad, D. Andrés Bello, en la instalación de este cuerpo el dia 17 de Septiembre de 1843." *Anales de la Universidad de Chile* 1 (1843–44): 139–152.

Bilbao, Francisco. *Obras completas de Francisco Bilbao.* Edited by Manuel Bilbao. 2 vols. Buenos Aires: Imprenta de Buenos Aires, 1866.

Briseño, Ramón [N.O.R.E.A, pseud.] *Curso de filosofía moderna, para el uso de los colegios hispano-americanos, y particularmente para el de los de Chile: extractado de las obras de filosofía que gozan actualmente de más celebridad.* 2 vols. Valparaíso: Imprenta del Mercurio, 1845–1846.

______. "Consideraciones sobre el panteísmo; su refutación y por consiguiente de los sistemas de Spinoza y Hegel." *Anales de la Universidad de Chile* 17 (1860): 459–472.

______. *Curso de filosofía moderna. Tomo segundo, que comprende la historia de la filosofía y el derecho natural.* Santiago: Imprenta Nacional, 1866.

______. *Derecho natural o filosofía del derecho. Curso compuesto para la enseñanza del ramo en la sección superior del Instituto Nacional de Chile.* 4th ed. Valparaíso: Imprenta del Mercurio, de Tornero y Letelier, 1870.

Cárter, Guillermo Juan. "El liberalismo." *Anales de la Universidad de Chile* 53–54 (1878): 87–141.

De la Cuadra, Jorge. *La filosofía de la realidad.* Santiago: Editorial Nascimento, 1949.

Egaña, Juan. *Tractatus de Re Logica, Metaphisica, et Morali. Pro Filiis et Alumnis Instituti Nacionalis Jacobo Politanae Erudendis J. E.* Santiago: Raimundo Rengifo, 1827.

Fernández Concha, Rafael. *Filosofía del derecho o derecho natural.* Santiago: Imprenta del Correo, 1877; 2d ed. 2 vols. Barcelona: Tip. Católica, 1887–88; 3d ed., 2 vols. Santiago: Editorial Jurídica de Chile, 1966.

______. *Del hombre en el orden sicológico, en el religioso y en el social.* 2 vols. Santiago: Imprenta de Emilio Pérez, 1900.

Finlayson, Clarence. *Dios y la filosofía.* Medellín: Universidad de Antioquia, 1945.

______. *Hombre, mundo y Dios: Visión cristiana de la existencia.* Bogotá: Instituto Colombiano de Cultura Hispánica, 1953.

______. *Antología.* Edited by Tomás MacHale. Santiago: Editorial Andrés Bello, 1969.

Frei Montalva, Eduardo. *La política y el espíritu.* 2d ed. Santiago: Editorial del Pacífico, 1946.

Giannini, Humberto. *Reflexiones acerca de la convivencia humana.* Santiago: Facultad de Filosofía y Educación, Universidad de Chile, 1965.

______. *El mito de la autenticidad.* Santiago: Ediciones de la Universidad de Chile, 1968.

______. *Desde las palabras.* Santiago: Ediciones Nueva Universidad, 1981.

______. *Tiempo y espacio en Aristóteles y Kant.* Santiago: Editorial Andrés Bello, 1982.

______. *La "reflexión" cotidiana: Hacia una arqueología de la experiencia.* Santiago: Editorial Universitaria, 1987.

Ginebra, Francisco. *Elementos de filosofía para uso de los colegios de segunda enseñanza.* 6th ed. 2 vols. Barcelona: Eugenio Subirana, Editor y Librero Pontificio, 1915–1916.

Gómez Lasa, Gastón. *Platón: El periplo dialógico.* Valdivia: Ediciones de la Universidad Austral de Valdivia, 1978.

______. *Platón: Aporías dialógicas.* Valdivia: Universidad Austral de Valdivia, 1978.

______. *Platón: Primera agonía.* Valdivia: Departamento de Extensión Académica, Universidad Austral de Valdivia, 1979.

______. *La institución del diálogo filosófico.* Valdivia: Universidad Austral de Valdivia, 1980.

______. *El expediente de Sócrates.* Valdivia: Universidad Austral de Chile, 1980.

González, Eugenio. *Introducción a la filosofía: Apuntes de clases.* Santiago: Instituto Pedagógico, Universidad de Chile, 1951.

Jourdain, Carlos. *Nociones de filosofía.* 2d rev. ed. Translated by Ramón Briseño. Valparaíso: Imprenta del Mercurio, 1870.

______. *Nociones de filosofía.* 3d ed. Translated by Ramón Briseño. Santiago: Librería de M. Servat, 1882.

______. "Una conversión a la Religión de la Humanidad." *Revista Chilena* 14 (1879): 228–246.

Lagarrigue, Jorge. "La filosofía positiva." *Revista Chilena* 2 (1875): 632–645.

Lagarrigue, Juan Enrique. *La Religión de la Humanidad.* 5th ed. Santiago: Fundación Juan Enrique Lagarrigue, 1926.

______. "Necesidad de una gran reforma en la enseñanza." *Revista Chilena* 10 (1878): 384–393.

Larraín Gandarillas, Joaquín. "Examen de varias cuestiones relativas a la instrucción pública." *Anales de la Universidad de Chile* 63 (1883): 501–973.

Lastarria, José Victorino. *Recuerdos literarios. Datos para la historia literaria de la América española y del progreso intelectual en Chile.* 2d ed. Santiago: Librería de M. Servat, 1885.

______. *Lecciones de política positiva.* Vol. 2 of *Obras completas.* Santiago: Imprenta Barcelona, 1909.

______. "Investigaciones sobre la influencia social de la conquista y del sistema colonial de los españoles en Chile." *Anales de la Universidad de Chile* 1 (1843–1844): 199–271.

Letelier, Valentín. *La lucha por la cultura: Miscelánea de artículos políticos y estudios pedagógicos.* Santiago: Imprenta y Encuadernación Barcelona, 1895.

______. *Filosofía de la educación.* Rev. and enl. ed. Buenos Aires: Cabaut, 1927.

Lois, Juan Serapio. *Elementos de filosofía positiva.* 2d ed. 2 vols. Copiapó: Imprenta de la Tribuna, 1906–1908.

Loyola, Pedro León. *Lógica formal.* 5th ed. Vol. 3 of *Curso elemental de filosofía.* Santiago: Imprenta Universitaria, 1935.

______. *Una oposición fundamental en el pensamiento moderno: Causalidad y evolución.* Santiago: Editorial Jurídica de Chile, 1954.

______. *Hechos e ideas de un profesor.* Santiago: Facultad de Filosofía y Educación, Universidad de Chile, 1966.

Mann, Wilhelm. "El espíritu general y los ramos de la enseñanza filosófica en el Liceo." *Anales de la Universidad de Chile* 137 (1915): 643–707.

______. "La enseñanza de la psicología y de la lógica en el Liceo." *Anales de la Universidad de Chile* 137 (1915): 939–977.

Marín, Ventura. *Elementos de la filosofía del espíritu humano escritos por Ventura Marín para el uso de los alumnos del Instituto Nacional de Chile.* 2 vols. Santiago: Imprenta de la Independencia, 1834–1835.

______. *Elementos de la filosofía del espíritu humano.* 3d ed. 2 vols in 1. Santiago: Imprenta Chilena, 1872.

Martínez Bonati, Félix. *La situación universitaria.* Santiago: Prensas de la Editorial Universitaria, 1965.

______. "La misión humanística y social de nuestra universidad." *Anales de la Universidad de Chile* 119 (1960): 114–137.

Millas, Jorge. *Idea de la individualidad.* Santiago: Prensas de la Universidad de Chile, 1943.

______. *Ensayos sobre la historia espiritual de Occidente.* Santiago: Editorial Universitaria, 1960.

______. *El desafío espiritual de la sociedad de masas.* Santiago: Editorial Universitaria, 1962.

______. "Discurso sobre la universidad y su reforma." *Anales de la Universidad de Chile* 127 (1963): 249–261.

______. *Idea de la filosofía.* 2 vols. Santiago: Editorial Universitaria, 1970.

______. *Idea y defensa de la universidad.* Santiago: Editorial del Pacífico; Coedición Corporación de Promoción Universitaria, 1981.

Millas, Jorge, and Edison Otero. *La violencia y sus máscaras.* Santiago: Ediciones Aconcagua, 1978.

Molina, Enrique. *De California a Harvard: Estudio sobre las universidades norteamericanas y algunos problemas nuestros.* Santiago: Sociedad Imprenta y Litografía Universo, 1921.

______. *Dos filósofos contemporáneos: Guyau-Bergson.* Santiago: Editorial Nascimento, 1925.

______. *Confesión filosófica y llamado de superación a la América hispana.* Santiago: Editorial Nascimento, 1942.

______. *Discursos universitarios.* 2d ed. Santiago: Editorial Nascimento, 1945; 3d ed. Santiago: Editorial Nascimento, 1956.

______. *De lo espiritual en la vida humana.* 2d ed. Santiago: Editorial Nascimento, 1947.

______. *Lo que ha sido el vivir.* Concepción, 1974. Unpublished.

______. *Epistolario de Enrique Molina Garmendia.* 14 vols. Compiled by Miguel Da Costa Leiva. Departamento de Filosofía, Vicerrectoría de Investigación, Universidad de Concepción, 1981–1982. Photocopy.

______. *La obra inédita de Enrique Molina Garmendia.* 17 vols. Compiled by Miguel Da Costa Leiva. Departamento de Filosofía, Vicerrectoría de Investigación, Universidad de Concepción, 1984. Typescript.

Mora, José Joaquín de. *Cursos de lógica y ética según la escuela de Edimburgo.* Lima: Imprenta de José Masías, 1832.

Munizaga Aguirre, Roberto. *Filosofía de la educación secundaria.* Santiago: Imprenta Rodolfo Quevedo O., 1947.

Otero, Edison, *Los signos de la violencia.* Santiago: Editorial Aconcagua, 1979.

______. "Vigencia y crisis de la filosofía." *Estudios Sociales* 18 (1978): 87–124.

Oyarzún, Luis. *Temas de la cultura chilena.* Santiago: Editorial Universitaria, 1967.

Pinto, Aníbal. "Consideraciones sobre el método filosófico." *Anales de la Universidad de Chile* 9 (1852): 154–167.

Rivano, Juan. *Entre Hegel y Marx: una meditación ante los nuevos horizontes del humanismo.* Santiago: Comisión Central de Publicaciones de la Universidad de Chile, 1962.

______. *Desde el abandono.* Santiago, 1963. Typescript.

______. *Desde la religión al humanismo.* Santiago: Editorial Universitaria, 1965.

______. *El punto de vista de la miseria.* Santiago: Facultad de Filosofía y Educación, Universidad de Chile, 1965.

______. *Contra sofistas.* Santiago: Encuadernadora Hispano-Suiza, 1966.

______. *Cultura de la servidumbre: mitología de importación.* Santiago: Editorial Santiago, 1969.

______. "El anteproyecto de estatuto orgánico de la Universidad de Chile: improvisación estructuralista." *Revista de Filosofía* 14, no. 1 (1969): 47–51.

______. *Lógica elemental.* Santiago: Editorial Universitaria, 1972; 2d ed. 1985.

______. *Filosofía en dilemas—El pensamiento de McLuhan.* Santiago: Prensa Latinoamericana, 1972.

______. *Un largo contrapunto.* Lund, 1986. Typescript.

Schwartzmann, Félix. *El sentimiento de lo humano en América; ensayo de antropología filosófica.* Vol. 1 Santiago: Universidad de Chile, 1950.

______. *El sentimiento de lo humano en América; antropología de la convivencia.* Vol. 2. Santiago: Universidad de Chile, 1953.

______. *Teoría de la expresión.* Santiago: Ediciones de la Universidad de Chile, 1967.

______. "Cultura nacional y mundialidad como forma de poder." *Atenea: Revista de Ciencia, Arte y Literatura* 442 (1980): 113–120.

______. "Carácter nacional e identidad nacional." *Revista de Santiago* 2 (1982): 27–34.

Soler Grima, Francisco. *Hacia Ortega.* Santiago: Facultad de Filosofía y Educación, Universidad de Chile, 1965.

Stahl, Gerold. *Elementos de metalógica y metamatemáticas.* Santiago: Editorial Universitaria, 1964.

______. *Elementos de metamatemáticas.* Santiago: Editorial Universitaria, 1973.

Torretti, Roberto. *Manuel Kant: Estudio sobre los fundamentos de la filosofía crítica.* Santiago: Ediciones de la Universidad de Chile, 1967.

______. "Poder político y opresión." *Revista de Filosofía* 9, nos. 1–2 (1962): 35–48.

Varas, José Miguel. *Lecciones elementales de moral.* Santiago: Imprenta de la Independencia, 1828.

Varas, José Miguel, and Marín, Ventura. *Elementos de ideología.* Santiago: Imprenta de la Independencia, 1830.

Vial Larraín, Juan de Dios. *Metafísica cartesiana*. Santiago: Editorial Universitaria, 1971.

______. "Acerca de la filosofía." *Revista de Filosofía* 8, no. 1 (July 1961): 91–113.

______. "Universidad y educación." *Finis Terrae* 35 (1962): 43–59.

______. "Consistencia metafísica de la filosofía." *Revista de Filosofía* 8, nos. 2–3 (November 1961): 45–55.

______. "Idea de la universidad." In *La universidad en tiempos de cambio*, 7–12. Santiago: Editorial del Pacífico, 1965.

______. "El designio histórico de la universidad." *Realidad* 16 (1980): 33–44.

______. *Una ciencia del ser*. Santiago: Ediciones Universidad Católica de Chile, 1987.

Secondary Sources

Abellán, José Luis. *Filosofía española en América, 1936–1966*. Madrid: Ediciones Guadarrama, 1967.

Alexander, Robert J. *The Tragedy of Chile*. Contributions in Political Science, No. 8. Westport, Connecticut: Greenwood Press, 1978.

Altbach, Philip G., ed. *University Reform: Comparative Perspectives for the Seventies*. Cambridge: Schenkman Publishing Company, 1974.

Amunátegui, Miguel Luis. *Don José Joaquín de Mora: Apuntes biográficos*. Santiago: Imprenta Nacional, 1888.

______. *Vida de don Andrés Bello*. Santiago: Imprenta Pedro G. Ramírez, 1882.

Amunátegui Solar, Domingo. *Los primeros años del Instituto Nacional, 1813–1835*. Santiago: Imprenta Cervantes, 1889.

______. *El Instituto Nacional bajo los rectorados de don Manuel Montt, don Francisco Puente y don Antonio Varas, 1835–1845*. Santiago: Imprenta Cervantes, 1891.

______. *El progreso intelectual y político de Chile*. Santiago: Editorial Nascimento, 1936.

______. *Recuerdos del Instituto Nacional*. Santiago: Ediciones de la Universidad de Chile, 1941.

Ardao, Arturo. "Assimilation and Transformation of Positivism in Latin America." *Journal of the History of Ideas* 24 (1963): 515–522.

______. "Bello y la filosofía latinoamericana." In Fundación La Casa de Bello. *Bello y la América Latina,* 179–191. Caracas: Fundación La Casa de Bello, 1982.

Astorquiza, Fernando. ed. *Bio-Bibliografía de la filosofía en Chile desde el siglo XVI hasta 1980.* Santiago: Universidad de Chile-Instituto Profesional de Santiago, 1982.

______. *Bio-Bibliografía de la filosofía en Chile desde 1980 hasta 1984.* Santiago: Universidad de Chile-Instituto Profesional de Santiago, 1985.

Atria B., Raúl, Eduardo Acuña A., Patricio Dooner D., Edmundo López H., and Ernesto Moreno B. *Actores sociales y cambio institucional en las reformas universitarias chilenas.* Santiago: Corporación de Promoción Universitaria, 1973.

Bader, Thomas. "Early Positivistic Thought and Ideological Conflict in Chile." *The Americas* 26 (February 1970): 376–393.

Barros Arana, Diego. *Un Decenio de la historia de Chile.* 2 vols. Santiago: Imprenta, Litografía y Encuadernación Barcelona, 1913.

______. "Fragmentos del discurso de Diego Barros Arana con motivo del cincuentenario de la universidad en 1893." *Boletín de la Universidad de Chile* 35 (November 1962): 42–44.

Blakemore, Harold. "Chile from the War of the Pacific to the World Depression, 1880–1930." In *The Cambridge History of Latin America* edited by Leslie Bethell, vol. 5, 499–551. Cambridge: Cambridge University Press, 1986.

Boas, George. *French Philosophies of the Romantic Period.* Baltimore: The Johns Hopkins Press, 1925.

Bonilla, Frank, and Myron Glazer. *Student Politics in Chile.* New York: Basic Books, 1970.

Bowers, Claude G. *Chile Through Embassy Windows: 1939–1953.* New York: Simon and Schuster, 1958.

Brunner, José Joaquín. *Informe sobre la educación superior en Chile.* Santiago: Facultad Latinoamericana de Ciencias Sociales, 1986.

Brunner, José Joaquín, and Angel Flisfisch. *Los intelectuales y las instituciones de la cultura.* Santiago: Facultad Latinoamericana de Ciencias Sociales, 1983.

Burnett, Ben G. *Political Groups in Chile: The Dialogue Between Order and Change.* Austin and London: University of Texas Press, 1970.

Burr, Robert R. *By Reason or Force: Chile and the Balancing of Power in South America: 1830–1905.* Berkeley: University of California Press, 1974.

Campbell, Margaret. "Education in Chile: 1810–1842." *Journal of Inter-American Studies* 1 (July 1959): 353–375.

Campos Harriet, Fernando. *Desarrollo educacional, 1810–1960.* Santiago: Editorial Andrés Bello, 1960.

Centro de Alumnos de Filosofía, Universidad de Chile. "La Reforma universitaria: espejismo y verdad." *Revista de Filosofía* 14, no. 1 (1969): 5–15.

______, ed. *En el límite.* Santiago: Talleres de R. Neupert, 1971.

______, ed. *En el límite 2.* Santiago: Talleres de R. Neupert, 1972.

Cifuentes, Abdón. *Memorias.* 2 vols. Santiago: Editorial Nascimento, 1936.

Collier, Simon. *Ideas and Politics of Chilean Independence, 1808–1833.* Cambridge: Cambridge University Press, 1967.

______. "The Historiography of the 'Portalian' Period (1830–1891) in Chile." *Hispanic American Historical Review* 57, no. 4 (November 1977): 660–690.

______. "Evolución política, institucional, social y cultural de Chile entre 1829 y 1865." In Fundación La Casa de Bello. *Bello y Chile,* vol. 1, 25–50. Caracas: Fundación La Casa de Bello, 1981.

______. "Chile from Independence to the War of the Pacific." In *The Cambridge History of Latin America.* Edited by Leslie Bethell, vol. 3, 583–613. Cambridge: Cambridge University Press, 1985.

Correa, Raquel, Malú Sierra, and Elizabeth Subercaseaux. *Los generales del régimen.* Santiago: Editorial Aconcagua, 1983.

Crawford, William Rex. *A Century of Latin American Thought.* Rev. ed. Cambridge: Harvard University Press, 1961.

Cristi, Renato. "El gesto filosófico de Lastarria." *Teoría* 5–6 (December 1975): 3–14.

Davie, George Elder. *The Democratic Intellect: Scotland and Her Universities in the Nineteenth Century.* 2d ed. Edinburgh: Edinburgh University Press, 1964.

Davis, Harold Eugene. *Latin American Thought: A Historical Introduction.* Baton Rouge: Louisiana State University Press, 1972. Reprint. New York: The Free Press, 1974.

Davis, Nathaniel. *The Last Two Years of Salvador Allende.* Ithaca and London: Cornell University Press, 1985.

De la Barra, Eduardo. *El embrujamiento alemán.* Santiago: Establecimiento Poligráfico Roma, 1899.

Donoso, Armando. *Bilbao y su tiempo.* Santiago: Talleres de la Empresa Zig-Zag, 1913.

Donoso, Ricardo. *Recopilación de leyes, reglamentos y decretos relativos a los servicios de la enseñanza superior.* Santiago: Imprenta de la Dirección General de Prisiones, 1937.

______. *Las ideas políticas en Chile.* Colección Tierra Firme, No. 23. Mexico City: Fondo de Cultura Económica, 1946.

______. "El Instituto Pedagógico: tres generaciones de maestros." *Journal of Inter-American Studies* 6 (January 1964): 5–16.

Dooner, Patricio, and Iván Lavados, eds. *La universidad latinoamericana: visión de una década.* Santiago: Corporación de Promoción Universitaria, 1979.

Drake, Paul W. *Socialism and Populism in Chile, 1932–52.* Urbana, Chicago, and London: University of Illinois Press, 1978.

______. "Chile." In *The Spanish Civil War, 1936–39. American Hemispheric Perspectives,* edited by Mark Falcoff and Frederick B. Pike, 245–290. Lincoln and London: University of Nebraska Press, 1982.

______. "El impacto académico de los terremotos políticos: Investigaciones de la historia chilena en inglés, 1977–1983." *Alternativas* no. 2 (January–April 1984): 56–78.

______. "Chile, 1932–1958." In *The Cambridge History of Latin America.* Edited by Leslie Bethell. Forthcoming. Cambridge: Cambridge University Press.

Echeverría Yáñez, José R. *La enseñanza de la filosofía en la universidad hispanoamericana.* Washington, D.C.: Unión Panamericana, 1965.

Edwards Vives, Alberto. *La fronda aristocrática: historia política de Chile.* 4th ed. Santiago: Editorial del Pacífico, 1945.

Encyclopedia of Higher Education. "University Reform," by Philip G. Altbach, 4263–4273.

Escobar, Roberto. *La filosofía en Chile.* Santiago: Universidad Técnica del Estado, 1976.

Eyzaguirre, Jaime. *Chile durante el gobierno de Errázuriz Echaurren.* 2d ed. Santiago: Empresa Editora Zig-Zag, 1957.

Fagen, Patricia Weiss. *Chilean Universities: Problems of Autonomy and Dependence.* Comparative Political Series, vol. 4. Beverly Hills: Sage Publications, 1973.

Farrell, Joseph P. *The National Unified School in Allende's Chile: The Role of Education in the Destruction of a Revolution.* Vancouver: University of British Columbia Press, 1986.

Feliú Cruz, Guillermo. *La fundación del Instituto Nacional.* Santiago: Imprenta Cultura, 1950.

———. *La Universidad de Chile: Universidad de América.* 2d ed. Santiago: Departamento de Extensión Cultural, Universidad de Chile, 1953.

———. "El Instituto Pedagógico bajo la dirección de Domingo Amunátegui Solar, 1892–1922." *Mapocho* 3 (1965): 11–43.

———. *Ramón Briseño: Vida y obra del primer bibliógrafo chileno, 1814–1910.* Santiago: Editorial Universidad Católica, 1966.

———, ed. *Estudios sobre Andrés Bello.* Santiago: Fondo Andrés Bello, 1966.

Fernández Larraín, Sergio. *Cartas a Bello en Londres, 1810–1829.* Santiago: Editorial Andrés Bello, 1968.

Ferrater Mora, José. *Diccionario de Filosofía.* 6th ed. 4 vols. Madrid: Alianza Editorial, 1986.

Figueroa, Virgilio. *Diccionario histórico, biográfico y bibliográfico de Chile.* 5 vols. Santiago: Establecimientos Gráficos Balcells, 1928–1931.

Fischer, Kathleen B. *Political Ideology and Educational Reform in Chile, 1964–1976.* Los Angeles: UCLA Latin American Center Publications, 1979.

Fleet, Michael. "Academic Freedom and University Autonomy in Chile." *Latin American Studies Association Newsletter* 8, no. 2 (June 1977): 23–38.

Flisfisch, Angel. "Elementos para una interpretación de los procesos de reforma en la Universidad de Chile, 1950–1973." FLACSO Documento Preliminar No. 19. Facultad Latinoamericana de Ciencias Sociales, September 1981.

Fogg, Stephen Lockhart. "Positivism in Chile and its Impact on Education Development and Economic Thought, 1870–1891." Ph.D. diss., New York University, 1978.

Frondizi, Risieri. "Tendencies in Contemporary Latin American Philosophy." *Inter-American Intellectual Exchange,* 35–48. Austin: University of Texas Press, 1943.

______. "¿Hay una filosofía Iberoamericana?" *Realidad* 3 (1948): 158–170.

Frondizi, Risieri, and Jorge J. E. Gracia. *El hombre y los valores en la filosofía latinoamericana del siglo XX*. Mexico: Fondo de Cultura Económica, 1975.

Fuentealba H., Leonardo. "Filosofía de la historia en Letelier." *Revista Chilena de Historia y Geografía* 127 (January–December 1959): 313–51.

Fuenzalida, Edmundo. "The Reception of 'Scientific Sociology' in Chile." *Latin American Research Review* 18, no. 2 (1983): 95–112.

Fuenzalida Grandón, Alejandro. *Lastarria y su tiempo*. Santiago: Imprenta Cervantes, 1893.

Galdames, Luis. *Educación económica e intelectual.* Santiago: Imprenta Universitaria, 1912.

______. *La Universidad de Chile, 1843–1934*. Santiago: Prensas de la Universidad de Chile, 1934.

______. *Valentín Letelier y su obra, 1852–1919*. Santiago: Imprenta Universitaria, 1937.

______. *Historia de Chile*. 13th ed. Santiago: Empresa Editora Zig-Zag, 1952.

Garretón, Manuel Antonio. *El proceso político chileno*. 2d ed. Santiago: Facultad Latinoamericana de Ciencias Sociales, 1983.

______. "Universidad y política en los procesos de transformación y reversión en Chile, 1967–1977." *Estudios Sociales* 26, no. 4 (1980): 83–109.

______. "The Political Evolution of the Chilean Military Regime and Problems in the Transition to Democracy." In *Transitions from Authoritarian Rule: Latin America,* edited by Guillermo O' Donnell, Philippe C. Schmitter, and Laurence Whitehead, 95–122. Baltimore and London: The Johns Hopkins University Press, 1986.

Garretón, Manuel Antonio, and Tomás Moulian. *La Unidad Popular y el conflicto político en Chile.* Santiago: Ediciones Minga, 1983.

Gill, Clark G. *Education and Social Change in Chile.* Washington, D.C.: U.S. Department of Health, Education, and Welfare, Office of Education, 1966.

Godoy Urzúa, Hernán. *El carácter chileno.* 2d ed. Santiago: Editorial Universitaria, 1976.

Góngora, Mario. *Ensayo histórico sobre la noción de estado en Chile en los siglos XIX y XX.* 2d ed. Santiago: Editorial Universitaria, 1986.

González, Eugenio. "El rol de la universidad en el proceso para el cambio social." *Boletín de la Universidad de Chile* 57 (June 1965): 4–7.

Gracia, Jorge J. E., ed. *Latin American Philosophy in the Twentieth Century: Man, Values, and the Search for Philosophical Identity.* Buffalo, N.Y.: Prometheus Books, 1986.

______. "Philosophical Analysis in Latin America." *History of Philosophy Quarterly* 1, no. 1 (January 1984): 111–122.

Gracia, Jorge J. E., and Iván Jaksić. "The Problem of Philosophical Identity in Latin America." *Inter-American Review of Bibliography* 34, no. 1 (1984): 53–71.

______. "Philosophical Bases of Unbelief in Latin America." *Encyclopedia of Unbelief,* edited by Gordon Stein, vol. 2, 385–393. Buffalo, New York: Prometheus Books, 1985.

Guirao Massif, Ana. *Historia de la Facultad de Filosofía y Humanidades de la Universidad de Chile hasta la fundación del Instituto Pedagógico, 1843–1889.* Vol 1 of *Memorias de los Egresados.* Santiago: Facultad de Filosofía y Educación, Universidad de Chile, 1957.

Hamuy, Eduardo. *El problema educacional del pueblo de Chile.* Santiago: Editorial del Pacífico, 1961.

Hale, Charles A. "Political and Social Ideas in Latin America, 1870–1930." In *The Cambridge History of Latin America,* edited by Leslie Bethell, vol. 4, 367–643. Cambridge: Cambridge University Press, 1986.

Halperín Donghi, Tulio. *Historia de la Universidad de Buenos Aires.* Buenos Aires: Editorial Universitaria de Buenos Aires, 1962.

______. *Historia contemporánea de América Latina.* 2d ed. Madrid: Alianza Editorial, 1970.

______. "Estilos nacionales de institucionalización de la cultura e impacto de la represión: Argentina y Chile." In *Represión y reconstrucción de una cultura: El caso argentino,* edited by Saúl Sosnowski, 27–48. Buenos Aires: EUDEBA, 1988.

Hanisch Espíndola, Walter, S. J. *En torno a la filosofía en Chile, 1594–1810.* Santiago: Universidad Católica de Chile, 1963.

______. *Rousseau, la ideología y la escuela escocesa en la filosofía chilena, 1828–1830.* Santiago: Instituto de Historia, Universidad Católica de Chile, 1968.

______. "Andrés Bello y su pensamiento filosófico en Chile, 1829–1865." In Fundación La Casa de Bello, *Bello y Chile,* vol. 1, 259–316. Caracas: Fundación La Casa de Bello, 1981.

______. "La Facultad de Teología de la Universidad de Chile, 1842–1927." *Historia* 20 (1985): 47–135.

Harrison, John P. "The Role of the Intellectual in Fomenting Change: The University." In *Explosive Forces in Latin America,* edited by John J. TePaske and Sydney Mettleton Fisher, 27–42. Columbus: Ohio State University Press, 1964.

Hojman, David E., ed. *Chile After 1973: Elements for the Analysis of Military Rule.* Liverpool: The University of Liverpool, 1985.

Huneeus Gana, Jorge. *Cuadro histórico de la producción intelectual de Chile.* Santiago: Biblioteca de Escritores de Chile, 1910.

Huneeus Madge, Carlos. *La reforma en la Universidad de Chile.* Santiago: Corporación de Promoción Universitaria, 1973.

Jaksić, Iván. "The Philosophy of Juan Rivano: The Intellectual Background of the University Reform Movement of 1968 in Chile." Ph.D. diss., State University of New York at Buffalo, 1981.

______. "Philosophy and University Reform at the University of Chile, 1842–1973." *Latin American Research Review* 19, no. 1 (1984): 57–86.

______. "The Influence of Positivism on Latin American Educational Thought: The Case of Chile and Valentín Letelier." In *Latin American Education: A Quest for Identity,* edited by Nancy J. Nystrom, 59–72. New Orleans: Roger Thayer Stone Center for Latin American Studies, Tulane University, 1985.

______. "Philosophia Perennis en tiempos pretorianos: La filosofía chilena desde 1973." *Cuadernos Americanos* 259, no. 2 (March–April 1985): 59–87.

______. "La vocación filosófica en Chile." *Cuadernos Americanos* (Nueva Epoca) 2, no. 8 (March–April 1988): 21–42.

Jobet, Julio César. *Valentín Letelier y sus continuadores: Darío Salas, Luis Galdames y Pedro Aguirre Cerda.* San José, Costa Rica: Editorial Universitaria, 1954.

______. *Doctrina y práxis de los educadores representativos chilenos.* Santiago: Editorial Andrés Bello, 1970.

Jorrín, Miguel, and John D. Martz. *Latin American Political Thought and Ideology.* Chapel Hill: The University of North Carolina Press, 1970.

Kilgore, William J. "The Development of Positivism in Latin America." *Inter-American Review of Bibliography* 19 (1969): 23–42.

______. "Notes on the Philosophy of Education of Andrés Bello." *Journal of the History of Ideas* 22 (October–December 1961): 555–560.

Kinsbruner, Jay. *Chile: A Historical Interpretation.* New York: Harper & Row, Publishers, 1973.

Kirberg, Enrique. *Los nuevos profesionales: Educación universitaria de trabajadores en Chile: UTE, 1968–1973.* Guadalajara: Instituto de Estudios Sociales, Universidad de Guadalajara, 1981.

Krebs, Ricardo, ed. *Catolicismo y laicismo: Las bases doctrinarias del conflicto entre la iglesia y el estado en Chile, 1875–1885.* Santiago: Ediciones Nueva Universidad, Pontificia Universidad Católica de Chile, 1981.

Labarca, Amanda. *Historia de la enseñanza en Chile.* Santiago: Imprenta Universitaria, 1939.

Levy, Daniel C. *Higher Education and the State in Latin America: Private Challenges to Public Dominance*. Chicago and London: The University of Chicago Press, 1986.

______. "Student Politics in Contemporary Latin America." *Canadian Journal of Political Science* 14 (June 1981): 353–76.

______. "Chilean Universities Under the Junta: Regime and Policy." *Latin American Research Review* 21, no. 3 (1986): 95–128.

Lipp, Solomon. *Three Chilean Thinkers*. Waterloo, Ontario: Wilfrid Laurier University Press, 1975.

Lipset, Seymour Martin, and Aldo Solari, eds. *Elites in Latin America*. New York: Oxford University Press, 1967.

Loveman, Brian. *Chile: The Legacy of Hispanic Capitalism*. New York: Oxford University Press, 1979; 2d rev. and enl. ed., 1988.

______. "Military Dictatorship and Political Opposition in Chile, 1973–1986." *Journal of Interamerican Studies and World Affairs* 28, no. 4 (1986–87): 1–38.

Lynch, John, ed. *Andrés Bello: The London Years*. Richmond, Surrey: The Richmond Publishing Co., 1982.

Maier, Joseph and Richard W. Weatherhead, eds. *The Latin American University*. Albuquerque: University of New Mexico Press, 1979.

Mann, Wilhelm. *Chile luchando por nuevas formas de vida*. 2 vols. Santiago: Prensas de la Editorial Ercilla, 1935.

______. "Jorge Enrique Schneider: Su acción en el progreso de la filosofía." *Anales de la Universidad de Chile* 117 (1905): 1–17.

Medina, José Toribio. *Historia de la Real Universidad de San Felipe de Santiago de Chile*. 2 vols. Santiago: Sociedad Imprenta y Litografía Universo, 1928.

Michaels, Albert L. "Chilean Politics and University Reform: 1964–1973." *Universities and the New International Order*, edited by Irving J. Spitzberg, vol. 4, 14–40. Buffalo, N.Y.: State University of New York at Buffalo, 1979.

Milliani, Domingo. "Utopian Socialism, Transitional Thread from Romanticism to Positivism in Latin America." *Journal of the History of Ideas* 24 (1963): 523–538.

Molina, Enrique. *La filosofía en Chile en la primera mitad del siglo XX.* Santiago: Editorial Nascimento, 1953.

Monguió, Luis. *Don José Joaquín de Mora y el Perú del ochocientos.* Berkeley and Los Angeles: University of California Press, 1967.

Montebruno, Julio. "Don Jorge Enrique Schneider." *Revista Chilena de Historia y Geografía* 101 (July–December 1942): 175–207.

Orrego Luco, Augusto. *Recuerdos de la escuela.* Santiago: Editorial del Pacífico, 1953.

______. "La resurrección del Latín." *Revista Chilena de Historia y Geografía* no. 101 (July–December 1942): 157–174.

Ortega y Gasset, José. *Misión de la universidad y otros ensayos afines.* 4th ed. Madrid: Editorial Revista de Occidente, 1965.

______. "Recuerdo del paso por Chile del filósofo José Ortega y Gasset." *Occidente* 301 (May–June 1983): 32–38.

Oviedo, Benjamín. *La masonería en Chile.* Santiago: Sociedad Imprenta y Litografía Universo, 1929.

Oyarzún, Luis. *El pensamiento de Lastarria.* Colección de Estudios Jurídicos y Sociales. Santiago: Editorial Jurídica de Chile, 1953.

______. "Lastarria y los comienzos del pensamiento filosófico en Chile durante el siglo XIX." *Revista de Filosofía* 1 (August 1949): 27–56.

Pacheco Gómez, Máximo. *La Universidad de Chile.* Santiago: Editorial Jurídica de Chile, 1953.

Pérez Rosales, Vicente. *Recuerdos del pasado, 1814–1860.* 6th ed. Santiago: Empresa Editora Zig-Zag, 1958.

Petras, James, and Robert Laporte. *Politics and Social Forces in Chilean Development.* Berkeley and Los Angeles: University of California Press, 1972.

Pontificia Universidad Católica de Chile. *La presencia de la filosofía en la Universidad Católica (1888–1973).* Santiago: Pontificia Universidad Católica de Chile, 1982.

Programa Interdisciplinario de Investigaciones en Educación. *Las transformaciones educacionales bajo el régimen militar.* 2 vols. Santiago: Programa Interdisciplinario de Investigaciones en Educación, 1984.

Ramírez Necochea, Hernán. *El partido comunista y la universidad.* Santiago: Ediciones de la Revista Aurora, 1964.

Ruiz Schneider, Carlos. "Moderación y filosofía: notas de investigación sobre la filosofía de Andrés Bello." *Teoría* 5–6 (December 1975): 15–39.

______. "Política de la moderación: notas de investigación sobre las ideas filosóficas y políticas de Andrés Bello." *Escritos de Teoría* 1 (December 1976): 9–26.

Sacks, Norman P. "José Victorino Lastarria: un intelectual comprometido en la América Latina." *Revista Chilena de Historia y Geografía* 140 (1972): 153–193.

Salazar Bondy, Augusto. *¿Existe una filosofía en nuestra América?* Mexico City: Siglo XXI, 1968.

Salcedo, Danilo. *La Universidad de Chile y su reforma inconclusa.* Santiago: Editorial Nascimento, 1975.

Sánchez Reulet, Aníbal. *Contemporary Latin American Philosophy.* Translated by Willard R. Trask. Albuquerque: The University of New Mexico Press, 1954.

Sater, William. *The Heroic Image in Chile: Arturo Prat, Secular Saint.* Berkeley and Los Angeles: University of California Press, 1975.

Sarti, Sergio. *Panorama della filosofia Ispanoamericana contemporanea.* Milan: Cisalpino-Golliardica, 1976.

Schutte, Ofelia. "Toward an Understanding of Latin American Philosophy: Reflections on the Formation of a Cultural Identity." *Philosophy Today* 31, no. 1/4 (Spring 1987): 21–34.

Schwartzmann, Félix. "La Philosophie au Chili." In *La Philosophie Contemporaine,* edited by Raymond Klibanski, 635–642. Florence: La Nuova Editrice, 1971.

Segall, Marcelo. "Un hegeliano en Chile: José Bruner, su vida y su época." *Boletín de la Universidad de Chile* 91 (April 1969): 45–53.

______. "Ideas, personajes y presencia filosófica de la olvidada escuela hegeliana chilena." *Boletín de la Universidad de Chile* 104 (August 1970): 28–42.

Sehlinger, Peter Joseph. "The Educational Thought and Influence of Valentín Letelier." Ph.D. diss., University of Kentucky, 1969.

______. "El desarrollo intelectual y la influencia de Valentín Letelier: un estudio bibliográfico." *Revista Chilena de Historia y Geografía* 136 (1968): 250–284.

______. "Cien años de influencia de la obra de Letelier." *Revista Chilena de Historia y Geografía* 139 (1971): 72–85.

Serrano, Sol. "Los desafíos de la Universidad de Chile en la consolidación del estado, 1842–1879." In *Historia, política y religión. Homenaje a Mario Góngora*. Santiago: Ediciones Universidad Católica, 1988.

______. "De la academia a la especialización. La Universidad de Chile en el siglo XIX." *Opciones* 13 (January–April 1988): 9–34.

Sigmund, Paul E. *The Overthrow of Allende and the Politics of Chile, 1964–1976*. Pittsburgh: The University of Pittsburgh Press, 1977.

Silva Castro, Raúl. "Don Eduardo de la Barra y la pedagogía alemana." *Revista Chilena de Historia y Geografía* 101 (July–December 1942): 208–235.

______. "El pensamiento de Bello en el discurso de instalación." *Boletín de la Universidad de Chile* 35 (November 1962): 28–32.

______. "El ensayo en Chile." *Journal of Inter-American Studies* 4, no. 4 (1962): 441–461.

Silvert, Kalman H., and Leonard Reissman. *Education, Class and Nation: The Experiences of Chile and Venezuela*. New York: Elsevier Scientific Publishing Co., 1976.

Smith, Brian H. *The Church and Politics in Chile: Challenges to Modern Catholicism*. Princeton: Princeton University Press, 1982.

Solberg, Carl. *Immigration and Nationalism: Argentina and Chile, 1890–1914*. Institute of Latin American Studies, The University of Texas at Austin, Latin American Monographs, no. 18. Austin and London: The University of Texas Press, 1970.

Sommerville, Hayra G. de; Laura Zagal Anabalón, Carlos Videla V., and Esteban Doña U. "Una fase importante de la enseñanza de la filosofía, de la psicología y de la pedagogía en la Universidad de Chile." *Anales de la Universidad de Chile* 100, nos. 45–46 (1942): 206–237.

Stabb, Martin S. *In Quest of Identity: Patterns in the Spanish American Essay of Ideas, 1890–1960*. Chapel Hill: The University of North Carolina Press, 1967.

Stoetzer, O. Carlos. "The Political Ideas of Andrés Bello." *International Philosophical Quarterly* 23, no. 4 (December 1983): 395–406.

Stuardo Ortiz, Carlos. "El Liceo de Chile: Antecedentes para su historia, 1828–1831." *Revista Chilena de Historia y Geografía* 114 (July–December 1949): 81–91; 115 (January–June 1950): 162–217; and 116 (July–December 1950): 50–91.

Sywak, William Walter. "Values in Nineteenth-Century Chilean Education: The Germanic Reform of Chilean Public Education 1885–1910." Ph.D. diss., University of California at Los Angeles, 1977.

Tocornal, Manuel Antonio. "La independencia de los profesores universitarios." *Revista Chilena de Historia y Geografía* 101 (July–December 1942): 153–156.

Torchia Estrada, Juan Carlos. *La filosofía en la Argentina.* Washington, D.C.: Unión Panamericana, 1961.

Valenzuela, J. Samuel, and Arturo Valenzuela, eds. *Military Rule in Chile: Dictatorship and Oppositions.* Baltimore and London: The Johns Hopkins University Press, 1986.

Vega, Miguel Angel. "El aporte alemán al progreso de Chile." *Anales de la Universidad de Chile* 116, nos. 109–110 (1958): 488–495.

Velasco, Fanor. "Recuerdos del Instituto Nacional." *Revista Chilena de Historia y Geografía* 51, no. 55 (1925–26): 39–56.

Vial Larraín, Juan de Dios. "Situación de la Filosofía en Chile." In *Las ciencias sociales en Chile, 1983: Análisis de siete disciplinas,* 117–125. Santiago: Corporación de Promoción Universitaria, 1983.

Vicuña Subercaseaux, Benjamín. *Memoria sobre la producción intelectual en Chile.* Santiago: Sociedad Imprenta y Litografía Universo, 1909.

Vidal Muñoz, Santiago. "Apuntes sobre la filosofía en Chile." *Cursos y Conferencias* 48 (March 1956): 39–60.

______. "La filosofía en Chile." *Cuadernos de Filosofía,* no. 6 (1977): 19–44.

Walter, Richard J. "The Intellectual Background of the 1918 University Reform in Argentina." *Hispanic American Historical Review* 49 (1969): 233–253.

Whitaker, Arthur P., ed. *Latin America and the Enlightenment.* Ithaca, N.Y.: Cornell University Press, 1965.

Woll, Allen L. *A Functional Past: The Uses of History in Nineteenth-Century Chile.* Baton Rouge and London: Louisiana State University Press, 1982.

Woodward, Ralph Lee, ed., *Positivism in Latin America, 1850–1900: Are Order and Progress Reconcilable?* Lexington, Mass.: D.C. Heath and Company, 1971.

Yeager, Gertrude Matyoka. *Barros Arana's "Historia Jeneral de Chile:" Politics, History and National Identity.* Texas Christian University Monographs in History and Culture. Fort Worth: Texas Christian University Press, 1981.

———. "Barros Arana, Vicuña Mackenna, Amunátegui: The Historian as National Educator." *Journal of Inter-American Studies and World Affairs* 19 (May 1977): 173–200.

Zapiola, José. *Recuerdos de treinta años (1810–1840).* 5th ed. Santiago: Biblioteca de Autores Chilenos, 1902.

Zea, Leopoldo. *Dos etapas del pensamiento en hispanoamérica: Del romanticismo al positivismo.* Mexico City: El Colegio de México, 1949.

———. *Pensamiento positivista latinoamericano.* 2 vols. Caracas: Biblioteca Ayacucho, 1980.

Zeitlin, Maurice. *The Civil Wars in Chile (Or the Bourgeois Revolutions That Never Were).* Princeton, N.J.: Princeton University Press, 1984.

Index